CONTENTS

STUDY
GUIDE

AGE 11-14

KEY STAGE 3

HISTORY

Peter Lane and Christopher Lane

- A clear introduction to the new National Curriculum

- Topic by topic coverage, with lots of diagrams and illustrations

- Frequent questions to test your knowledge

- Index and glossary of terms

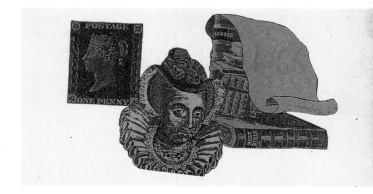

First published 1992
Reprinted 1992, 1994, 1996, 1997, 1998, 2000 (twice), 2001, 2002
Revised 1995

Text: © Peter Lane and Christopher Lane 1992

Illustrations: Ian Foulis Associates, Peter McClure

© Letts Educational Ltd
The Chiswick Centre, Chiswick High Road
London W4 5TF
020 8996 3333

Printed in Great Britain by
Bath Press Colourbooks, Glasgow

British Library Cataloguing in Publication Data
A CIP record for this book is available from the British Library

ISBN 1 85758 938 6

Acknowledgements
Thanks go to David Bell and Robert Medley, the advisers on this book.

The authors and publisher gratefully acknowledge the following for permission to reproduce illustrations and extracts:

Aerofilms Ltd p14; B T Batsford Ltd pp18, 19, 20, 21, 34, 50, 78; *The Making of America*, BBC Publications 1968 pp178, 182, 183, 184, 185; The Bodleian Library, Oxford pp 18, 20, 21, 40, 41; The British Library pp17, 18, 19, 28, 43, 46, 70; The British Library: Add 42130 folio 208 p18 (pic 4); *Slaves Fell the Ripe Sugar*, Antigua, 1823 by W. Clark p166, *The Crusher Squeezes Juice from the Cane*, Antigua 1823 by W. Clark p166, *Slaves Ladle Steaming Juice from Vat to Vat*, Antigua, 1823 by W. Clark p167, all from British Library/Bridgeman Art Library, London; reproduced by courtesy of the Trustees of the British Museum pp8, 34, 68, 98; City of Bristol Museum and Art Gallery p57; reproduced by kind permission of City of Bristol Record Office, owned by Bristol City Council, reference 04720(1) p33; Bulloz pp84, 86, 87, 90, 102; Commissioner of Public Works in Ireland p41; Communist Party Library p122; The Corporation of London Records Office p10; Country Life p60; Rude, Paris, Arc de Triomphe, 'La Marseillaise', © DACS 1995 p102; Dudley Library p124; the collection of the Duke of Roxburghe p44; Edinburgh University Library p66; English Heritage pp14, 42; Mary Evans Picture Library pp50, 51, 60, 74, 88, 96, 108, 110, 126, 130, 132; Explorer p82; The Fotomas Index pp32, 48, 70, 72, 94; John Frost Picture Library p140; Photographie Giraudon p36; Sonia Halliday Photographs pp28 (pic 5), 30 (pic 3); *A History of Dahomey* by A Dalziell, 1793 p170 (pic 1); Michael Holford Photographs pp8, 9, 16, 17, 28; Hulton Deutsch Collection Ltd pp20, 21, 22, 31, 120, 130, 138, 150, 158, 160, 164, 176; The Illustrated London News p118; Imperial War Museum, London pp 133, 136, 137, 138, 140, 141, 144, 150, 156, 158; *Paths of Glory*, 1917 by CRW Nevinson (1899-1946), Imperial War Museum, London/Bridgeman Art Library p134; A F Kersting pp37, 54; Laing Art Gallery, Newcastle upon Tyne (Tyne and Wear Museums) p32; Library of Congress p179; Louisiana State Museum p168; The Mansell Collection pp14, 34, 38, 44, 45, 46, 47, 60, 62, 65, 68, 73, 76, 102, 106, 110, 112, 114, 116 (pics 1, 3), 118, 122, 128, 138, 140, 146, 148, 170, 171, 172; *I Hope the Game Finishes Soon*, Musee de la Ville de Paris, Musee Carnavalet/Giraudon/Bridgeman Art Library, London p80; The National Museum of Wales p42; The National Museum of Labour History p116; The National Portrait Gallery, London pp31, 48, 62, 63, 64, 68; New York Public Library p174 (pic 1); Novosti (London) 1992, *Panfilov Guardsmen's Exploit* (fragment) by V R Panfilov p132; reproduced from the 1:250 000 Ordnance Survey Salisbury Central map with the permission of the Controller of Her Majesty's Stationery Office © Crown copyright p27; Picturepoint p28; Plymouth City Museum and Art Gallery p56; Popperfoto pp146, 160; The Public Record Office, Richmond p10; The Royal Commission on the Historical Monuments of England © RCHME Crown Copyright pp26 (pic 3), 30, 31, 37; *Trade Emblems of the Associated Shipwrights Society*, Trades Union Congress, London/Bridgeman Art Library, London p120; by courtesy of the Centre for the Study of Cartoons and Caricature, University of Kent at Canterbury: Low, David, *Evening Standard* 27th July 1945 p160; Low, David, *Evening Standard* 19th January 1933 p146; *Evening Standard* pp154, 164; *Vicky: A Memorial Volume*, Allen Lane, The Penguin Press, 1967 p160: all copyright Solo Syndication & Literary Agency Ltd; The Master and Fellows of Trinity College Cambridge pp36, 49; The University of Reading, Rural History Centre pp106, 124; courtesy of the Trustees of the V&A Museum pp56, 66; Wilberforce Museum pp174 (pic 2), 177; Woodmansterne Ltd pp9, 24, 30, 43, 54.

Material from the National Curriculum is Crown copyright and is reproduced by permission of the Controller of HMSO.

I ntroduction

S UCCESSFUL STUDYING AT KEY STAGE 3

During Key Stage 3 of the National Curriculum, you will have to study the following subjects:

English, Mathematics, Science, Technology, a modern foreign language (usually French or German), Geography and History.

This stage of your education is very important because it lays the foundation which you will need to embark upon your GCSE courses. The National Curriculum requires you and all 11–14 year olds to follow the same programmes of study, which define the knowledge and skills you will need to learn and develop during your course.

At school, your teachers will be monitoring your progress. At the end of Key Stage 3, your performance will be assessed and you will be given a National Curriculum level. Most students should reach level 5 or level 6, some may reach levels 7 or 8, or perhaps even higher. In English, Mathematics and Science, you will have to take a National Test towards the end of your last year at Key Stage 3. The results of your tests, also marked in levels, will be set alongside your teachers' assessment of your work to give an overall picture of how you have done.

How this book will help you

This book is designed for you to use at home to support the work you are doing at school. Think of it as a companion or study guide to help you prepare for class work and homework. Inside the book, you will find the level descriptions which will be used to assess your performance. We have included them in the book so that, as you near the end of Key Stage 3, you will be able to check how well you are doing.

Reading the book, and doing the questions and activities will help you get to grips with the most important elements of the National Curriculum. Before you begin to read the book itself, take a few moments to read the introductory sections on 'History in the National Curriculum' and 'How to use this book'.

HISTORY IN THE NATIONAL CURRICULUM

All pupils will study History at Key Stage 3 (Years 7, 8 and 9) and the National Curriculum ensures that all pupils are taught a broad outline of both British and World History.

You will study four core units, which are covered in this book.

They are:

1) Medieval realms: Britain 1066–1500.
2) The making of the United Kingdom: Crown, Parliament, people 1500–1750.
3) Britain 1750–1900.
4) The 20th-century world.

These units will be taught chronologically. Year 7 pupils (age 11 and 12) will study core unit 1. Year 8 pupils (age 12 and 13) will study core unit 2 and year 9 pupils (age 13 and 14) will study core units 3 and 4.

In addition to the core units, you will study two supplementary units; one from each of the two categories A and B:

- Category A is a unit involving the study of an era or turning point in European History before 1914. Examples of these units are:
  - The Roman Empire.
  - The Crusades.
  - The French Revolution.

- Category B is a unit involving the study of a past non-European society. Examples of these units are:
  - Black Peoples of America.
  - Imperial China from the First Emperor to Kubla Khan.
  - The civilizations of Peru.

During your Key Stage 3 education, you will be taught and assessed according to **one** Attainment Target called HISTORY. Under this target you will be helped to develop and communicate your historical knowledge and understanding and shown how to use and interpret a variety of historical sources.

By setting a variety of work, your teachers will assess the level which you have achieved within the target. This level will be included in your end of year school report. You will find the level descriptions at the back of this book, just before the glossary.

By the end of Key Stage 3, not only will you be familiar with many different periods in British, European and World History, you will have been learning how to think and act as an historian.

Good luck and enjoy National Curriculum History!

H OW TO USE THIS BOOK

If you look at the contents page you will see that this book includes the four compulsory (core) study units as laid down in the National Curriculum.

This book also includes two supplementary units. From Category A we have offered **The French Revolution**. From Category B we have offered **Black Peoples of America**.

The study units have been broken down into a number of topics each of which is covered on two pages, called a 'double-page spread'. Each double-page spread consists of three sections.

1) **An introduction text** describing the main events involved in the topic. This text will give you the background knowledge which you need to know about the particular topic.
2) **Two kinds of historical sources:** written extracts and illustrations.
3) **A 'Now test yourself' section** in which you answer questions on the text and the sources. Sometimes in these questions you are asked to look back at earlier double-page spreads so that you can discover how events often have long-term causes and effects.

Studying history

You will find that your teacher will tackle the topics covered in this book in the core study units and possibly also in the two supplementary units. Since it may be difficult for you to take your school text book home, you will find this book useful in giving you extra information and sources to help you with your homework and revision for class tests. If you are set a project or a 'personal enquiry' task, this book will help you to work at home, or on your own at school.

You should get used to using local libraries and, especially, the advice of the library staff to help you with your work at school.

Libraries will be able to offer you a catalogue of books, help in getting any book you may need through the inter-library lending system and help in finding out the addresses of local places of interest, local Records Offices and local branches of the Historical Association, whose members may well be able to help you with your work.

You might find it useful to have either a folder or an exercise book in which to keep your answers to the various questions. You should also look at the level descriptions at the back of the book and think about what these level descriptions are looking for when writing your answers.

It is hoped that you will enjoy both using the material offered in this book and thinking about the history involved. As you work your way through the book you will not only develop your knowledge of the past, but also an historian's skill in dealing with historical evidence.

*M*edieval realms: Britain 1066–1500

WE THREE KINGS OF ENGLAND ARE

Who was to succeed 'the saintly Edward' when he died on 5 January 1066? Earl Harold of Wessex, Edward's brother-in-law, England's leading nobleman and Edward's choice, was crowned on 6 January after the Council (*picture 1*) had elected him as their king (*extract A*).

1. A Saxon King and his Witan.

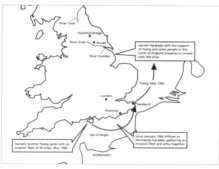

2. Harold's problems January–September 1066.

King Hardrada of Norway said that Harthacnut, King of England in 1042, promised the crown to his family. He was supported by the King of Scotland and Harold's brother, Tostig, the favourite of their sister Queen Edith. Harold finally defeated both of his rivals at the Battle of Stamford Bridge on 25 September 1066.

William, Duke of Normandy, said Edward had promised *him* the crown (*extract B*) and that Harold had sworn to support him (*extract C and picture 3*). Harold said that the oath had been made under pressure: he feared that he would be kept in prison or killed if he had not taken the oath.

The Pope believed William, who took six months to prepare an invasion (*picture 4*). On 27 September he landed at Pevensey but rushed to Hastings, a better harbour from which to sail if he was defeated. He built a motte and bailey castle (page 14, *picture 1*) and waited for Harold, who had gone to Yorkshire to defeat Hardrada and Tostig.

The Battle of Hastings took place on 14 October 1066, and the Normans were victorious (*extract D and picture 5*). William took his time getting to London (*picture 6*) where he was crowned on Christmas Day and where he built a motte and bailey Tower of London (*picture 7*) as a refuge and stronghold.

The **Bayeux Tapestry** (*pictures 3–5*) is a strip cartoon, about 69 metres (230 feet) long. It is sewn in wool on linen. Bishop Odo of Bayeux (William the Conqueror's brother) had it made for him by English needlewomen: it still hangs in Bayeux and is a valuable source for historians.

The **Anglo-Saxon Chronicle** (*extract A* and pages 10–11 and 20–21) is not one document but a series of records written in English between 900 and 1150. It is the oldest set of records in any European language, other than Latin. Some of the records were written at Winchester, others at Canterbury and Peterborough.

3. Harold promising the crown to Duke William.

4. Preparing the invasion fleet.

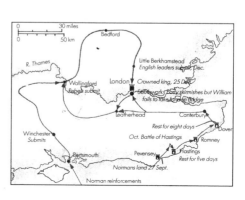

6. March of the Norman army, October–December 1066.

5. To quell rumour of his death, William removes his helmet crying, 'Look at me well! I am still alive and by God's grace I shall yet prove victor.'

7. The White Tower, Tower of London.

EXTRACT A
Edward gives the Crown to Harold

And Earl Harold succeeded to the throne just as the King had granted it to him and as he had been chosen to the position.

(*Anglo-Saxon Chronicle*, c 11th century)

EXTRACT B
Edward promises the Crown to William

In 1063 Edward gave William, whom he loved like a son, and whom he had already named his heir in 1051, a more serious pledge. He sent Harold to William to confirm his promise by oath.

(William of Poitiers writing in 1073 or 1076)

EXTRACT C
William's account of Harold's visit: a speech made at Hastings, 1066

'On the journey, Harold was in danger of being taken prisoner by Guy of Ponthieu. I rescued him by threat of war. Through his own hands he made himself my subject and gave me a firm pledge about the throne of England.'

(Quoted by William of Poitiers)

EXTRACT D
A Norman account of the Battle of Hastings

The English were as brave as we were. With their battle-axes and with men hurling spears and stones, they repelled our attacks when we came to close quarters, and they killed many of our men shooting missiles from a distance. Indeed our men began to retreat; disobeying Harold's orders, the English footmen chased them from the field. It was only William's courage which saved us. Three times he had horses killed beneath him; each time he leapt to the ground and killed the footman who had killed his horse. Fighting on foot he split shields, helmets and coats of mail with his great sword. Seeing his men fleeing, he took off his helmet and cried, 'Look at me well! I am still alive and by God's grace I shall yet prove victor.' This inspired his tired men who gathered for a final charge in which Harold was killed. Seeing this, the English fled as quickly as they could, leaving the bloodstained battleground covered with the flower of youth and nobility of England.

(William of Poitiers)

Now test yourself

Knowledge and understanding

Using the text and *extracts B, C and D* give:
(a) one reason why William thought he should be king; (b) one reason why Harold thought he should be king; (c) the reasons for William's victory over Harold.

Using the sources

1 How can *each* of the *pictures 2, 4, 5 and 6* be used by historians writing about the battles of 1066 between Harold and William?
2 Which of these pictures is most useful? Explain your answer.

J UST WILLIAM

Some of Harold's followers were angry at William's success (*extract A*) and others refused to accept Norman rule. William had to cope with many rebellions (*picture 1*). So how did he manage to impose Norman rule on England?

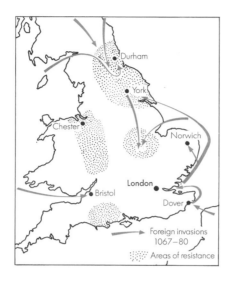

1. Revolts and invasions, 1067–80.

Foreign invasions 1067–80

Areas of resistance

❶ He promised to follow 'saintly Edward's' laws and customs (*picture 2*).

❷ He acted as owner of all the land. He kept a quarter for himself, gave the Church a quarter, and rewarded Normans with most of the rest.

❸ He, and his Norman barons, built castles from which they imposed their rule on the surrounding areas (pages 14–15).

❹ Although his barons had sworn an oath of loyalty to him, William knew that, in Edward's England and his own Normandy, powerful landowners had challenged their overlord's power. They relied on the support of the knights to whom they had sub-let some of their land, and from whom they got an oath of loyalty. So, in 1086, William made every landowner swear an oath of loyalty to him personally (*extracts B, C and D*).

❺ William spent Christmas 1085 at his Gloucester estate: he and other landowners went from one estate to another to 'live off the produce of their land'. It was at Gloucester that William decided to find out exactly what went on in his kingdom (*extract E*). His shire officers worked so efficiently that by the time he came to Salisbury in August 1086 they could give him the pages of sheepskin, sewn together to form a book, which contained all the details he had asked for. The book was so complete that it was soon called the Domesday Book because people compared it with what might happen on the Last Day of Judgement.

4. A page from the Domesday Book.

2. William I's charter to the citizens of London.

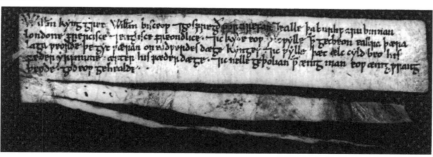

3. A knight taking an oath to his king.

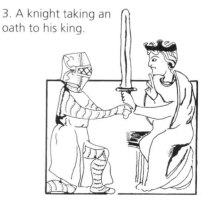

Interpretations by later historians. Edward Freeman (*extract C*) was a famous historian who gave his own views (or interpretations) of past events. Such views are called secondary sources, although historians will have studied many primary sources during their research. Other similar secondary sources will be found on pages 19 (*extract C*), 23 (*extract A*) and 36 (*extracts A and C*).

EXTRACT A
An angry Saxon bishop on William's success

'Such was the feebleness of the wretched people that after the first battle they never tried to rise up for their freedom. It was as though that when Harold fell so, too, fell the whole strength of the country.'

(Quoted in *Social History of England*, A. Briggs, 1983)

EXTRACT B
The Oath of Salisbury, 1086

William came to Salisbury on 1 August. There came to him all the landowners of England, no matter whose vassal they might be. They all submitted to him and became his vassals, and swore oaths of allegiance to him, that they would be loyal to him against all other men.

(*Anglo-Saxon Chronicle*, c11th century)

EXTRACT C
The significance of the Oath of Salisbury

On that day England became for ever a kingdom, one and indivisible, which since that day no man has dreamed of parting asunder.

(The historian Edward Freeman, 1868)

EXTRACT D
A baron's oath to the King

I become your man from this day forward, for life and limb and loyalty. I shall be true and faithful to you for the lands I hold from you.

EXTRACT E
The Domesday Book's origins

After this, the King met with his council to discuss this country – how it was occupied and with what sort of people. Then he sent his men over all England into every shire, and had them find out how many hundred hides there were in the shire, what land and cattle the King himself had in the country, what taxes were due in each year from the shire. He had a record made of how much land his archbishop had, and his bishops, abbots, earls … what or how much everybody had who occupied land in England, in land or cattle, and how much money it was worth. So very closely did he have it investigated that there was not a hide or virgate of land, not one ox or cow or pig which was left out of his record.

(*Anglo-Saxon Chronicle*)

EXTRACT F
Making the Domesday inquiry at Ely

The King's officials met the priest, the reeve and six men from each village. They inquired what the manor was called, and who held it in the time of King Edward; who holds it now; how many hides there are, how many ploughs, villeins, cottars, slaves, freemen; how much woodland and meadow; how many mills; what the estate is worth now. And it was also to be noted whether more could be taken from the estate than is now being taken.

(*The Domesday Book*)

EXTRACT G
An extract from the Domesday Book, 1086

Eaton Constantine
King William owned Eaton Constantine.
Earl Roger of Montgomery, as Tenant-in-Chief, holds the manor of Eaton Constantine from King William.
Rainald the Knight holds the manor of Eaton Constantine from Earl Roger of Montgomery.
Rainald kept the demesne farm which four cottars (slaves) worked with two ploughs.
Rainald let one villein and four bordars (poor peasants) work on small plots.

(*The Domesday Book*)

Now test yourself

Knowledge and understanding

Read the text and *extracts B, C and F*. (a) Why did William strengthen the feudal system in England? (b) In what ways did the Normans (i) change some aspects of life in England *but* (ii) leave other aspects unchanged?

Using the sources

(a) What do you learn from *extracts E, F and G* about the way William hoped to use the Domesday survey? (b) Make a list of the questions which you think the Domesday commisssioners asked in each village.

THE FEUDAL SYSTEM

What was the feudal system?

- *Feud* was the land given to someone in return for service to its owners.
- The feudal system described the way in which owners of land (king, nobles, churchmen and peasants) were linked to one another.

Some historians still claim that William I imposed a new system of organization on the country called the feudal system. In fact, there was a strong feudal system in Anglo-Saxon times (*extract A*). There was no way in which a king could control the whole of England in the 9th century. Saxon kings had put parts of their country under the rule of important followers (called earls). These earls had to provide the king with soldiers in time of war and promise to be loyal. The earls gave some parts of their land to thegns or knights who had to form part of the earl's armed force in time of war. These knights gave part of their land to peasants or farmers.

'Every man had his lord' in this system. Each lord had to protect his 'subject' against lawbreakers and invaders.

William's 'system'

We have seen that William divided the land among his followers, keeping about one-quarter for himself (*picture 1*). He knew that his more powerful followers (barons) might rebel in spite of oaths of loyalty. So while he gave these 200 men large amounts of land, he made sure their holdings were divided up, with, for example, one baron owning land in Wiltshire, Middlesex, Hertfordshire, Sussex and Surrey. This kept the barons going around their estates and made it hard for them to raise a rebel army.

He allowed three barons to have larger holdings at Hereford, Shrewsbury and Shropshire, hoping that they would hold back the threat from Wales.

1. Castles of the Norman conquest and royal dwellings and royal forests at the end of the 12th century.

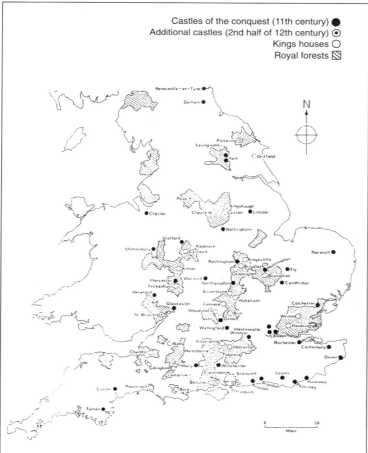

Castles of the conquest (11th century) ●
Additional castles (2nd half of 12th century) ◉
Kings houses ○
Royal forests ▨

What was new about William's 'system' and rule?

- He was ruthless in putting down any uprising. In 1067 one of his barons, Eustace of Boulogne, sided with a Saxon rising in Kent. William's army destroyed the rebels. In 1068 he crushed rebellions in Devon and Gloucester, and defeated the Saxon earls Edwin and Morcar – but when they gave in to him, he allowed them to keep their land. In 1069 Edgar of the old line of Wessex kings joined King Swein of Denmark in a Northern rebellion. William took two years to put down this rising, destroying most of the northern counties as he did so (*extracts C and D*).
- He had all landowners swear the Oath of Salisbury (page 11, *extracts B and C*). Saxon kings had received oaths of loyalty only from their earls who had received such oaths from their thegns. Now all landowners swore loyalty to the king.

The feudal system did not stay exactly the same throughout the Middle Ages. England continued to be ruled by the monarchy. The barons, including some abbots, were still the most powerful people after the king, followed by the knights and the peasants. However, during the Middle Ages the way people thought and behaved gradually changed which caused the feudal system to decay (see page 22).

EXTRACT A
Anglo-Saxon 'feudal' system

Laboratores (workers) are they who provide us with sustenance, ploughmen and farmers devoted to that alone.
Oratores (people who pray) are they who intercede for us to God and promise Christianity among people, a spiritual toil devoted to that alone for the benefit of us all.
Bellatores (fighters) are they who guard our boroughs and also our land, fighting with weapons against the oncoming army.

(Aelfric, Abbot of Eynsham, medieval historian, c 1066)

EXTRACT B
The knights' feudal duties, 1100

Knights have their lands in return for military service. They should not have to pay any rents or taxes for their lands. In return, they should be equipped with a coat of mail, and enough horses and weapons, so that they can defend the kingdom.

(Coronation Oath of Henry I, 1100)

EXTRACT C
A Norman description of the Northern rebellion, 1069

They captured York and pulled down the castle and seized the treasure in it. They killed hundreds of Normans and took many of them to their ships.

(William of Poitiers, 1071)

EXTRACT D
A Norman description of William's treatment of the North

The royal forces approached York, only to learn that the Danes had fled. The King ordered his men to repair the castles in the city. He himself continued to comb forests and remote mountainous places, stopping at nothing to hunt out the enemy hidden there. He cut down many in his vengeance; destroyed the lairs of others; harried the land, and burned homes to ashes. Nowhere else had William shown such cruelty. He made no effort to control his fury and punished the innocent with the guilty. In his anger he ordered that all crops, herds and food of every kind should be brought together and burned to ashes, so that the whole region north of the Humber might be stripped of all means of sustenance. As a result of this such a terrible famine fell upon the humble and defenceless people that more than 100,000 Christian folk of both sexes, young and old alike, perished of hunger.

(Roger Wace)

Now test yourself

Knowledge and understanding

Explain (a) how the way the feudal system worked under the Saxon kings was both (i) similar to and (ii) different from the feudal system under the Normans; (b) how William dealt with his enemies.

Using the sources

Study *extracts B, C, D* and *picture 1*. (a) Do you agree that these sources are useful and reliable for historians writing about the way the Norman Kings controlled England? (b) Do you agree that the evidence on pages 10–11 and 12–13 show that William was a ruthless King? Explain your answer.

BARONS IN THEIR CASTLES

Saxons were forced to build William's first castle at Hastings, as a place of retreat if he was attacked by the defeated Saxons (*picture 1*). They dug a large circular ditch, throwing the earth up to form a mound (motte). On top they built a fort from timbers brought in the invasion fleet. Then they dug a ditch to enclose a larger area (bailey) where, later, they put huts for the castle servants, a blacksmith's forge, chapel, bakery and so on.

1. Digging the ditch for William's first castle at Hastings.

2. Motte and bailey castle at Elsdon, Northumberland. The ditch is still visible, the wooden castle long gone.

3. The 12th century Norman keep at Castle Hedingham.

Around the motte and bailey castle, they put a wooden fence for protection. A wooden bridge linked the motte and the bailey (*picture 2*). Later this was replaced by a drawbridge which could be raised in an emergency.

William's barons built similar castles on their new estates as refuges in case they were attacked by the Saxons (page 12, *picture 1*). By 1070 about 400 had been built. Later, when they felt safe, the barons replaced their wooden castles with stone ones. Wooden ones could more easily be set on fire by an enemy, and, in any case, wood got wet and eventually rotted. Many of these early castles have disappeared (*picture 2*); many more are mere ruins.

The first stone castles were fairly simple (*picture 3*). The tower was called a *keep* since people kept their goods there. Its walls could be more than 3 metres thick. Inside there were few rooms (*picture 4*) and little comfort: the damp air and winds came through the narrow slits (*winds eyes*) making the stone building even colder. Later castles were much larger and had stone defensive walls around the castle area. These had defensive towers which became more rounded and more difficult to attack as builders became more skilled and learned from Arab builders. Walls and keeps were given crenallated battlements – men hid behind the higher parts and threw missiles through the gaps. Edward I's Welsh castles were even more developed (pages 42–3, *pictures 3 and 4*).

Castles were easy to defend as long as food and water lasted. Attackers used various methods to try to break down walls. A wheeled belfry (*picture 5*) put across a filled-in moat allowed miners to dig beneath the walls (*sapping*). They then filled the dug-out area with wood, which was lit to dry out the mortar holding the stones together and make the wall collapse. Other men used the belfry's *drawbridge* to get over the wall, while archers fired at the defenders from the top of the belfry. Here the defenders had the easier task, sheltered by the castle walls (*extracts A and B*).

During the 14th century, attackers learned to use gunpowder to fire metal balls at walls and defenders. Castles became less easy to protect and many nobles gave them up and built more comfortable country houses (page 54, *pictures 1 and 2*).

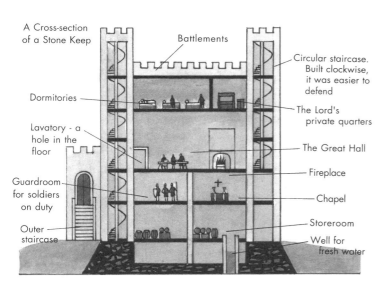

4. An artist's impression of the interior of a keep such as Hedingham (*picture 3*).

5. An artist's impression of attackers using a belfry.

EXTRACT A
How King Stephen captured Exeter Castle, 1136

Its castle is on a high mound protected by towers of stone and strong walls. Inside, Baldwin had a strong garrison to man the walls and towers. They taunted the King and his men as they approached the walls. They made some unexpected sorties and fell upon the Royal army. At other times they shot arrows and threw missiles from above.

The King built lofty wooden towers from which he attacked the defenders, day and night. He got his slingers to annoy the enemy by hurling stones. He used miners to dig under the fortifications. He had all types of machines built, some of great height (to see what went on inside the castle), others level with the foot of the walls to batter them down. The besieged destroyed these machines: all the cleverness spent on their building was wasted – until the water supply ran out.

(Adapted from an eyewitness account in a medieval chronicle)

EXTRACT B
An attack on Rochester Castle, 1215

As well as firing stones from catapults and slings, and arrows and bolts from handbows and crossbows, the knights and their men made many attacks. When some men tired, fresh ones took their place, and gave the defenders no rest. At last the King used miners. Many of the royal troops had been killed, and his siege machines were useless. Soon the miners undermined most of the wall. By now the defenders' food was running out; they even ate their horses.

(Adapted from an eyewitness account in a medieval chronicle)

Now test yourself

Knowledge and understanding

Using the text, extracts and pictures, explain (a) why the Normans built castles when they came to England; (b) how castles changed in their appearance through the Middle Ages; (c) how they could be both (i) attacked and (ii) defended.

Using the sources

Study *extracts A and B* and *pictures 1–5*.
(a) How can each of the pictures help us to write about the history of castles? (b) Do the extracts help us to understand why castles became less easy to defend?

BARONS AND KNIGHTS LIVED TO FIGHT

On page 12 we saw that Saxon kings and their Norman successors gave large parts of their land to their more important followers, e.g. the Norman barons. We also saw that these barons gave parts of their landholdings to some of their followers called knights. If you play chess you will know that the piece called a knight usually has a horse's head. This is because, in earlier times, the word knight meant servant (or follower) on horseback.

1. Servants with the knight's armour.

In return for his grant of land, a knight had to spend forty days every year in the king's army, bringing his own horse, weapons and band of foot soldiers (page 13, *extract B*). You will see that the knights made up the cavalry (or horsemen) of an army, while his followers made up the infantry (or foot soldiers).

Picture 1 shows servants bringing the Norman knight his armour. The trousers and long coat were made of iron rings linked together – this was chain mail. The helmet had a piece covering the nose. Later on, as craftsmen became more skilled, armour improved and the whole body was covered by a metal suit. Some suits weighed about 30kg, so knights' horses had to be powerful animals. The knights' main weapons were the lance – a long thin spear – and the sword. You can see both of these in *picture 1*. Later on knights had very well-developed and strong metal lances. On their shields, and on a flag on the end of their lances, each knight had his own badge (or coat of arms) which was designed and coloured by important officials called heralds. They worked to strict rules (called heraldry) so that everyone knew to whom each design belonged.

The knight's main feudal duty was to fight his lord's enemies. He knew that he might die in battle, but he also knew that he was much more likely to be captured if his lord's side lost a battle. If he was captured by an enemy knight, his family or his villagers would pay a ransom to persuade his captor to let him go free.

Knights' sons were prepared from an early age to become knights themselves. At 7 years of age they were sent to live in another nobleman's castle. They had to be his personal servant, or page: they waited on him at table and helped him to dress. In return the lord taught the page how to behave, wear armour, ride and use a sword and lance (*picture 2*).

At the age of 15 the page became a squire. Now he had to follow his lord into battle, the hunting field and in the tournament (*extract A*). He had to guard his lord from attack, look after his horse, carry his shield and help dress him in his armour (*pictures 1 and 3*).

When he was 21 years old the squire could become a knight if his lord or the king decided that he was fully prepared. The young man spent the night before his knighting in prayer (the vigil). He was supposed to think about his knightly duties – to be kind to women in particular and to everyone in general, to be brave and honest, to be loyal to his lord and king, and gentle with his inferiors. After the vigil, his baronial master, or perhaps the king, took the young man to the other knights in the castle, palace, battlefield or tournament and tapped him on the shoulders with a sword, presented him with his spurs to wear behind his heels, and informed everyone that the young man was now to be called Sir, followed by his name.

There were many years when knights were not called on to go to war for their lord. During the autumn and winter the war-trained knights, their squires and pages kept themselves busy hunting in the nearby forests. During the spring and summer they took part in mock battles, called tournaments, to stop them getting bored. These were like real battles except that only blunt weapons were used. *Extract A* makes a tournament sound like a carnival. However, even with blunt weapons, some tournaments got out of hand, and in one more than sixty knights were killed, while others were trampled to death.

Because of such dangers, knights then invented the joust. This took place in the same type of field and with the same sort of spectators as described in *extract A*. But in the joust, two knights rode against each other. Each had his lance which was about 3 metres long, which was used to try to knock the opponent off his horse. The defeated knight had to give his horse and armour and pay a ransom to the winner.

When a king went on a Crusade, or wanted to fight a long war in Europe, he needed followers who would stay longer than the forty days' service which his knights owed him. So, from the 13th century onwards, kings began to allow knights to pay them shield money (or scutage from the Latin for shield) instead of coming to serve for forty days. This gave kings enough money to pay those knights who were willing to serve for as long as a war lasted. These were mercenaries (from the Latin word for reward).

2. A knight practising with his sword and lance.

3. Knighthood.
1 The squire of the knight holds his shield
2 The squire helps the knight to dress
3 The King ties the knight's sword, the squire puts on his spurs.

EXTRACT A
A tournament at Smithfield, 1390

It was to take place on Monday. Sixty knights were going to tilt with blunt lances against all comers. The prize was a rich crown of gold. On Tuesday squires were going to tilt against others of their rank. Their prize was a war horse saddled and bridled.

On Sunday afternoon sixty decorated war horses, each ridden by a squire, processed out of London. Following them came sixty noble ladies riding highly decorated ponies, each leading a knight in armour. This procession moved through London to Smithfield where the Queen of England, her ladies, as well as the King were waiting. Servants led the ladies to the pavilions prepared for them. The knights waited until the squires had brought their war horses. When the tournament began many were unhorsed, and many more lost their helmets. The joust went on until night came. Then everyone went to the feast.

On Tuesday the squires tilted until nightfall, in the presence of the King, Queen and all the nobles. Supper was, again, at the Bishop's palace, and the dancing went on until daybreak. On Wednesday knights and squires all jousted together. The rest of the week was spent in feasting and dancing.

(*Chronicles*, Jean Froissart, c 1390)

Now test yourself

Knowledge and understanding

1 Make a list of the stages in the life of a young man on his way to becoming a knight and explain what his life was like at each stage.

2 Look at *picture 1* and page 38, *picture 2*. (a) How does the armour of William's knights (*picture 1*) compare with the armour of a knight in the late Middle Ages? (b) Why did armour change over the years?

Using the sources

1 Do you think the sources and text in this topic show that being a knight was all about fighting? Give evidence to (a) support and (b) disprove that idea.

2 How can we use the pictures in this topic to help us understand (a) the duties of squires and knights; (b) the customs of the time?

To THE MANOR BORN

William's barons rewarded their followers with grants of land. These were the manors where people produced almost everything they needed. *Picture 1* is a medieval plan of a manor. In the centre is the manor house and the lord's private estate (demesne) with some outbuildings – chapel, stables, kitchens, barns, perhaps a mill, and a forge (*picture 2*). A wall gave the lord some privacy. To the north, three houses represent villagers' homes. Elsewhere you can see forests, animals to be hunted for food, and fields (pages 20–21). Villagers had to make various payments for their share of the fields (*extract A*). The manor house was usually stone built, with defence in mind. Inside, a large hall contained a grand table (*extract B*), stools or chairs. The rest of the house was poorly furnished: rushes on stone floors, a few beds, some chests for clothes – and little else. The house was the centre of an industrial estate and, for two or three hundred years, the place where the lord acted as judge in the manor court (*extract D*) with the help of a jury of 12 men.

Villagers' houses were small. The single room on the ground floor had a partition behind which animals were kept – a cow or two, a couple of pigs, chickens and so on. Some villagers made a bedroom from the loft which they reached by a ladder: others slept on the ground floor. They had little furniture – wooden dishes, a cooking pot and a few simple stools.

Both lord and villagers drank ale or wine: water was usually unfit to drink. For the villagers, the basic food was black bread which they had for breakfast at sunrise, for dinner at 10.00 am (with cheese or eggs) and for supper at 4.00 pm (with soup or stew). For most of the year they ate salted meat, mainly bacon from their pigs. Everyone hunted (*picture 6*) and fished to find extra food. Unlike the lord (*extract B*) villagers often had little to eat, and if there was a bad harvest, many died of starvation.

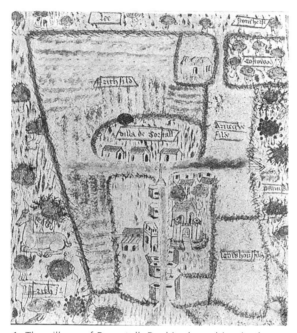

1. The village of Boarstall, Buckinghamshire, in the 15th century.

3. The barn at Godmersham – once the great hall of the manor.

4. Sir Geoffrey Luttrell and his family entertaining two Dominican friars.

8. Entertainers and musicians would perform for guests at castles and manor houses – particularly at festival times.

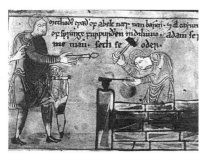

2. A 14th century blacksmith.

5. A lady hunting

6. Ladies at the end of a stag kill.

EXTRACT A
Manorial rolls

'These give us details of how manorial estates were run. On one the villeins each had a virgate of land (about 14 acres), for which they had to plough, sow and till half an acre of the lord's demesne: they had also to give such services as the lord's bailiff would demand, pay a quarter of seed-wheat at Michaelmas, a peck of wheat, four bushels of oats and three hens on 12 November, and at Christmas a cock, two hens and two-penn'orth of bread. There were also cash payments – a halfpenny on 12 November and a penny whenever they brewed ale. Each villein had also to reap three days at harvest time, but for this he received ale and a loaf of bread, and as large a sheaf of corn as he could carry home on his sickle.'

(Quoted in *Upper Class*, P. Lane, 1972)

EXTRACT B
Eating with the lord of the manor, c 1390

His bread, his ale were finest of the fine
And no one had a better stock of wine.
His house was never short of bake-meat pies,
Of fish and flesh, and these in such supplies
It positively snowed with meat and drink,
And all the dainties that a man could think.
According to the seasons of the year
Changes of dishes were ordered to appear.
He kept fat partridges in coops beyond,
Many a bream and pike were in his pond.
And in his hall a table stood arrayed
All ready all day long, with places laid.

(Geoffrey Chaucer, 1340–1400)

EXTRACT C
A hand-made world

It was a hand-made world throughout, a world without power, a world in which all things were made one by one, a world dependent upon human muscular power and the muscular power of draught animals, a slow world.

(E. Gill, quoted in *The Making of the English Landscape*, W.G. Hoskins, 1955)

EXTRACT D
At a manorial court, 1249

It was presented that Robert Carter's son by night invaded the house of Peter Burgess and in felony threw stones at his door so that the said Peter raised the hue. Therefore let the said Robert be committed to prison. Afterwards he made fine with 2s.
All the ploughmen of Great Ogbourne are convicted by the oath of 12 men … because by reason of their default [the land] of the lord was ill-ploughed whereby the lord is damaged to the amount of 9s … And, Walter Reaper is in mercy for concealing [not giving information as to] the said bad ploughing. Afterwards he made fine with the lord with one mark.

(*Select Pleas in Manorial Courts*, F.W. Maitland, 1889)

Now test yourself

Knowledge and understanding

1 In what ways was life on the manor (a) different from *but* (b) similar to life where you live today?
2 How did the lives of well-off lords compare with those of the ordinary villagers?

Use of sources

1 How do *each* of the pictures and extracts help you to understand what life on the manor was like?
2 Read *extract D*. How do you think that (a) Robert Carter, (b) the ploughman and (c) the lord felt after they had attended the manorial court?

D OWN ON THE FARM

In the Midlands and East Anglia manor farms consisted of three huge, unhedged (open) fields (*picture 1*), common land, and the surrounding forest. Each field went through a three-year cycle (rotation, *picture 2*). In year one it grew wheat or rye, in year two oats or barley, and in year three it was left unploughed (fallow) to give the land a chance to recover.

Villagers were given portions of land for their own use. The reeve (*picture 5*) divided the land so that no one was luckier than another, and so no one person had all the good land, while another had all the stony land. Each field was split into strips of about 200 metres by 20 metres and each villager had a number of strips in different parts of each field: some had 50, others only five, depending on whether they were freemen or cottars.

The villagers' year was a seasonal one (*picture 10*): in the spring the reeve supervised the preparation of the soil (*pictures 3, 4 and 9*); sowing of seed was done by men carrying bags of seed which they threw out by hand. In the summer came harvesting (*picture 5*). Then, when the corn ears had been flailed from the straw, each villager took their corn to be ground (*picture 8*). Villagers resented paying the lord for the use of the mill (*extract E*).

Villagers grazed their animals on the large common, and used the forest as a source for firewood and wattles to build their hut walls; for food – nuts, berries and gamebirds; and as the place where pigs could forage.

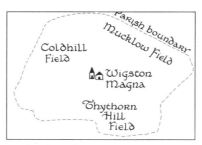

1. The three-field system, Wigston Magna, Leicestershire.

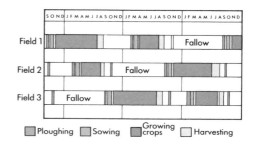

2. Rotation of the three-field system.

3. A two-oxened plough.

4. Horse-drawn harrow and plough.

5. Reeve supervising peasants at harvest time.

6. Shepherds keeping watch.

7. Bee catching.

8. Carrying corn to the mill.

9. Breaking up the soil.

10. Harvesting – from a medieval calendar.

EXTRACT A
The ploughman's view of life

I work very hard. At dawn I drive the oxen in the field and yoke them to the plough. However harsh the winter, I dare not stay at home, for fear of my lord. Every day I have to plough an acre or more. I have a boy who drives the oxen with a goad, and he is always hoarse from cold and shouting. I fill the ox-bins with hay and water, and I clear out the dung.

(*Aelfric*, Abbot of Eynsham, medieval historian, c 1066)

EXTRACT B
Diseases and hardship, 1131

In that year there was such a great animal plague as had never been before. It affected cattle and pigs; in a village that had 10 or 12 ploughs in action there was not one left. The man who had two or three hundred pigs was left with not one. Hens died, and meat, cheese and butter became scarce.

(*Anglo-Saxon Chronicle*)

EXTRACT C
Ploughman and shepherds

The art of the ploughman is in knowing how to make a straight furrow with the oxen. Ploughmen ought to encourage their oxen with melody and song. They must feed their animals, sleep with them at night, rub them down, make sure their food is not stolen. They should not be allowed to have a candle unless it is in a lantern. Shepherds should be intelligent, watchful and kind men who will not harry the sheep by their bad temper … should have a good barking dog and sleep with their sheep at night.

(*Fleta*, a Latin tract, 1289)

EXTRACT D
Dairymaids and swineherds

The dairymaid ought to be faithful and of good reputation, keep herself clean, know how to make cheese and salt cheese. The bailiff and reeve ought to inspect the dairy often.
The swineherd ought to be on manors where swine can be kept in the forest or woods or waste or in marshes without cost to the manor. During the winter there ought to be a pigsty where the swine can be kept day and night.

(*Husbandry*, Walter of Henley, c 1280)

EXTRACT E
The jolly (but wicked) miller

(a) There was a jolly miller once, lived on the river Dee;
He worked and sang from morn till night; no lark more blithe than he

(*Love in a Village*, Isaac Bickerstaffe, 1762)

(b) … a master hand at stealing grain.
He felt it with his thumb and knew
Its quality and took three times his due.

(*The Canterbury Tales*, Geoffrey Chaucer, c 1390)

(c) 'What is the boldest thing in the world?'
'A miller's shirt, because it clasps a thief daily by the throat.'

(A medieval riddle)

Now test yourself

Knowledge and understanding

Read the text and *extract B*. (a) Make a list of the (i) various jobs that had to be done on the farm; (ii) possible reasons for food shortages, some of which are mentioned in the extract. (b) Why did the lords of the manor suffer less than the peasants during times of food shortage?

Using the sources

Study the extracts and pictures. (a) What were the main problems facing medieval farmers? (b) Why were all the jobs done on the farm important? (c) Are these sources equally useful to historians writing about life on the farm? Give reasons for your answer.

THE BLACK DEATH AND SOCIAL CHANGE

By 1300 the population was three times greater than in 1066. To produce more food, parts of forests were cleared and marshes were drained (*picture 1*). Increased demand for cloth exports led to an increased demand for wool. Many landowners enclosed parts of the open fields behind hedges or stone walls, so that 'sheep could safely graze'. This helped speed up the process of commutation, by which peasants paid for their land with money instead of work-service (*extract A*).

In 1348 the people of England were attacked by a plague brought from abroad by black rats infected with plague-carrying fleas. People found large lumps under their armpits and their bodies covered with red and black spots (hence the Black Death).

1. The Somerset Levels: once marshy land drained between the 10th and 14th centuries.

It spread quickly (*extract B*): one-third of the population died. Some places were left with no inhabitants (*extract C*). Everywhere there were too few people to do the farm work. Some thought the disease was caused by the smell from diseased people: they hoped to be saved by carrying flowers. Others prayed (*picture 2*); many sold all they had (*extract D*) which pushed prices down. More land was turned into sheep farms which needed fewer workers. Some lords tried to attract workers by offering high wages (*extract E*) and peasants demanded the end of work-service (*extract A*).

Parliament passed laws to try to turn back the clock. In 1349 the Statute of Labourers ordered workers to return to their original manor. This Act and another in 1351 tried to force workers to accept lower wages (*extract F*). But even landowners ignored these laws: workers had enjoyed their freedom and the better living standards resulting from higher wages and falling prices (*extract G*).

The long decline of feudalism

On pages 12–13 we saw that feudalism involved the relationship between owners of land and their inferiors based on the rights and duties of both the landowner and the inferior towards each other. Money played little part in the relationship.

However, this system of land organization began slowly to change in the 12th century (*extract A*). The move to 'a cash economy' was given a further push in the 13th century when kings encouraged their barons and knights to give them a money payment (called shield money or scutage) instead of performing their forty days' military service a year (page 17).

Meanwhile Parliament's efforts angered the peasants. This helps to explain their part in the Peasants' Revolt (pages 38–9). This, in turn, marked another stage in the decline of feudalism.

2. Praying for a plague victim.

3. An insciption telling the horror of the plague: 'miserable … wild … distracted'.

EXTRACT A
'Commutation' – or money rents in place of work-service

In the 12th century many lords accepted money rents instead of work-service. Serfs still had to pay some work-service; they might even have to work on the lord's demesne for certain days if he chose to renew his claim. But reeves had learned that the demesne would be better cultivated by hired men, working the year round, than by the unwilling work of villeins taken from working on their own strips.

(*Medieval English Wool Trade*, E. Power, 1941)

EXTRACT B
The coming of the Black Death, 1348

The plague penetrated the coasts from Southampton and came to Bristol; there almost the whole population died, very few kept their beds for more than three days, or even half a day. In the small parish of St Leonard in Leicester more than 380 died; in the parish of Holy Cross more than 400, and so in each parish a great number.

(Henry Knighton, *Chronicle II*, Rolls Series, c 1363)

EXTRACT C
Deserted monasteries, parishes and villages

After the pestilence many buildings, great and small, fell into ruins in every borough and village, for lack of people; many places became deserted, all having died who lived there.

(Henry Knighton, c 1363)

EXTRACT D
The immediate fall in prices after the Black Death

There were falling prices everywhere because of fear of death. Few people cared about money or anything. You could buy a horse, once worth 40 shillings, for 6 shillings; sheep and cattle wandered over fields and crops failed because there was no one to look after them.

(Henry Knighton, c 1363)

EXTRACT E
Rising wages, 1348

In the autumn no one could get a reaper for less than 8 pence or a mower for less than 12 pence. So, many crops perished in the fields. But there was still such an abundance of corn that no one bothered.

(Henry Knighton, c 1363)

EXTRACT F
The Statute of Labourers, 1349

Because many people have died in this plague, some workers will not serve unless they get excessive wages. We have decided that anyone not earning a living from a craft or fully employed on his own land shall be bound to work for any lord who asks him to work, and shall receive the wage that used to be paid in 1347.

(Close Roll 23, Edward III, 1349)

EXTRACT G
Lords and labourers ignore Parliament and the law

The King sent laws that labourers should not take more than they had earned previously. But the workers would not listen. And if any lord wanted workers, he had to give them what they asked for. He had either to lose his crops, or satisfy the greed of the labourers.

(Henry Knighton, c 1363)

Now test yourself

Knowledge and understanding

1 List and explain the main reasons for the spread of the Black Death.
2 How did the Black Death affect (a) the size of the population; (b) manors and monasteries; (c) prices and workers' wages; (d) relationships between landlords and workers?

Using the sources

1 How do *extracts B, C D* and *picture 2* help you to understand how tragic the Black Death was for some people? Explain your answer.
2 Does *extract A* give a full explanation of how the feudal system changed in the 14th century? Explain your answer.

BISHOPS AND THEIR CATHEDRALS

Medieval kings wanted the Church to help keep the country peaceful (*extract A*). William I brought men from France to become bishops and abbots. They were great landowners and barons: the Bishop of Durham guarded the northern border; the Bishop of Winchester (*extract B*) had more knights than any earl. The Archbishop of Canterbury (*extract E*) was 'the First citizen of the Kingdom'. Kings had to make sure that such men were loyal to them (*extracts B, D, and E*).

1. Durham Cathedral: the nave.

2. Lincoln Cathedral: Angel Choir.

The country was divided into a number of dioceses, each with its bishop, with the Archbishop of Canterbury as the Primate (or chief bishop). Dioceses were divided into deaneries and, lower down, into parishes. Bishops set up schools in their dioceses: they licensed teachers and made sure that they taught what the Church, the king and lords wanted people to learn (*extract A*). Each bishop had his seat (cathedra) in his own church (or cathedral).

The first cathedrals, built in the 11th century, copied the Roman style and are known as Romanesque. They had thick walls, massive columns, round arches and few windows (*picture 1*). In the 13th century builders learned how to use thinner columns and walls, with pointed arches: walls were supported on the outside by flying buttresses. This Gothic style allowed for more windows and ceilings (*picture 2*). Later builders developed the decorated style (*picture 3*) and the perpendicular style.

Bishops ruled their dioceses and estates, and helped to run the country as government ministers or ambassadors. Some had too little time for Church work and some of their priests became greedy and lazy. Such behaviour was attacked by the writer Chaucer in *The Canterbury Tales*, by rebels in the Peasants' Revolt (pages 38–9) and by the Lollards (pages 30–31).

3. Exeter Cathedral showing decorated style.

4. King's College Chapel, Cambridge (1450–1500). This fan vaulting has been called 'the perfection of perpendicular Gothic'. Notice, too, the large windows.

EXTRACT A
Religion and the control of the peasants

The priest should ask the peasants whether they have cheated by not paying their full tithes to the church; whether they have been obedient to their lord; whether they have done all the work they should for the lord; whether they have broken into a neighbour's land with plough or animal. They must be told that it is a sin to work hard only when their lord is present and to be idle when he is absent, and they must not grumble when he corrects them.

(From a handbook for the medieval clergy, c 1380)

EXTRACT B
Henry II names a new Bishop of Winchester, 1173

'Greetings to my faithful monks of Winchester: I order you to hold a free election, but I forbid you to elect anyone except Richard, Archdeacon of Poitiers.'

(Quoted in *Thomas Becket, Archbishop of Canterbury*, A Duggan, 1952)

EXTRACT C (see page 30, *picture* 4)
St Bernard opposes church decoration

'What business have these useless monkeys, fierce lions, semi-human figures? Everywhere there is such a variety of shapes and forms that it is more pleasant to look at the marble than the books, and to spend the day like that and not on meditating on Divine Law.'

(Quoted in *Civilisation*, K. Clark, 1969)

EXTRACT D
Politician-bishops

William Longchamp started as a clerk, became Chancellor in 1189 and Justiciar in 1190, the most powerful posts in the government. As Regent, he ruled when Richard I went to the Crusades. In 1190 he became Bishop of Ely and papal legate, which gave him control of the Church in England. He was overfond of power and used it to benefit his family. One monk wrote: 'The laity found him more than a king, the clergy more than Pope, and both found him a tyrant.'

(*Religion*, H. Bodey, 1973)

EXTRACT E
Electing a new Archbishop of Canterbury, 1313

The prior and chapter of Canterbury unanimously elected Thomas de Cobham, a learned noble. But, while the old Archbishop was dying, the Pope had said that he would name the successor. The King asked the Pope to transfer the Bishop of Worcester to Canterbury. So, Thomas was not chosen, even though the chapter named him: the King paid the Pope to name Worcester. So, instead of a learned man we had an illiterate one. That's what money does for the Church.

(*The Life of Edward II*, N. Denholm-Young, 1957)

Now test yourself

Knowledge and understanding

1 Make a list of the ways in which, as time went on, cathedrals (a) changed in style; (b) remained unchanged in purpose.
2 Explain (a) why the Church was important in the Middle Ages; (b) why it became unpopular; (c) why English kings wanted to get control of the Church (*extracts B and E*).

Using the sources

(a) Read *extract C*. What do you think the author of this extract would have said about the view of the art historian, Kenneth Clark, that church art and decorations were aids to prayer and devotions? (b) How do you explain these differences of opinion? (c) Do pictures 1–4 show that historians ought to visit these places in order to understand the religious faith of medieval people? Explain your answer.

Monasteries

Anglo-Saxon monasteries followed the rule of St Benedict, 'the father of monasticism' (*extract A*). In 910 Benedictines at Cluny in France started a stricter form of life – Cluniac monasteries, such as the one at Lewes (*extract B*), were set up in England after 1066. In 1098 other Benedictines started an even stricter monastery at Citeaux in France. Some of these Cistercians came to England and founded monasteries: their most famous houses were Rivaulx and Fountains in Yorkshire. By the time of the Black Death there were over 600 monasteries and the same number of convents in England, some with over 700 inhabitants.

Most were built to a similar pattern: Fountains Abbey (*picture 1*) lay in a sheltered valley, the stream providing water for kitchens, lavatorium (washing place) and for taking away sewage. The most important building was the church: many of these are our cathedrals (page 24, *pictures 1–3*). The cloister was the covered passageway, where the monks read, heard lectures and wrote (*picture 2*). Each morning the monks met to read a chapter of their rule and, in the chapter house (*picture 3*), reached decisions about work to be done. They slept in the dormitory which had a staircase to the church. Meals were taken in silence in the frater. Other buildings included the abbot's private house where he entertained important visitors and the infirmary where monks and neighbours were treated.

Some boys joined monasteries as young as 7 years old. Most joined the novitiate (for newcomers) when they were older (*picture 4*). After a year, and provided he was 16 years old, a person could take vows of poverty (he would own nothing), chastity (or purity), obedience (to superiors) and stability (to stay in the same monastery for life).

In his simple clothes (*extracts A and C*) the monk prayed six times a day in the church: at 2.00 am (Matins), 7.00 am (Prime), 9.00 am (Tierce, or third prayer), 12.00 noon (Sext), 5.00 pm (Vespers, or evening prayer) and 7.00 pm (Compline, or final prayer). In between there was work in the kitchen, farm or library, building (*picture 5*), choir practice and so on. However, in time, many monks failed to live up to these ideals (*extracts D and E*). At Salisbury for example the monks became more concerned with the development of towns on their lands (*picture 6*).

1. Ground plan of Fountains Abbey.

2. A monk working on a manuscript.

3. The Chapter House of Westminster Abbey where the men elected from the counties and towns met as a separate 'House' of common people from early in the 14th century.

4. Taking monastic vows.

5. Monks at work.

6. Salisbury today.

EXTRACT A
From the Rule of St Benedict, 529

We are going to set up a home to serve God and we will never leave it. Eight times a day we will praise God. No one shall own anything – no book, pen, nothing. Monks shall be silent at all times, but especially after Compline. The normal clothes shall be a cloak and hood, a scapular for working time, shoes and stockings.

EXTRACT B
Founding a Cluniac house at Lewes, Sussex

My wife and I wish to fund some religious houses for our sins and souls. We give the monks a church built of stone, and as much land and beasts and goods as will keep 12 monks there.

(William de Warren, Earl of Surrey, 1077)

EXTRACT C
A novice on his hard but peaceful life, Rivaulx Abbey, 1239

'Our food is scanty, our clothes rough; our drink is from the stream and our sleep often on our book. Under tired limbs there is only a mat; when sleep is sweetest we must rise at the bell's call. There is no room for self-will, idleness or misbehaviour. But everywhere is peace and serenity.'

(Quoted in *Religion*, H. Bodey, 1973)

EXTRACT D
Dispute between merchants and the Abbot of Bury St Edmunds, 1304

Before the King's judges at the town of St Edmund, the merchants claim the right to form a guild and to make laws about their town. They agree the Abbot is lord of the town, but claim that they are free citizens who ought to be able to rule their town. The Abbot claimed that they had no such right and wanted to take away his control. The judges rule in the Abbot's favour, award him £200 in damages and send the leading merchants to jail.

(From a document in the British Museum)

EXTRACT E
Luxurious eating in a later monastery

'He described with relish the number of well-cooked dishes and sauces he had eaten with the monks at Canterbury. He had no appetite left, he said, for the main course of vegetables, and he praised also the wine, mead and fruit juice that went with the meal.'

(Quoted in *Food*, S. Ferguson, 1971)

Now test yourself

Knowledge and understanding

Using the text, *extracts A–C* and *picture 4* explain (a) why many people took up the monastic life; (b) how monasteries changed the lives of those who joined them *and* those who lived outside the monasteries.

Using the sources

1 How does *extract E* give a different view of monastic life from that given in *extracts A and C*? Why were there different views about monasteries in the Middle Ages?

2 Do you agree that the pictures in this topic are useful to historians trying to understand medieval monastic life? Why?

MURDER IN THE CATHEDRAL

Many people went on pilgrimages to places linked to their faith, such as Canterbury (*picture 2* and *extracts A and B*). Like modern 'fans' they collected badges (*picture 1*) from places they visited.

1. Pilgrimage badge from Canterbury.

The murder of Thomas Becket, Archbishop of Canterbury, was the result of the continual rows between kings and the Church (*extract C*). William I allowed the Church to have its own Courts of Justice where people of 'the clerical order' were tried if accused of crime. Henry II, trying to widen his power, wanted such 'clerics' to be sent to his courts for sentencing. That is why he had his friend Thomas Becket made Archbishop of Canterbury: Becket was already Chancellor, or chief minister. But Becket quarrelled with Henry over the courts question (*picture 3*) and fled to France. When the Archbishop of York crowned Henry's son as 'king-to-be', Becket excommunicated him and his supporters, cutting them off from the Church's life, a serious matter in Catholic England. Henry's anger at this led him to call for Becket's murder (*extracts F and G* and *picture 4*). The King had to bow before the storm of protest against the killing and accept punishment at Becket's cathedral (*picture 5*).

2. Pilgrims sharing a meal.

Shortly afterwards two new orders were founded. Francis of Assisi (1182–1226) founded an order whose men were to lead poor lives (*extract H*); Dominic (1170–1221) founded an order to give the Church highly intelligent leaders. Both of these orders aimed at reminding monks, nuns and other religious people about the real purpose of religious life. Dominic's intelligent followers were a challenge to ignorant monks, while Francis's poverty was a challenge to the worldly lives led by too many monks, nuns and priests (page 31, *extracts B and C*). Because too few were willing to change their lifestyles, the demand for church reform grew – and was one reason for the Reformation under Henry VIII (pages 50–51).

3. Becket arguing with Henry.

4. The murder of Thomas Becket.

5. Henry's penance at Canterbury.

EXTRACT A
Becket's shrine

I saw the magnificent tomb of St Thomas at Canterbury – beyond belief … entirely covered with plates of pure gold covered with all sorts of valuable jewels.

(*The Italian Relation of England*, Camden Society, c 1500)

EXTRACT B
Chaucer's pilgrims

Then people long to go on pilgrimages
And palmers long to see the stranger strands
Of far off saints, hallowed in sundry lands,
And specially, from every shire's end
In England, down to Canterbury they wend.

(*The Canterbury Tales*, c 1390)

EXTRACT C
Kings versus Popes

The King of England, though he does not always behave as devoutly as we wish, has not destroyed the churches of God: he tries to govern in peace and justice; he has not done anything to hurt the Papacy; he is more worthy of honour and approval than other Kings.

(Pope Gregory, 1081)

EXTRACT D
Becket warns Henry II when he becomes Archbishop, 1162

'If you were to ask of me anything which I could not bear quietly, the love you now bear me would turn to bitter hatred.'

(Quoted in *Thomas Becket, Archbishop of Canterbury*, A. Duggan, 1952)

EXTRACT E
Becket gives in to Henry II – but not quite, 1169

Thomas knelt before Henry and repeated the formula by which he accepted the King's power. Then he added the fatal clause, 'except for the honour of God and the rights of the Church and of my clerical order'.

(*Thomas Becket, Archbishop of Canterbury*, A. Duggan, 1952)

EXTRACT F
Henry's anger leads to murder

When news of the bishops' excommunication by Thomas reached Henry, he was at Sur-le-Roi near Bayeux. His anger burst through his reserve and he shouted words he was always after to regret. 'What sluggards and knaves have I fed in my house that they are faithless to their lord, and let him be tricked so infamously by one upstart clerk.'

(*Kings of Merry England*, P. Lindsay, 1935)

EXTRACT G
Becket's murder

In fury the knights called out, 'Where is Thomas Becket, traitor to the King?' He came down and in a clear voice said, 'I am here, no traitor to the King, but a priest. Why do you seek me?' 'Forgive the people you excommunicated,' they cried. 'I will not,' he answered. 'Then you shall die,' they cried. 'I am ready to die for my Lord, so long as the Church can have its freedom.'

(Edward Grim's eyewitness account, quoted in *Materials for the History of Becket*, 1875)

EXTRACT H
Francis of Assisi warns his followers against riches, 1226

Let all the brethren beware of accepting churches, houses or anything else provided for them unless they conform to Holy Poverty, to which we are vowed in our rule, always lodging as strangers and pilgrims.

(The Last Testament of Francis of Assisi)

Now test yourself

Knowledge and understanding

Make two lists showing which of the following causes of Becket's death were (a) long term and (b) short term: (i) disputes over Church courts; (ii) the Church's wish to be independent of the king; (iii) Henry's anger at the excommunication of his supporters; (iv) the wish of the knights to win the king's favour.

Using the sources

1 Do the text, pictures and extracts show that 'religion was losing its hold over the people' at this time? Give reasons for your answer.
2 Is *extract C* more useful than *extracts D and E* to historians trying to explain the quarrel between Church and kings in the Middle Ages? Why?

FOR AND AGAINST THE CHURCH

The manorial (or parish) church was the second largest building in the village (page 18, *picture 1*) and town churches were also impressive buildings. In 1086 Norwich had 1000 houses, 20 churches and 40 chapels. The Saxons had built small, wooden churches. The early Normans replaced these with stone buildings. Between 1150 and 1250 their descendants built thousands of churches, many with spires rising above the town (*picture 1*).

The Church had an important part in medieval life. On Sundays and 100 Holy Days (holidays) the Church banned working; everyone went to Mass on those days, and learned about their faith from wall paintings (*picture 2*), Biblical stories shown in stained glass windows, sermons and the priest's advice, although this often favoured the lord (page 25, *extract A*). Priests received some training before their ordination and many ran schools for parish children.

The priest's income came from crops grown on church land (the glebe), from fees paid for baptisms, weddings and funerals, and from tithes or tenths; everyone had to give the priest one-tenth of what they produced or earned.

There were good and bad priests (*extracts A and B*). During the 14th century many people criticized the Church. Wycliff (*picture 6*), a priest-lecturer at Oxford, attacked the lives of worldly bishops, greedy monks (page 27, *extracts D and E*) and ignorant priests. He wanted a simpler Church and people called him a Lollard, a European word for religious critic. Many craftsmen as well as Oxford lecturers supported him. In 1381, the year of the Peasants' Revolt (page 38) he was driven from Oxford because he attacked the Church's teaching on the Eucharist: his earlier attacks had been on Church discipline only. Wycliff died in 1384. Because some Lollards had been active in the Peasants' Revolt, Parliament passed an Act for the burning of heretics (*extract D* and *picture 7*); Parliament saw a link between religious and social unrest (page 53, *extracts C and D*).

1. Parish church of St. Wilfred, Scrooby.

2. Stories from the Bible shown on a wall painting.

3. Part of a window at Canterbury Cathedral showing demons taking the wicked to hell.

4. A carving from Beverley Minster showing bear baiting.

5. A carved font, Castle Frome.

6. John Wycliff.

7. Lollards burnt at the stake.

EXTRACT A
Geoffrey Chaucer's good priest

A holy-minded man whose good was known
There was, and poor, the parson of a town.
Yet he was rich in holy work and thought;
Truly he knew Christ's gospel and it preached
Within his parish, and all it reached.
He proved his goodness in adversity.
He'd hate to write out of the tithe or holy fee.

Indeed, he much liked beyond any doubt,
To give to poor parishioners all about,
From his own goods and gifts at Eastertide
For those with wants he'd put it all aside.

(*The Canterbury Tales*, c 1390)

EXTRACT B
Langland's unworthy priest

I have been priest and parson for thirty winters past.
But I cannot solfa sing, nor read a Latin life of saints:
But I can find a hare in a field or in a furrow,
Better than construe the first Psalm or explain it to the parish
I can hold a friendly meeting. I can cast a shire's accounts,
But in mass-book or Pope's edict I cannot read a line.

(*Piers the Ploughman*, William Langland, c 1370)

EXTRACT C
Lollards against unworthy priests

At Leicester a priest called William of Swynderby preached against the clergy saying they were bad, and, as other Lollards said, people need not pay tithes to the impure or those too ignorant to teach and preach. Lollards said that tithes were a voluntary gift and that to pay evil clergy was to agree with their wickedness. The Bishop heard about this and banned William from preaching and excommunicated all who listened to him. So he put up a pulpit near the High Street chapel and more people came to hear him than had done so before he was excommunicated.

(*Chronicles*, Henry Knighton, c 1395)

EXTRACT D
The burning of heretics, 1401

Because of the heresies of the Lollards, Parliament decreed that no one should preach publicly without a Bishop's permit, and that no one shall preach doctrine contrary to the Catholic faith. If anyone is found guilty of any heretical teaching, and refuses to stop preaching, the sheriff of the county or mayor of the town shall have them burned in public as a warning to other heretics.

(Adapted from an Act for the burning of heretics, 1401)

Now test yourself

Knowledge and understanding

Use the text and *extracts A, B, C and D* to make *three* lists showing (a) why the Church was important to medieval people; (b) why some people attacked the Church; (c) how such attackers were dealt with.

Using the sources

1 In what ways do *extracts A and B* give differing views about priests?
2 Why do you think there were these different views in medieval times?
3 Do the pictures in this topic provide useful evidence about the faith of medieval people? Give reasons for your answer.

LET'S GO TO TOWN

The Domesday book named over 100 small towns: the Danes had built defensive burghs, from which we get burgess (citizen) and borough; Saxon defensive centres had names ending in ham or ton. Towns also grew as ports, convenient river crossings and market centres. During the 12th and 13th centuries over 140 new towns were built. Some grew around castles, cathedrals and monasteries which employed craftsmen (page 27, picture 6), some were built by landowners who were paid land rents and tolls (or taxes) on goods coming to market (*picture 1*) and from fines paid at the local court. The people, or burgesses, still paid the usual feudal work-service to their landowning lord.

1. Table of toll charges levied at Braydon, Lane Gate, Carlisle.

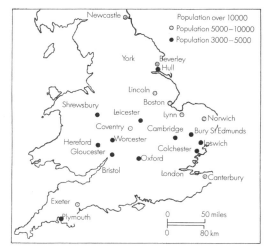

2. Main English towns in the late 14th century.

The small towns (*picture 2*) had defensive walls (*extract D* and *picture 3*) with gates (*picture 4*) which were opened at dawn to allow in 'foreigners' coming to market, and closed again at sunset when 'foreigners' had to leave. In the towns were craftsmen who made things (pages 34–5) and merchants who sold things and who united in a merchant guild (or society) which was a social club, religious body and welfare society but, above all, an economic organization. Its officers inspected the market (*picture 5*), checked weights and measures, and the quality of workmanship (pages 34–5).

The rich merchants tried to get their landowner to give them a charter freeing them from his control. Kings were always willing to sell such charters (*picture 6* and *extract B*); the Church was less willing. A borough charter allowed the burgesses to elect a council and mayor (*picture 7*) to run the town free from feudal control.

3. Defensive walls around Exeter.

4. Bargate, Southampton in the early 19th century.

5. A 15th century market place.

6. Townspeople receiving a charter in the 15th century.

7. Swearing in the mayor of Bristol.

EXTRACT A
The Normans saw England as a wealthy country

'England is a land which is fertile and rich because of the wealth which its merchants have increased by bringing in riches. Treasures have been gathered there which are remarkable for their number, quality and workmanship.'

(Quoted in *Historical Atlas of Britain*, Falkus and Gillingham, 1981)

EXTRACT B
Henry III grants a charter to the Borough of Gloucester, 1227

By this charter we grant to our burgesses of Gloucester the whole borough, in return for an annual payment of £55. Their merchants' guild is exempt from appearing at any outside court, and from any tolls when entering any town throughout the land. They however have the right to charge tolls on any foreign merchants entering their borough. If a villein escapes from his lord and stays in Gloucester for a year and a day, then he shall become free, and his lord may not reclaim him.

(Charter Roll, Henry III, 1227)

EXTRACT C
Two monasteries fight over having a market, 1201

The King allowed the monks of Ely to set up a market at Lakenheath. We wrote asking them to stop it. They refused. We took them to court and the King decided against them. But the monks refused to accept the decision. So the Abbot of Bury St Edmunds ordered his bailiff to take a force of 600 men to pull down the market and arrest the wrongdoers. They did so. But the Bishop of Ely complained to the Justiciar and Parliament at this arrogance by the Abbot. This stirred many to indignation against the Abbot.

(Chronicles of Jocelin of Brakeland concerning the monastery of St Edmund)

EXTRACT D
An Italian's view of London, 1497

It is defended by handsome walls on the northern side. Within these is a strongly defended castle on the banks of the river where the King lives. There are also other great buildings, and especially a beautiful bridge which has on it many shops of stone and even a large church. The streets are so badly paved that they get wet whenever it rains, or when the water slops from the buckets being carried by animals. Then evil-smelling mud forms which lasts nearly the year round. So the people spread fresh rushes on the floors of their houses on which they clean their shoes when they come in.

(*Itinerarium Britanniae*, Andreas Franciscus, 1497)

Now test yourself

Knowledge and understanding

1 What were the most important (a) reasons for the growth of towns in the Middle Ages; (b) benefits of this growth to kings, merchants, craftsmen and landowners?
2 How did medieval towns (a) differ from; (b) resemble the farming communities of the time?

Using the sources

1 How do *extracts A and D* show (a) the differences; (b) similarities of opinions about English towns?
2 How do you explain why the author of *extract D* both praises *and* criticizes London?
3 Are the pictures helpful to historians writing about medieval towns?

CRAFTS AND CRAFTSMEN

Towns were centres for trade and industry. Goldsmiths and silversmiths made goods for use in manor house, castle, cathedral and abbey. Blacksmiths (*picture 1*) made tools, gates, armour and delicate clocks. There were many other craftsmen – weavers, tailors, makers of harness and saddles, jewellers, shoemakers and so on.

Most workers lived in small wooden houses like the villeins' cottages. Craftsmen had a workroom and shop facing the street (*picture 2*). People doing the same craft lived near one another: names of medieval streets read like a list of occupations – Baker Street, Butchers' Row and so on.

1. A blacksmith in the 12th century.

The noise from the workrooms and from the traders' shouting added to the confusion caused by cattle, horses and donkeys. Blood from slaughterhouses and butchers' shops, fish heads from fishmongers, coloured sludge from dyers and rubbish from other shops made streets dangerous and dirty (page 33, *extract D*).

Like the merchants, craftsmen had their guilds, one for each craft. Members paid a weekly fee to guild officers and in return had welfare benefits (*extract A*). Guild officers made sure that members upheld the honour of the craft (*picture 3*): they examined workshops and goods being made and sold; they laid down the hours when work was allowed, and the number of apprentices a craftman could have.

2. In the workroom and shop.

3. A craftsman, who had been selling goods at too high a profit, in the pillory.

A boy became an apprentice to a master craftsman who taught him the 'mysteries' of the craft. After about seven years as an unpaid apprentice, guild officers allowed him to become a journeyman – a person paid by the day (*le jour* in French). When he had enough money to buy his own tools, he could ask to be recognized as a master. In *picture 4* you can see an officer examining the work of a journeyman mason. He is making his masterpiece which, if good enough, will allow him to become a master mason.

Master craftsmen tried to keep down their journeymen's wages. They also pushed up the fees that new masters had to pay when promoted from being journeymen. Disputes between masters and workers were common (*extract C*). However, all members worked together to produce their craft's mobile stage on which members acted out a Biblical story. These stories were called 'mystery plays'. In some towns, as many as 40 such carts took part in the entertainment, which lasted all day.

4. Examining the work of a journeyman mason.

5. The house of Thomas Paycocke, cloth merchant, Coggeshall, Essex. He died in 1461. His large, comfortable home was a sign of his economic success, his social status and his political power in the town.

EXTRACT A
Rules of the Guild of Tanners of London, 1346

1 To each pay towards the cost of keeping a candle burning in the Church of All Hallows near London Wall.
2 To give 7 pence a week from guild funds to members too old or ill to work.
3 To allow only apprentices to work in this trade.
4 Not to steal apprentices from one another.
5 To fine anyone breaking our rules, the first time 2 shillings, the second 40 shillings … the fourth time to banish him from the trade.
6 To permit the guild officers to confiscate bad work.

(Guildhall Letters)

EXTRACT B
Wage rates, 1425

To William Hykkedon, working for four days making an entry from the parlour to the Prior's hall, 16 pence; to John Coventry, with two servants, tiling the room for 4 days, 3 shillings and 4 pence.

(Account Roll, Maxted Priory, 1425)

EXTRACT C
Dispute between Master Saddlers and their journeymen, 1396

Masters say that serving-men, without their masters' agreement, have held meetings in various places. These inconvenience the masters, and worse might happen if the rulers of the city do not stop it. The men say that they have met for many years on 15 August, the Feast of the Assumption, to hear Mass. The masters argue that these meetings have only been going on for 13 years and that they were not held during the last few years. They claim that the men had been meeting to try to force up wages. Formerly a man worked for 40 shillings a year and his keep; now they ask for 100 shillings and keep. Decision by the City Council, 19 July, that the men have to be governed by their masters, that they do not form a brotherhood or hold meetings.

(Guildhall Letters)

Now test yourself

Knowledge and understanding

1 Write a paragraph about *each* of the following aspects of the lives of craftsmen: (a) Why the streets were dangerous and dirty. (b) The part crafts guilds played in the lives of craftsmen. (c) The reasons for disputes between masters and journeyman workers.
2 Do you agree that the relationship between masters and journeymen was *both* similar to *and* different from relationships between landowners and villeins in the countryside (see pages 20–21)? Why?

Using the sources

1 Do you think that *pictures 1–4* are useful for historians writing about the life and work of craftsmen in medieval towns? Explain your answer.
2 Read *extracts A–C*. Is *extract A* more useful than *extracts B and C* in helping you to understand what life was like for workers and masters in the Middle Ages? Explain your answer.

WOOL – ENGLAND'S INDUSTRIAL FUTURE

For many centuries England's main export was wool, highly valued by clothmakers in Flanders, Germany and Italy. The main sheep-rearing areas were the Cotswolds, the Yorkshire Dales, East Anglia, the Mendips and the south west. Manorial lords, especially the great abbeys, earned huge sums from their sale of wool, which encouraged many to enclose land for sheep-rearing (page 22 and page 51, *extract B*).

1. Taking the wool to market.

2. Spinning.

3. A happy scene of women weaving contrasted with the tortures of hell: from a medieval manuscript.

4. How cloth was made: carding.

After the sheep had been sheared, the wool was put into packs and taken to the nearest market town (*picture 1*). Before export, it was gathered into large sacks which were stamped by one of the 400 members of the group called the Merchants of the Staple, appointed by kings to supervise the export of wool and the collection of the export tax, which accounted for three-quarters of all the taxes collected by Edward III.

Exporters did not pay for the wool in cash (gold). A system developed by which merchants promised to pay in the future. This credit system had been used in Europe for many years. It was, and still is, the basis for almost all later industrial growth (*extract A*).

Edward III's advisers saw that European manufacturing countries grew rich by using England's raw material. He invited Flemish spinners (*picture 2*) and weavers (*picture 3*) to teach their crafts to the English. They also taught the English how to make cloth (*picture 4*) and England became the world's leading cloth exporter. In time the export of wool was banned (*extract B*).

Clothiers bought the wool and gave it to villagers to spin, weave and make cloth in their homes, in what became known as the domestic system (pages 108–9). Clothiers made huge profits, part of which they spent on great houses (*picture 5*) and part on paying for large churches, which can still be seen in the Cotswolds and East Anglia as a reminder of this former wealth (*picture 6* and page 30, *picture 1*).

EXTRACT A
The Merchant Staplers develop a new system of payment

When the wool reached Calais, the foreign buyer paid a certain sum in cash and gave bills (promising to pay in the future). These bills were accepted as promises to pay by other traders. The trade custom of passing bills from one creditor to another is at least 500 years old.

(*The Economic History of England*, E. Lipton, 1931)

EXTRACT B
Henry VII bans the export of English wool, 1489

For the increase of making of cloth within this land, the King, with the advice of Parliament, has decreed that no one from this first of March shall buy wool in any county of England unless it is for the making of yarn or cloth within this kingdom, and that no foreigner or agent acting for a foreigner be allowed to offer to buy English wool.

(*An Act to keep English wool for English clothiers, 1489*)

6. Merchants had the money to pay craftsmen for ornate works – like a ceiling boss.

EXTRACT C
Capitalism and the breakdown of the guild system

The guild system was not favourable to the build up of capital. It was limited in outlook to the local borough and its structure was too tight. It gave way to a system which allowed for expansion and change. This we call merchant capitalism with its domestic industry. The merchant capitalist broke down old barriers. He defied the chartered town by giving out work to the country.

(*Great Britain from Adam Smith to the Present Day*, C.R. Fay, 1950)

5. Banqueting room built for a rich wool merchant, 1470.

Now test yourself

Knowledge and understanding

1. List and explain the reasons for the growth of the wool trade.
2. How did this growth affect (a) manorial lords; (b) merchants; (c) clothiers?
3. Do you think that the changes Edward III brought to the wool trade come under the heading 'rapid change'? Why?

Using the sources

1. Read *extract C*. List three ways in which merchant capitalists were different from the guildsmen.
2. How useful are *pictures 1–6* for helping us to understand the lives of people in the medieval wool trade? Explain your answer.

WE WON'T PAY THE POLL TAX, 1381

To understand why there was a 'Great Revolt' in 1381 we have to look at long-term causes and immediate ones.

1. Richard II at Blackheath, approaching the rebels in his royal barge

- **Peasant discontent.** The feudal system had begun to decay in the 12th century (page 23, *extract A*) as landowners took money-rent in place of feudal services and began to employ paid labourers. After the Black Death (1348–49) this became widespread (page 23, *extracts F and G*). Landowners controlled Parliament and they tried to turn back the clock by passing Statutes of Labourers in 1349 (page 22, *extract F*) and 1351. This angered the peasants.
- **Ex-soldiers' discontent.** Many ordinary people played an important part in the victories over the French in the 1340s and 1350s (*extract A*). They had grown in self-esteem and confidence.

Some had prospered as farmers: the trials of rebels in 1381–2 showed that many of them farmed as much as 200 acres. They were unwilling to be pushed around by a landowners' Parliament. Other former soldiers had become prosperous craftsmen in chartered boroughs where they enjoyed their freedom. They, too, resented attempts by landowners to win back feudal dues. This helps to explain why the people of London opened the city gates to the rebels in 1381.

- **Religious discontent.** Many people, including some landowners, were angered by the over-rich bishops, abbots and monks (page 27, *extracts D and E*; page 29, *extract H* and page 31, *extracts B and C*). They supported the preaching of reforming priests such as John Ball and the arguments of men like Wat Tyler (*extract C*).
- **The immediate cause** of the uprising was taxation. In 1377 the French landed an army on the Isle of Wight and their navy attacked towns along the coast of southern England. The government needed extra taxes to pay for larger armies. The first poll tax came in 1377: everybody over the age of 15 had to pay 4 pence. There was another such tax in 1379 and a third in 1381 when the tax was 12 pence per person. This was the spark which lit the fire of revolt. Many people hid in the forests to escape the tax collectors: others fought the tax collectors. Then, in April 1381, the Chancellor Archbishop Sudbury was allowed to send armed forces to compel payment of the tax. The revolt followed.

2. The death of Sudbury.

3. Richard and Tyler at Smithfield. Tyler (left) is being attacked while Richard rides over to the rebels.

30 May: Commissioners stoned at the manor of Fobbing, Essex.

2 June: Chief Justice sent to punish villagers – attacked by army of men from south Essex, led by Farringdon. They marched on to London.

4 June: Essex men camped out at Mile End.

2–4 June: Rioting in Rochester, Kent – castle attacked and prison opened.

7 June: Wat Tyler led Kentish rebels at Maidstone and marched on London.

12 June: Kentish men camped at Blackheath. Richard II went to meet them but retreated to the Tower (*picture 1*).

13 June: Tyler and Lollard John Ball spoke to the rebels (*extract C*).

14 June: Mob stormed into London – attacked Savoy Palace, home of Richard II's uncle, John of Gaunt. The King met Tyler at Mile End and announced the abolition of villeinage, the power of the craft guilds and wage-fixing by Parliament, and an amnesty for all rebels. Tyler demanded the punishment of the King's advisers, but he rejected this. The Essex men killed Archbishop Sudbury (*picture 2*).

15 June: After a night's rioting in London, Richard and Tyler met again, at Smithfield (*picture 3*). The King was angry at Sudbury's death. Tyler demanded the right to remain as head of his 'army'. Richard refused. Tyler became angry and one of the King's men called Tyler 'a thief'. He drew his dagger and tried to stab London's Mayor, who was saved by his coat of mail. He and another then stabbed Tyler who fell in front of his men. Richard bravely faced the rebels, asked them to accept him as their leader, reminded them of his promises and invited them to go home. They did so, and the revolt was over. The King then punished the rebels' leaders. Tyler was dragged from St Bartholomew's Hospital, beheaded and his head placed on London Bridge, where rebels had put Sudbury's head some days before. Armed forces were sent to arrest other leaders in Kent and Essex and to crush any local risings.

22 June: Richard told some Essex men: 'Villeins you are and shall remain.'

2 July: Richard cancelled all his promises to Tyler and the rebels.

EXTRACT A
The success of the common soldiers against the French

'They made all France afraid. And although they are not called "Master" as gentlemen are, or "Sir" as knights are, but only "John" and "Thomas" and so on, yet they have been found to have done great deeds at Crecy and Poitiers.'

(Quoted in *Illustrated History of England*, G.R. Trevelyan, 1926)

EXTRACT B
Fear of social unrest, 1380

It seems to me that laziness has put the lords to sleep and they do not guard against the folly of the common people, but allow that nettle to grow which is too violent in its nature. If God does not help us, the nettle will suddenly sting us.

(John Gowe, 1330–1408, writing in 1380)

EXTRACT C
Equality for all, 1381

We are men formed in Christ's likeness, but we are kept like beasts. No lord should have lordship: it should be divided among all men, except for the King's own lordship.

(Wat Tyler at Blackheath, 13 June 1381)

When Adam delved and Eve span, Who was then the gentleman?

(John Ball, 13 June 1381)

Now test yourself

Knowledge and understanding

1 Using the text and extracts, list the causes of the Peasants' Revolt in order of their importance. Explain your choice.

2 What were the effects of the Revolt in (a) the short term; (b) the long term?

Using the sources

(a) How can we check the accuracy of *pictures 1, 2 and 3*? (b) Do you agree that these pictures are useful to the historian? (c) Do the pictures support the statements made in the text? Explain your answer.

IRELAND – BRITAIN'S OTHER 'ISLAND'

Six kings ruled six Irish provinces, each of which had many tribes with their own kings. Traditionally a High King of Ireland claimed tribute from other kings. The last High King was Brian Boru, King of Munster, who died in 1014 while defeating the Danes at Clontarf. His rival, the King of Leinster, aided the Danes who, after 1014, ruled Dublin, Waterford and Limerick. Four kings – of Leinster, Munster, Connaught and Ulster – fought for Boru's crown.

1. The marriage of an Irish king to his country.

In 1154 Henry II persuaded Pope Adrian IV to give him authority to conquer Ireland. In 1166 he had his chance. MacMurrough (Leinster) had stolen the wife of O'Rourke of Breffney, a neighbour of O'Connor (Connaught). All the kings condemned MacMurrough and banished him (*extract A*). He asked for Henry's help. He sent de Clare (Strongbow), Earl of Pembroke (page 42) to lead an army of chain-clad knights, supported by Welsh archers (page 43, *extract C*). The unarmoured Irish, with their Danish battle-axes (*picture 4*) were no match for them. The English took Wexford, Waterford and Dublin.

In 1175 Henry forced O'Connor to sign the Treaty of Windsor. This allowed him to act as Henry's deputy in Ireland, where English power was limited to the area around Dublin (page 67, *extract A*) where officials set up what they said was an Irish government (*picture 6*). Their rule never extended to the far west and deep south where Celtic tribal chiefs ruled the people. Nor did they control the ambitious barons. Strongbow, for example, married the only child of the King of Leinster and so became king himself; Hugh de Lacy married the daughter of O'Connor, the last High King and gained influence in Connaught. After an Irish uprising (1177) other barons seized land. De Courcy, Fitzstephens and Butlers were among the gainers, building castles, abbeys, churches and Normanizing Ireland.

2. Cross of the Scriptures, Clonmacnoise.

The English and Norman lords and knights who went to Ireland married native girls, as did their sons and grandsons. They adopted the Irish language, dress and customs so that they became completely Irish. This was seen to be the case when the proclamation of Henry III as king (1207) had to be read in Gaelic to the Irish Parliament because only one Norman-Irish baron would have understood it if it had been read in English.

During the 14th century, three great earldoms were created for the Norman-Irish barons. Two of these went to the Fitzgerald family – the earldoms of Desmond and Kildare. The third, the earldom of Ormond, was given to the Butler family. By 1490 the English government controlled only a small area around Dublin – the so-called *Pale* (*picture 7* and page 67, *extract A*).

Why had the English allowed their control over Ireland to weaken? First, it was a poor country from which little could be got. Second, there were more pressing problems – wars with France, for example. Only when rebels used Ireland as a base from which to attack the new Tudor monarchy did England try to regain control of that other 'island' (page 67, *extract B*).

3. The Cross of Cong.

5. Hugh de Lacy's castle, Carlingford.

6. The Irish 'government' sitting around the exchequer.

Key:
Anglo-Irish Chiefs
Celtic Chiefs

O'Donnell
De Burgh
O'Neill
De Burgh (= Burke)
O'Connor
De Lacy
The Pale
Dublin
O'Kelly
Fitzgeralds, Earls of Kildare
O'Brien
De Clare
Butlers, Earls of Ormonde
Fitzgeralds, Earls of Desmond
McCarthy

7. Ireland and its earldoms.

4. Irishmen in combat.

EXTRACT A
One view of Diarmait MacMurrough

O King of Heaven, dreadful is the deed that has been done in Ireland today. Diarmait, son of Donchad MacMurchada, King of Leinster and the Foreigners or Dublin Danes, has been banished over sea by the men of Ireland. Alas, alas, O Lord, what shall I do?

(*The Book of Leinster*, c 1166)

EXTRACT B
Edward I, who 'united' the British Isles

Now are the islanders all joined together,
And Scotland reunited to the royalties
Of which King Edward is proclaimed lord.
Cornwall and Wales are in his power,
And Ireland the great at his will.
There is neither King nor prince of all the countries
Except King Edward who has thus united them:
Arthur never had the fiefs so fully.

(*Chronicle of Peter Langtoft*, 1297)

Now test yourself

Knowledge and understanding

Explain the reasons for (a) Henry II's victories over the Irish; (b) the reasons why the English never controlled all of Ireland.

Using the sources

1 Do you agree that the evidence in this topic shows that (a) the Irish assimilated the Normans *or* (b) the Normans assimilated the Irish *or* (c) both? Explain your answer.

2 What do the pictures tell you about the nature of Irish kingship?

E DWARD I AND THE CONQUEST OF WALES

William I created three powerful Lords of the Marches – at Chester, Shrewsbury and Hereford – to prevent any invasions from Wales where kings (*picture 1*) ruled over a number of provinces such as Powys (*picture 2*). It was these lords who invaded Wales and set up almost independent lordships. At first they built motte and bailey castles (*extract C*) but later replaced these with fortresses such as Pembroke Castle (*picture 3*), where de Clare (Strongbow) created an earldom in 1109, over which earls had sovereign rights until 1536.

1. A Welsh king from a 13th century manuscript.

During the 13th century the Welsh fought back. Llewelyn 'the Great' of Gwynedd gained control of most of Wales from English kings, so that in 1216 all Wales accepted his overlordship. However, when he died, civil war broke out until his grandson, Llewelyn Fawr, regained control. In 1267 Henry III acknowledged him as Prince of Wales (*extract E*).

Edward I tried to control Wales. When Llewelyn refused to accept him as overlord, he invaded Wales (1276–7) and defeated the Welsh. When they rebelled, he led a second invasion (1282–3) during which Llewelyn was killed. To ensure his control over Wales, Edward built eight great coastal castles. His son, the future Edward II, was born in one (Caernarfon) in 1284: 1000 men worked on the building of another for many years (Harlech) while Beaumaris (*picture 4*) is described as 'a masterpiece of medieval fortification'.

In 1284 Edward issued the Statute of Rhuddlan which divided Wales into three northern counties (Anglesey, Caernarfon and Merioneth) and two southern ones (Cardigan and Carmarthen). The rest of Wales was ruled by Norman barons. The Statute put English clergy in charge of the Church, replaced Welsh law with English law and made English the official language – not spoken by the majority. In 1301 Edward made his eldest son 'Prince of Wales' (*picture 5*) hoping that this Caernarfon-born Englishman would be accepted as true heir to Llewelyn. Later uprisings showed that the Welsh were not that easily fooled.

2. The provinces of Wales at the time of William I.

3. Pembroke Castle.

THE LEGEND OF KING ARTHUR AND THE KNIGHTS OF THE ROUND TABLE

The English thought that the Welsh were 'Celtic barbarians'. It is true that they were economically backward, living much as the Saxons had lived in England in the 8th century. In 1139, a Welsh writer, Geoffrey of Monmouth, wrote *The History of the Kings of Britain*. He described a Romano-Celtic 'King' Arthur who was descended from Aeneas, the mythical founder of Rome. King Arthur's court at Camelot was known for its learning, chivalry and high living.

This attempt to give the Welsh some pride in their supposed ancestry was taken over by later Norman-English writers who claimed that Arthur's Camelot had been in England, not Wales, and that his knights' Round Table was to be found in Winchester and not in some Celtic stronghold.

4. Beaumaris Castle.

EXTRACT A
A tricky coastline, 1188

We went along the seashore towards the River Neath and its quicksands. My packhorse, which had gone along the shore, sunk into the quicksands. It was got out only with great difficulty but the baggage was badly damaged. Although Prince Morgan, of that county, was our guide we were often in peril. We tried to rush through the quicksands, whereas we ought to have gone more slowly. The fords across the river change with every tide, so we did not try to cross by foot but took a boat.

(*Description of Wales*, Gerald of Wales, 1188)

5. Edward I making his son Prince of Wales.

EXTRACT B
Norman Marcher lords fighting in Wales, 1188

The Norman soldier is different from the Welsh. In Normandy the battle is on the level, here on rough ground. There they take prisoners, here they kill them. In their flat country their heavy armour is useful: here, fighting in narrow passes and in woods, it is a handicap. Their troops march only with the greatest difficulty.

(Gerald of Wales)

EXTRACT C
Dangers from Welsh archers, 1188

Two Normans were crossing a bridge to get to safety in a tower built on a mound of earth. The Welsh chased them. Their arrows pierced the thick oaken door of the tower. William de Braose told me that one of his men was wounded by an arrow which passed through his thigh and its protective armour and through the saddle, killing the horse. Their bows are designed to inflict severe wounds in a close fight.

(Gerald of Wales)

EXTRACT D
Welshmen in battle, 1188

They are very fierce at the start. But if the enemy resist and they have to retreat, they become confused. They run away and do not try to fight back. Their only tactics are either to chase an enemy or to run away: they do not fight long battles or in hand-to-hand conflict. They harass enemies by ambushes and night attacks.

(Gerald of Wales)

EXTRACT E
Llewelyn ap Gruffydd, 'the Last' (1246–82)

And the King granted that the Prince should receive the homage of the barons of Wales, and that the barons should put themselves and their followers wholly under the Prince, and that there should be Princes of Wales from that time on.

(Chronicles of the Princes, 1267)

Now test yourself

Knowledge and understanding

1 How did the conquest of Wales (a) differ from; (b) resemble the conquest of Ireland?
2 Explain how the effects of the English invasions (a) took place immediately; (b) took longer to come about.

Using the sources

1 Do you agree that the author of *extracts A–D* was biased towards the Normans *or* towards the Welsh? Give reasons for your answer.
2 Are *pictures 3 and 4* helpful to historians writing about the conquest of Wales by the Normans? Explain your answer.

SCOTLAND FOR EVER – ALMOST

The Romans had built Hadrian's Wall to hold back the Scots and to mark the northern limit of their own conquest of Britain. On their side of the wall, the Scots lived in two 'natural' kingdoms (*extract A*) with the Lowlanders claiming to rule parts of northern England into which they often went raiding. William the Conqueror did not try to conquer Scotland, but, in answer to the raids, he sent an army which defeated the Scots and forced their king to do him homage as overlord.

In 1097 Scotland's two kingdoms were united. King David I (1124–53) (*picture 1*) invited the Normans into Scotland where they built castles, churches and abbeys and provided David with knights for his army. While they paid homage to David as overlord, many Scots married Norman women and did homage to English kings for lands they held in England.

These intermarriages did not stop raids into England. In 1174 the Scottish king William the Lion (1165–1214) was defeated by an avenging English army and forced to accept Henry II as overlord. The English king Richard I later sold back that overlordship for money needed to pay for one of his Crusades abroad.

Edward I hoped to unite the two countries by a marriage. Alexander III of Scotland (page 47, *picture 3*) agreed that his heiress, his granddaughter Margaret, would marry Edward's son, the Prince of Wales (page 43, *picture 5*). Unfortunately, the 6-year-old Margaret died in the Orkneys while on her way from Norway. Edward's plan had failed.

The Scots then helped him. On Alexander's death (1286) thirteen Scots claimed the throne. Civil war followed. The thirteen agreed to ask Edward to choose Alexander's successor. He chose John Balliol (1292–6) as King of Scotland and got him to promise that he would take Edward as overlord. However, when Balliol refused to supply men and money for Edward's French wars, the English invaded Scotland, defeated Balliol and took the Coronation Stone from Scone to Westminster. English officials were left in charge of the country.

William Wallace (*picture 2*) then led a guerilla war against the English. In 1297 he captured the English headquarters at Stirling and drove the conquerors out of Scotland. In 1298 Edward sent fresh armies which defeated Wallace at Falkirk. Wallace went into hiding, was betrayed by a fellow Scot and was executed (*extract B*).

In 1306 Robert Bruce, one of the claimants to the throne in 1286, had himself crowned at Scone and declared war on England. Defeated at Perth, he fled to Rathlin, off the Irish coast. When Edward II became King of England (1307), Bruce returned to Scotland, where he received support and was then able to defeat the English. Only Stirling

1. King Malcolm IV (right) and his grandfather King David I, shown on a charter granted by Malcolm to Kelso Abbey in 1159.

2. Statute of Sir William Wallace at Stirling.

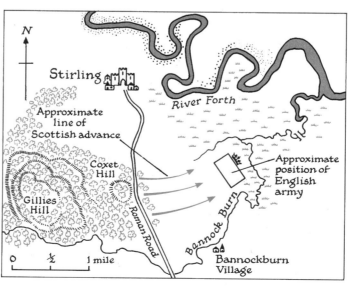

3. A plan of the Battle of Bannockburn.

and Bothwell remained under English control. Edward II sent 20,000 soldiers to defend Stirling. Although Bruce had only 7000 men, he won the Battle of Bannockburn (*extract C* and *picture 3*). After more years of fighting, the English finally signed the Treaty of Northampton (1328) in which Bruce was recognized as King of an independent Scotland.

Several of Bruce's successors on the Scottish throne married English brides. In 1503 the first Tudor king of England, Henry VII, negotiated the marriage of his daughter, Margaret to King James IV of Scotland. Their great-grandson was to become James VI of Scotland and James I of England.

5. Henry VII's daughter, Margaret Tudor, shown at prayer. She is wearing robes decorated with the royal arms of both England and Scotland.

EXTRACT A
The Scottish countryside, 14th century

Scotia has areas of land bordering on the sea, pretty level and rich, with green meadows, and fertile and productive fields. In the uplands and the highlands, fields are less productive. There the country is ugly, with moors and marshy fields. It is however full of pasturage for cattle, and has good grazing in the glens along the water-courses. This region has many wool-bearing sheep, horses, cattle and wild beasts; it is rich in milk and wood and is wealthy in fish.

(*Chronicles of the Peoples of Scotland*, John Fordun, 1381)

EXTRACT B
The execution of William Wallace, 1305

Wallace, a man without pity, a robber given to sacrilege, arson and murder, more hardened than Herod, madder than Nero, was condemned to a cruel but deserved death. He was drawn through London's streets at the tails of horses to an unusually high gallows. There he was hung. He was taken down while still alive: he was then mutilated, his bowels torn out, his head cut off, his body divided into four, and these quarters sent to four principal parts of Scotland.

(*Chronicle of Lanercost*, 1320)

EXTRACT C
The Battle of Bannockburn, 1314

When both sides were ready, the English archers were put in front of the line of knights. The Scottish archers fought with them but were soon put to flight. As the two armies drew closer, the Scots knelt to say the Lord's prayer before they advanced. They had two columns side by side in front of a third led by Robert Bruce. The great English horses charged the pikes of the Scots and there was the great noise of broken spears and fatally wounded horses. There was a stalemate: the English at the rear could not reach the Scots because the front line was in the way. So the rear fled, leaving many nobles, and great numbers of footmen dead. Then came another disaster. To get at the Scots the English had crossed a great ditch into which the tide flows. Now, when they wanted to re-cross it, many nobles and horses fell in. Some escaped only with great difficulty, while many never got out at all. Thus was Bannockburn spoken about by the English for many years. I got the account from a trustworthy person who was there.

(*Chronicle of Lanercost*, 1320)

Now test yourself

Knowledge and understanding

1 Next to each of the following dates, write the major event in the history of English–Scottish affairs: 1174; 1287; 1292; 1298; 1306; 1307; 1314; 1328.
2 What was (a) similar; (b) different about English attacks on Scotland compared to the attacks on Wales?

Using the sources

Read *extracts A B and C*. (a) Do they contain (i) statements of fact *or* (ii) opinions *or* (iii) both? (b) Which author shows his anti-Scottish bias? (c) How would a pro-Scottish writer describe Wallace's execution? (d) What other primary sources should we look at to get a fuller list of reasons for the Anglo-Scottish wars?

THE SLOW AND UNCERTAIN GROWTH OF PARLIAMENT

Early Norman kings had a Great Council (*picture 1*) which they called when they needed advice. Other than this, they were almost dictators.

Their power was challenged during John's reign (1199–1216). He had lost most of the English 'empire' in France, quarrelled with the Pope, angered people by stealing Church property and offended the barons by his high taxes. In 1215 the barons, led by the Archbishop of Canterbury, made him sign the Magna Carta (*picture 2*) which listed the rights which kings had earlier given to freemen. It said nothing about ordinary people or Parliament, but it showed that kings could be challenged.

1. The king in Council.

Henry III (1216–72) was only 9 years old when he was crowned. His brother-in-law, Simon de Montfort, ruled on his behalf until Henry was 16. Then the King angered barons by high taxation and by having Frenchmen as advisers. In 1258 de Montfort led the barons who forced Henry to set up a permanent Council and to call regular Parliaments. De Montfort did not trust Henry (*extract A*) so he strengthened his position by calling for the election of two knights to represent each county and two burgesses from each chartered borough. This was the beginning of Parliament (page 26, *picture 3*).

Edward I (1272–1307) accepted these ideas (*extract B*). In 1295 he called what is known as 'the Model Parliament', so giving Royal blessing to that body (*picture 3*). Medieval Parliaments only met when kings decided to call one, which was when they needed money to fight wars. Edward's wars led to several Parliaments and during the Hundred Years' War (1337–1435) Parliaments met more regularly.

Richard II (1367–99) tried to turn back the clock (*extract C*): he abolished laws passed by previous kings and Parliaments and bribed members of Parliament (MPs) to support him. He thought he was king by divine right (*extract D*). In 1399 he was overthrown by barons who supported Henry Bolingbroke's rising.

During the Wars of the Roses Parliaments gained confidence: more MPs came from the 'new men' grown rich by trade, willing to challenge the Church (page 30) and kings. Henry VIII's Reformation increased the power of Parliament (pages 50–51).

So, how powerful were medieval monarchs?

- The coronation ceremony was meant to show that the king (or queen) was God's representative on earth, with power coming directly from God. However, several kings were deposed and others challenged by barons (King John), the Church (Henry I and Henry II, as well as John) and even by the ordinary people (as during the Peasants' Revolt).
- The monarch was 'the provider of justice' with power to punish wrongdoers. However, during medieval times, many new kinds of judges were appointed (by the kings themselves) and new royal courts set up so that the power to punish tended to pass from king to judges – and juries.
- The monarch was the owner of huge amounts of land which gave a large income. However, much of this land was given away to favourites or sold, while the king's need for money increased as the cost of war increased.
- The king was the lawmaker: he chose the people who were to help him govern the country and, with them, he decided what Acts of Parliament were needed. However, his leading barons had expected to be consulted, even in the 11th century and, after that

2. The Magna Carta.

time, they demanded the right to be consulted – as King John had to learn.

- Parliaments only met when the monarch decided to call one, and they were sent packing when the monarch felt that he did not need any more advice. However, the king needed Parliament's permission to increase taxes or raise new ones, which meant that Parliament's power increased.

In general, the powers of the monarchy began to decline after 1066, although an efficient and ruthless king could exert more power than inefficient and weak ones.

EXTRACT A
The nobles force Henry III to admit wrongdoing, 1258

The King acknowledged the truth of the accusations at last, and he humbled himself, admitting that he had been too often misled by evil advice. He promised and swore a solemn oath at the altar of St Edward that he would fully correct his old ways, and show kindness to his subjects. But because of his earlier crimes it was impossible to believe him. But the nobles had not yet learned how to tie a King down so that he would keep his promises. This was a very difficult matter: so Parliament was dismissed for the time being.

(*Greater Chronicle*, Matthew Paris, 1258)

EXTRACT B
Edward I agrees that he needs the consent of taxpayers, 1297

And we have granted, for us and our heirs, that we will not take any taxes from our realm without the consent of all the realm.

(*Confirmation of the Charters*, 1297)

EXTRACT C
Richard II wants to be free of parliamentary control, 1397

The Crown of England hath been so free at all times that it hath been in no earthly subjugation in anything touching the crown.

(Statute of Praemunire, 1397)

3. Edward I in Parliament. King Alexander of Scotland is to the left, Prince Llewelyn of Wales on the right.

EXTRACT D
The King as God's annointed and 'untouchable', 1399

And shall the figure of God's majesty
His captain, steward, deputy elect
Anointed, crowned, planted many years
Be judg'd by subject and inferior breath?

(The Bishop of Carlisle in *Richard II*, William Shakespeare, 1595)

Now test yourself

Knowledge and understanding

Read the following list of reasons for the growth of Parliament's powers: John's quarrels with the Barons; de Montfort's quarrel with Henry III; Edward I's wars; the Wars of the Roses; the growth of trade. Which do you think were the three most important reasons? Why?

Using the sources

Read *extracts A, B, C and D*. (a) Do they show that Parliament was (i) weak; (ii) strong; (iii) a mixture of both? (b) Does Shakespeare (*extract D*) support the rights of Parliament or the king? Explain your answer.

The making of the United Kingdom: Crown, Parliament, people 1500–1750

THE TUDORS AND THEIR PARLIAMENTS

Henry VII (1485–1509) spent little money and rarely needed to call Parliament to ask for 'unusual taxes'. Henry VIII (1509–47) had to call for money for his wars against France and Scotland (page 62): he used Parliament to pass the laws he needed to make his break with Rome legal (pages 50–51).

Most Parliaments did what monarchs wanted. Henry VIII got his Reformation; Edward VI's Parliaments passed anti-Catholic laws; Mary got her Catholic laws through. Elizabeth I (1558–1603) called many Parliaments. It was during this reign that MPs first challenged the sovereign's rights, and so prepared the way for the more serious disputes with the Stuarts (pages 64 and 68).

1. Henry VIII opens Parliament, 1512.

2. Edward VI and his councillors allowed the Church more freedom. Henry VIII is shown ruling from his grave in an attempt to stop reform; the Pope is shown crushed by the English Prayer Book.

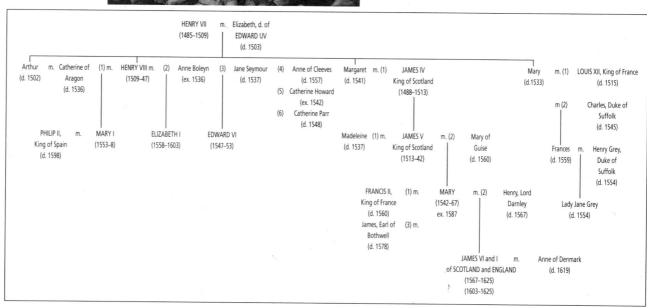

3. From Tudors to Stuarts, 1485–1625.

4. Queen Elizabeth I presiding over Parliament.

EXTRACT A
Elizabeth I scolds a restless Parliament, 1566–7

It does not become a subject to compel a sovereign. It is for me, the Anointed Queen, to provide for the succession and the country's future. I will never be forced to do anything to lessen my royal power, and the Sovereign's right to decide policy.

(Elizabeth I's message to the Commons, 1567)

EXTRACT B
Another clash, 1571

Her Majesty said that they would do well not to meddle with matters of state except those she put before them.

(The Lord Keeper to the Commons, April 1571)

EXTRACT C
A short but rebellious session, February–March, 1576

It is certain, Mr Speaker, that no one is without fault. Not even our noble Queen. Since, then, Her Majesty has committed great faults, some of which are dangerous to herself and to the State, love forces me to utter them for the sake of Her safety.

(Peter Wentworth, MP, at the opening of the Commons, February 1576)

EXTRACT D
Parliamentary freedom and the religious question, 1593

Elizabeth I: 'Your privilege is the freedom to say 'yes or no' and to give reasons for your opinion. This is a liberal privilege, and not a licence to you to say what you like. You cannot claim, under the pretence of liberty, the right to encroach on the royal control of the Church, on the succession to the throne, and on policy in general. You, my Commons, are overbold when you use God's name as the excuse for criticizing my Government.' *Peter Wentworth, MP:* 'Sweet is the name of liberty. Parliament is a place where we may speak freely about all the griefs of the country. I will not refer Christian doctrine to the bishops. To do that would make the Bishops into "Popes".'

(Adapted from quotations in *A History of England*, K. Feiling, 1974)

EXTRACT E
Parliament speaks out against Elizabeth's favourites, 1601

Mr Martin: 'The country groans under the burden of monopolies of starch, tin, fish, cloth, oil, vinegar … *Mr Hakewill of Lincoln's Inn called out:* 'Is not bread there? It will be before the next Parliament.'

(Commons debate, 20 November 1601)

EXTRACT F
Which 'expert' is right?

Elizabeth dissolved Parliament on 2 January 1567. Henry VIII had never lost a head-on clash with Parliament. Elizabeth had.

(*Elizabeth I*, J. Ridley, 1987)

The declaration of 2 January 1567 marked a decisive moment in the relations between the Queen and Parliament. After this, there was never any question but that it was she who directed the ship of state, Parliament meeting to give her their counsel, advice and consent.

(*Freedom's Own Island*, A.S. Bryant, 1986)

Now test yourself

Knowledge and understanding

1 Read the text and extracts. How does a study of the religious changes of the 16th century support the view that 'Tudor parliaments usually did what monarchs wanted'?
2 What were the long-term causes of the growth of the power of Parliament (see page 46)?

Using the sources

1 Read *extracts A–D*. Do these extracts fully agree about the powers of Parliament and Queen? Explain your answer.
2 How useful are *pictures 1–3* to historians writing about what Tudor Parliaments were like? Explain your answer.

HENRY VIII AND A NEW CHURCH – OR AN OLD ONE?

1. By attacking the work of Martin Luther, Henry VIII earned the title 'Defender of the Faith'.

In 1520 Martin Luther attacked Catholic beliefs. Henry VIII's attack on Luther (*picture 1*) won him the papal title of Defender of the Faith. Why then did he lead the Church in England away from allegiance to the Pope?

In 1509 he married Catherine of Aragon, widow of his elder brother, Arthur, who had died (1502). By 1527 he had a daughter, Mary, but not the son to whom he wanted to leave the Crown: he was also in love with Anne Boleyn. He sent his Archbishop, Cardinal Wolsey, to ask the Pope to let him divorce Catherine. When the Pope refused, Henry sacked Wolsey and appointed Thomas Cranmer as his Archbishop. Together they pushed the break with Rome through Parliament (1531–6). The most important stages in that break took place in:

1533: Parliament forbade appeals in Church matters being sent for papal decision. Cranmer now dissolved Henry's marriage (May), married him to Boleyn (June) and baptised their child, Elizabeth (September). The Pope excommunicated Henry and his supporters – cut them off from Catholic life.

1534: Parliament named Henry Supreme Head of the Church. Most Church leaders in England accepted this. The few who didn't were executed (*extract D*).

1535: A Treasons Act was passed, allowing Henry to punish any opponents.

1536: An Act allowed the closure of smaller monasteries. Henry put down the uprising known as the Pilgrimage of Grace (*picture 2*).

2. Executing rebels who took part in the Pilgrimage of Grace.

Henry then closed all monasteries (1537–9) and took all their land. The sale of this land gave him an income of £100,000 a year for some years, double his usual income. The land was bought cheaply by MPs, courtiers and other influential people, who were then anxious to maintain the break with Rome. Henry continued to burn Lutherans (*picture 3*) and in 1539 pushed through an Act accepting Catholic teaching on the Mass, the Eucharist, the non-marriage of clergy and confession. He died, as he thought, 'a good Catholic'.

'Revolutions devour their children' Henry VIII made what he thought were only moderate changes in Church life. But, once change had begun, it went on – in spite of him (page 48, *picture 2* and page 53, *extracts A and B*).

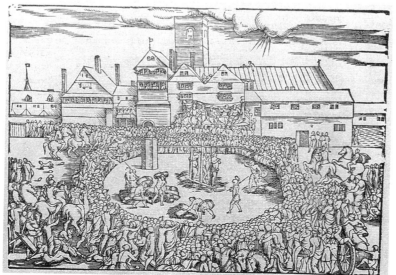

3. Burning Lutherans.

EXTRACT A
Wealthy monasteries

In the diocese of Bath there are two convents, one for monks, named Glastonbury, and the other for women, named Santsbury. The abbot of the former has a yearly income of more than £25,000 and the abbess of the other above £10,000.

(Letter by Italian Ambassador to London, 1500)

EXTRACT B
Thomas More's attack on greedy monks, c 1520

Certain abbots do not content themselves with their usual yearly revenue from their lands. They now leave no ground for tilling; they enclose all pastures; they throw down houses as they make everything sheepland.

(*Utopia*, Thomas More, 1516)

EXTRACT C
Lords and bishops ask the Pope to give Henry his divorce, 1530

If the Pope is unwilling, we are left to find a remedy elsewhere. Some remedies are extreme ones, but a sick man seeks relief in any way he can find.

(Letter signed by bishops and lords, sent to the Pope at Henry's request, 1530)

EXTRACT D
Thomas More refuses to accept Henry as Supreme Head of the Church

Sir Richard Rich: Master More, you are learned in the law. Pretend that an Act of Parliament said that I was King. Would you accept me as King?
Sir Thomas More: Yes.

Rich: Suppose an Act of Parliament said that I was Pope. Would you accept that?
More: Master Rich, Parliament may well meddle with the state of princes and make you King. As to your second question: suppose Parliament made a law that God was not God. Would you accept that?
Rich: No Parliament can make any such law.
More: No more can Parliament make the King Supreme Head of the Church.

(Interview during More's trial, 1535)

4. Henry VIII's seizure of spiritual power from the Pope increased the power of the Crown. He was helped by Cromwell (whom he had executed in 1540) and Cranmer (who, under Mary, first confessed he had been wrong in helping Henry, but then withdrew his confession and was burnt at the stake). Fisher, Bishop of Rochester, supported the Pope (Clement) and with More (extract D) was executed by Henry in 1535. In 1935 both More and Fisher were made saints of the Catholic Church.

Now test yourself

Knowledge and understanding

1 'The break with Rome' had many causes. (a) Make a list of the long-term causes of hostility towards the Church (see pages 30, 38, 51). (b) Do you think there would have been a break with Rome if Henry VIII had not wanted a divorce? Explain your answer.
2 What were the effects of Henry's religious policies on (a) the Church; (b) his wealth; (c) rich English families.

Using the sources

1 Read *extracts A and B*. Which is the more valuable as evidence of what monks were like in Henry VIII's time? Why? What other sources should historians use when writing about monks in England?
2 (a) Use *pictures 1–3* to describe how Henry VIII dealt with both Catholic and Protestant opponents of his religious policies? (b) What sort of person do you think these pictures show Henry to have been?

RELIGIOUS UNIFORMITY

Henry VIII's 1539 Act outlawed the teachings of Lutherans and Calvinists (*extract D*). Before he died, Henry ordered that his infant son should be helped by a Council of equal numbers of Catholics and Reformers (page 48, *picture 2*). But extremists seized power, banning the Mass (*extract A*), producing an anti-Catholic Prayer Book (*extract B*) and plundering churches (*pictures 1 and 2*).

When Mary became Queen (1553) she tried to restore 'the old faith', but greedy MPs and courtiers refused to allow the restoration of the monasteries. Like her father, she persecuted religious opponents: because of her unpopular marriage to Philip of Spain, this offended many people who saw it as Spanish policy. Most politicians, like the Cecils, and Princess Elizabeth, saved their lives and wealth by accepting Mary's religious changes.

When Elizabeth became Queen (1558) she tried to find a middle way (a *via media*). Many Catholics accepted this (*extract C*): others wanted a full return to Rome. It was easy to show that these were pro-Spanish traitors who deserved to be punished. On the other hand, her policy failed to satisfy the Protestant extremists (*extract D*) who had their supporters in the Commons (page 49, *extract D*). They would trouble her Stuart successors (pages 64–5).

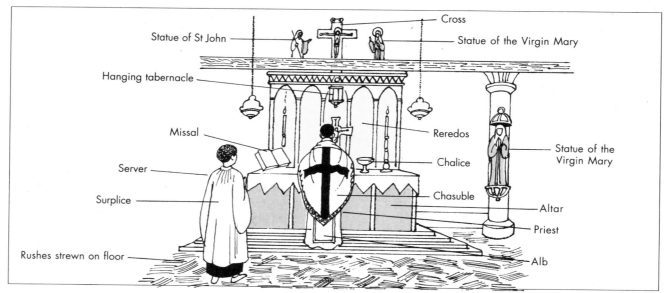

1. Inside a Catholic church.

2. Inside an Anglican church.

The extremist members of the Anglican Church were called *Puritans* (*extract D*). They wanted a 'purer' or simpler form of religion. They opposed Elizabeth's *via media* and the Book of Common Prayer, claiming them as 'too like Catholicism'. Elizabeth had many Puritans arrested and some executed, but their numbers grew.

When James I became king the Puritans expected some support from him. Their Scottish friends, the Presbyterians, had gained control of the Church in Scotland, and English Puritans hoped that James would reform the English Church along Puritan lines. He did not do so and they were disappointed (page 63, *extract C*).

EXTRACT A
Edward VI forbids Mary Tudor to have Mass said, 1547

My duty most humbly remembered unto your Majesty ... I trusted that you would have allowed me your poor sister to have the traditional Mass, which the King, your father and mine, with all his predecessors had; wherein I was brought up from my youth to which my conscience binds me, as also the promise made to the Emperor by your Majesty's Council which agreed that in so doing I would not offend the Laws. And when I last had an audience with you and told you that I would prefer that you should take my life rather than forbid me the Mass, your Majesty made me a very gentle answer...

(Letter from Princess Mary, 1547)

EXTRACT B
Mary Tudor refuses to use Cranmer's Book of Common Prayer, 1549

You hope that I will not refuse God's word. I cannot tell what you mean by God's word. But what is called God's word now was not God's word in my father's day. You would not have dared call that (book) God's word in my father's day.

(Princess Mary to Nicholas Ridley, Bishop of London, 1549)

EXTRACT C
Elizabeth I looks for a religious middle way, 1558

To unite the people of the realm in one uniform order' everyone was obliged to attend their parish church on Sunday; non-attendance was to be punished by a modest fine and, if persisted in, by imprisonment. In Elizabeth's Act of Uniformity and in the Thirty-Nine Articles which laid down guidelines for the Anglican Church, there was no abuse of Pope or Rome, while the words of the Cranmer's Communion Service left people free to accept or reject the Catholic teaching about the Real Presence of Christ in the Eucharist. Elizabeth's own attitude towards this beautiful but unprovable teaching was shown in some lines which she is said to have written:
'Twas Christ the word that spake it, He took the bread and brake it;
And what the word did make it, That I believe and take it.'

(*Freedom's Own Island*, A.S. Bryant, 1986)

EXTRACT D
Critics of the Elizabethan Church, 1598

There is a sect in England called Puritans. These, following Calvin's teachings, reject all ancient ceremonies, they do not allow any organs or altars in their places of worship. They oppose any differences in rank among churchmen, such as bishops, deans, etc. They were first named Puritans by the Jesuit Sandys. They do not live separately but mix with those of the Church of England in the colleges.

(*Travels in England*, P. Hentzner, 1598)

Now test yourself

Knowledge and understanding

1 Show how, after Henry VIII's death, religious laws and practices became (a) sometimes more Protestant than they had been; (b) sometimes more Catholic.
2 Why were the Puritans an important group of people in the 16th and 17th centuries and how did the monarchs deal with them?

Using the sources

1 Read *extracts A and B*. (a) Where in these extracts are there statements of fact? Where do they include someone's opinion?
2 Look at *pictures 1 and 2*. (a) How can we use these pictures to show similarities and differences between the Church in Henry's time and Elizabeth's time? (b) Are these drawings good guides to what happened to the Church in Tudor times? Why?

THE COUNTRYSIDE – CHANGED YET UNCHANGING

During this period most people lived in small villages and worked on the land. Their lives were very similar to those of their ancestors (pages 20–21). Of course there were some changes. Books were published to tell farmers about new crops such as the turnip, potato and clover, some of which enriched the soil, or gave winter food for animals, and provided a better diet for the people. The books also told farmers about improved tools (e.g. better spades and scythes) and how to improve the soil by marling (adding lime and clay to light soil) and manuring.

Most of these improvements depended on the work of reforming landowners. Many were the politicians who had gained from the sale of monastic lands (page 50). They bought land to show that they were members of the 'upper class' and because they hoped to make money from it (*extract A*).

1. Hatfield House, Hertfordshire, home of the Cecils, advisers to Elizabeth I and James I.

Many of them put hedges around what had been large open fields and common land (page 22): this enclosing (*extract A*) cost money: hedges had to be planted around the enclosure, ditches dug to drain the large enclosed field and new grasses sown to provide pasture for cattle and, most often, for large flocks of sheep. It was only the rich who could afford to spend the large sums of money needed for enclosure – from the sale of wool to the growing number of clothiers, the rich became even richer (*extract C*).

Some old landowners either could not afford to spend the money needed, or perhaps did not want to: they then sold their estates to 'improvers', such as Bess of Hardwick (*extract B*).

After 1650, as the population of England began to grow, there was an increased demand for food. So some landowners ploughed up their enclosed fields or enclosed more land which they ploughed. Here they grew wheat, barley and rye from which bread was made. They also grew clover and turnips, which they learnt to do from Dutch farmers. These provided food for sheep and cattle during wintertime. This meant that there was a greater supply of fresh meat, milk and butter.

These new landowners also built great country houses. Hatfield (*picture 1*) and Longleat (*picture 2*) were typical. Bess of Hardwick (*extract B*) supervised the building of four such large houses, the most famous being Hardwick Hall. These owners paid for huge windows, which made their homes much lighter than the gloomy castles, and for many fires (and chimneys – a feature of these buildings). They bought furniture designed by great craftsmen, had their portraits painted by English or foreign artists and bought expensive clothes, gold plate and other things which showed their wealth.

However, enclosures meant that many people were driven off the land. In the past such poor

2 Longleat House, Wiltshire.

people would have been looked after by the monasteries, the guilds or the local church. Now the government had to pass a series of Poor Laws which, by 1601, had created a system by which every parish was responsible for its poor: church leaders had to collect a Poor Rate, build a workhouse, and provide work and a dole for the poor.

3. Whipping a vagrant back to his home parish.

But what if someone left their parish to look for work? Such a person, if unemployed or sick, might become a burden to another parish. So the law allowed 'wandering beggars' to be branded with a 'V' for vagrant, to be whipped from parishes other than their own (*picture 3*) and forced back to that parish. In 1662 an Act of Settlement forbade people to leave their parishes. If this Act had remained in force, the later growth of industrial towns would not have happened (page 104–5).

EXTRACT A
New and improving landlords

These owners of old monastic lands now improve their soil by liming, marling, draining, hedging and enclosing. Their hearts, hands, eyes and all their powers concur in one thing – to force the earth to yield her utmost.

(John Norden, mapmaker, on the squires of the West Country, c1580).

EXTRACT B
A female 'improver': Bess of Hardwick (1518–1608), Countess of Shrewsbury

She was proud, furious, selfish and unfeeling, a builder, a buyer and seller of estates, a money-lender, a farmer and a merchant of coals, leads and timber. She kept close accounts and was a terror to her servants.

(*Country Life*, K. Butcher, 1970)

EXTRACT C
Bishop Latimer's protest against the new landowners, 1549

My father was a yeoman. He had no land of his own but rented a farm of three or four pounds a year at the most. Here he tilled as much land as employed six men. He had land for 100 sheep, and my mother milked 30 cows. He put me to school, otherwise I would not be preaching before your Majesty now. He married off my sisters, giving them five pounds each. He gave hospitality to poor neighbours, and alms to other poor. And all this from that farm. Today the tenant has to pay 16 pounds a year, or more; he is unable to do anything for his children or the poor. All the raising of rents and rearing of sheep and cattle bring profit only to the landowner.

EXTRACT D
A wealthy country

In England there are more things to produce riches and manufacture than in any two countries in the world. There is great wool, the most and best tin and lead, and flesh to feed the workers, and corn enough for the life of man, and the safest and best harbours.

(*Englands' Improvement*, Andrew Youranton, 1677).

Now test yourself

Knowledge and understanding

1 Make a list of the changes made in English farming in this period.
2 What were the most important consequences of those changes for (a) poor people; (b) the appearance of fields; (c) landowners' homes.
3 Look back at pages 18–21 (a) What were (i) the similarities and (ii) differences between farms of the 11th century and farms of the 16th and 17th centuries.

Using the sources

1 How can *extracts A, B and D* be used to explain why England was becoming a rich country in this period?
2 Why are *pictures 1–3* useful to historians writing about (a) the pleasant and (b) harsh aspects of life in Elizabethan England.

OVERSEAS TRADE AND COLONIES

1. The Drake Cup, presented in 1582.

2. An English gentleman – the sort who commanded ships around the world.

3. The charter of the Hudson's Bay Company, May 1670.

Turkish conquests in Asia Minor and the Balkans closed the old Mediterranean routes to the Far East. Europeans had to look for new routes: the Portuguese found a new way via the Cape of Good Hope; the Spaniards sailed west. Both countries founded empires in South and Central America. England played little part in this exploration.

After 1551 there was a drop in European demand for English cloth and merchants had to look for new markets. Adventurous sailors such as Humphrey Gilbert, Francis Drake (*picture 1*), Martin Frobisher and others (*picture 2*) faced great dangers as they sailed their small ships, knowing that Spanish and Portuguese fleets might attack them.

Even when trading with Europe, merchants had formed the Company of Merchant Staplers and the Company of Merchant Adventurers (pages 36–7). Elizabethans formed such companies to trade with the wider world. Each company had its royal charter (*picture 3*), giving its members the monopoly of trade in a certain area. Merchants formed 'joint stock ventures' and received a share of profits: a person who put in £100 received twice the profit of the one who put in £50:

- The Muscovy Company (1553) traded with Russia (*extract A*).
- The Eastland Company (1578) traded in the Baltic.
- The Levant Company (1581) traded in the eastern Mediterranean.
- The East India Company (1600) traded in the Far East (*extract C*).

Some people thought England did well from this trade (*extract B*). Spain and Portugal resented England's growth. Spain also did not like any English intrusion into its slave trade with Spanish America.

During the 17th century Britain fought wars against France and Holland over foreign trade and Britain's search for colonies. Its first colonies were small ventures on the eastern seaboard of North America. Private investors received royal charters giving a company the right to take over a certain area: so the Virginia, Massachusetts and other companies were formed.

Merchants from Bristol and Liverpool also developed the profitable triangle of trade (*picture 4*) based on the slave trade (pages 168–9). The Treaty of Utrecht (1713) ended a long period of wars with France and Spain and gave Britain a monopoly of that cruel trade (*extract D*).

By 1750 trade with colonies in North America, the West Indies and Asia gave some merchants large profits which would be used to finance the first stages of the Industrial Revolution (pages 108–9).

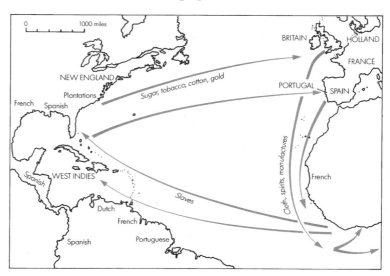

4. The 'triangle of trade' (pages 168–9)

5. Broad Street quay, Bristol, in the 18th century.

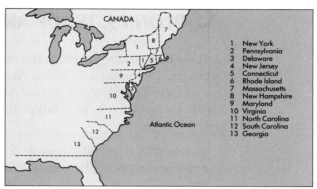

6. The American colonies, 1770.

EXTRACT A
The Muscovy Company's exports from Russia, 1560

5th May 1560. The goods we want you to prepare for our ships to carry are wax, tallow, oils, flax, cables and ropes, and furs, mainly sables. We look for a trade worth £3000.

(Directors of the Muscovy Company to their agent in Russia, Anthony Jenkinson, 1560)

EXTRACT B
England, the most successful trading nation, 1589

The English in searching every quarter of the globe have excelled all the nations. For which of our people, before this reign, had ever seen the Caspian Sea, dealt with the Emperor of Persia or Constantinople? Who, before her Majesty won for her merchants great privileges, ever found English agents in Syria, Aleppo, Babylon, Basra, and which is more, at Goa? What English ships before this anchored in the River Plate, went through the straits of Magellan, travelled the coast of Chile, went to the Philippines in spite of the enemy? When before did our merchants trade with the princes of the Moluccas and bring home the goods of China?

(Richard Hakluyt, 1589)

EXTRACT C
Jehangir Khan, ruler of India, to King James I, 1614

The letter of friendship which you sent, and the presents, I have received from your ambassador, Sir Thomas Roe. I have given command to all my dominions to receive all the merchants of the English nation, that wherever they choose to live, they should be treated well; that they be free to sail or buy as they wish; and at whichever port they arrive, neither Portugal nor any other shall dare to attack them.

EXTRACT D
The Treaty of Utrecht, 1713, and the Assiento

This peace was beneficial to Great Britain: several advantages were gained – Hudson's Bay, the island of St Christopher's, all Novia Scotia, Minorca, Gibraltar and all that Assiento trade which allows us alone the privilege of sending ships to trade with Spanish America and of taking there 4,800 slaves a year.

(Somers Tracts, 1715)

Now test yourself

Knowledge and understanding

1 Which individuals or groups were responsible for developing English trade with (a) Russia; (b) the Baltic; (c) the eastern Mediterranean; (d) India; (e) South America?
2 Make two lists to show (a) the short-term and (b) the long-term effects of the setting up of merchant companies.

Using the sources

1 How can each of the extracts be used to help historians write about the development of English trade?
2 Does *extract B* give an accurate account of the extent of English trade at this time?
3 How can the pictures be used to help us learn about (a) merchants' wealth; (b) Francis Drake; (c) British trade with America and Africa; (d) the trading ports?

COLONIES, TRADE AND TWO REVOLUTIONS

Britain had gained some colonies in the 17th century (page 56). The most important were the 13 colonies in North America (page 57, *picture 6*), each of which had its own elected parliament. However, a British governor could set aside any decisions made by a state (or colonial) parliament. The British government made sure that:

1 colonies did not start any industry to compete with a British one: so no American woollen or iron industries and no Irish woollen industry were founded.

2 colonies supplied Britain with goods which could not be produced in the home country. North America supplied timber, tobacco and pig iron; the East Indies and India sent spices, coffee, tea and silks; from the West Indies came sugar, rum and timber. Many of these goods were made into manufactured products near Bristol (page 57, *picture 5*), Liverpool (page 61, *extract A*), Glasgow or London, which became important industrial centres. More people were employed – in harbour work, warehouses, manufacturing and transport – at or near these ports. They then had money to spend on home-made goods and so provided one spur to the first Industrial Revolution (page 108).

Many of the imported goods were re-exported to Europe. This increased the demand for banks to look after the financing of import and export trades. The growth of local banking systems was an important help to the first industrialists (page 108; see also page 37, *extract A*).

Europe had once been the main market for British goods, but the colonies grew in importance as markets (*extract A*). This was a second spur to the first Industrial Revolution: the domestic system (page 109, *extract A*) was unable to provide enough goods.

The West Indies grew in importance (*extract A*). Its sugar plantations, like the cotton and tobacco plantations of North America, depended on the work done by the millions of slaves carried from Africa in British slave ships (page 56, *picture 4*).

The search for new colonies and the defence of existing ones led to a series of wars with France, Spain and Holland.

1698–1713. War with France and Spain ended with the Treaty of Utrecht (1713) (page 57, *extract D*).

1730–48. War with France and Spain was due mainly to rivalry with France in India and Canada and with Spain in America. It was a dress rehearsal for the next and more important war.

1756–63. The Seven Years' War was fought in Europe where Frederick of Prussia looked after British interests, while Britain drove the French from both India and Canada, won fresh colonies in the West Indies and took Florida from Spain.

These wars had been very costly, and after 1763 the British had to leave an army in North America to guard the colonies against attacks by the native American Indians. With the removal of the threats from France (in Canada) and Spain (in Florida), the colonists felt less need of British help. They also disliked British attempts to force them to pay internal taxes to meet part of the costs of their defence.

1764–70. Successive British governments tried to impose taxes on sugar imports into the colonies and on newspapers, advertisements and legal documents in the colonies, only to find that the colonists boycotted the taxed goods and formed organizations to protest against 'taxation without representation'.

1770. A Boston mob attacked a British army patrol, which fired on the mob, leading to the 'Boston Massacre' and to increased hatred of Britain in the colonies.

1772. A British revenue ship, the *Gaspée*, ran aground off Providence, Rhode Island. Americans rowed out and burnt it which increased British hostility.

1773. When the British allowed the East India Company to sell tea in the colonies at less than the price of smuggled tea, angry Americans boarded three tea ships in Boston harbour and tipped their cargo of tea overboard (December).

1774. In retaliation, the British closed the port of Boston, dismissed its Assembly (parliament) and put the colony of Massachusetts under military government.

1775. The colonists of Massachusetts organized an army, collected military stores at Concord and joined with other colonies in a Continental Congress to present a united front to the British government. When British soldiers went to seize the arms dump at Concord, they were met by colonists at Lexington and 244 British soldiers were killed. This was the start of the American Revolution.

1775–83. The British had little chance of winning the war that followed. The Americans fought for a cause, for their homes and families. They had, in their Congress, a government to organize the war and in George Washington, they had an inspiring leader. The British, on the other hand, had to bring supplies on a six-week voyage across the Atlantic where French, Dutch and Spanish navies attacked British shipping.

In 1781 most of the British army surrendered to a Franco–American army at Yorktown. After this, the British fought to regain control of the seas and to hold on to their West Indian colonies.

1783. The Treaty of Versailles ended the War of American Independence, which had been demanded in the Declaration of Independence (1776). However, even after gaining their independence, Americans continued to buy large amounts of British goods (*extracts A–C*).

EXTRACT A
British exports and imports (%)

	Exports			Imports		
	1750	1770	1797	1750	1770	1800
Europe	77	49	38	55	45	43
North America	11	25	22	11	12	7
West Indies	5	12	25	19	25	25
East Indies and Africa	7	14	13	15	18	25
Total in £m	9.5	9.6	21.6	7.7	12.2	28.3

(Compiled from custom house ledgers, PRO customs)

EXTRACT B
The importance of the American market, 1812

Those in Birmingham that are totally employed in the American trade are 50,000 excluding the nail trade which employs another 20,000 in the American trade. About two-thirds of all people are employed in the export trades, including trade to the United States.

(Joseph Shaw, Chairman of Birmingham Chamber of Foreign Commerce in evidence to a Parliamentary Committee, 1812)

EXTRACT C
Sheffield and the American trade, 1821

What is the population of Sheffield? According to the 1811 census about 53,000. *How many are employed in the American trade?* 4000 men and 2000 women and children: about 6000 in all. *How many work in the home trade?* 6000 men and 1000 women and children. *How many work in the foreign trade, excluding the American trade?* 2000 men and 1000 women and children. This trade includes trade with Spain, Portugal, the West Indies, South America and Canada. *What proportion of Sheffield goods go to America?* About one-third of all our manufactures; the home market takes about one-half.

(John Bailey, Sheffield exporter and home producer to a Parliamentary Committee, 1812)

Now test yourself

Knowledge and understanding

1 Show why the colonies were important to Britain (a) as markets for goods; (b) suppliers of raw material; (c) helping the growth of the banking system

2 Explain (a) how the search for colonies caused war between European countries; (b) the reasons why the American colonists overthrew British rule.

Using the sources

1 Read *extracts B and C*. (a) Do these show that Adam Smith was right to describe Britain as 'a nation of shopkeepers'? (b) How reliable do you think the statements in these extracts are likely to be and how do you think they can be checked?

2 How useful is *extract A* to historians writing about the effects of the colonies on Britain's economy? Explain your answer.

TOWNS, TRADE AND WEALTH

1. London in 1600.

2. St Peter's Hospital, Bristol: a typical town house from c1600.

Most people lived in villages (page 54) but some towns grew in this period (1500–1750). London (*picture 1*) spread on both sides of the Thames; Norwich, the second largest town, grew with the cloth trade; Exeter (page 32, *picture 3*) was the centre of the West Country cloth trade, as was Bristol (page 57, *picture 5*), which also gained from the growth of colonial trade and slavery (pages 168–9). Liverpool (*extract A*) developed rapidly; Leicester (*extract E*) was a typical small town – in 1700 its population was 3000.

Older towns showed their medieval origins: walls and gates (pages 32–3, *pictures 3 and 4*), market crosses and lack of water supply (*extracts D and E*). In old and newer towns, wealthy people showed off their wealth in larger and more comfortable houses (*picture 2*), with the furniture made by great craftsmen, and in their fashionable clothes (*extracts B and C*).

However, towns and even new houses were all too often very dirty. In 1660 the country suffered another Black Death, or plague, with London suffering more than the rest (*extract F*). Even so, businessmen continued to meet in their coffee houses (*picture 3*), another outward sign of the industrial growth which formed the basis for the later Industrial Revolution.

Towns were not only dirty; they were also dangerous places in which to live. The unemployed, and other hungry people, often turned to crime, and since there was no organised police system, they often got away with it. There were also groups of (often) drunken toughs who attacked people in the streets which were unlit at nighttime, making the escape of the attackers even easier. And on many occasions mobs were roused by political or religious fanatics and rampaged through the streets, looting and burning as they went.

3. Meeting in the coffee house.

You have all manner of news there: you have a good fire which you may sit by as long as you please: you have a dish of coffee: you meet your friends for the transaction of business, and all for a penny if you don't want to spend more.

(*Memoirs*, Maximilian Misson, 1719)

EXTRACT A
Liverpool: a wonder of the age

Mostly new houses of brick and stone after the London fashion. It was a few fishermen's houses, and now is a large fine town with very handsome streets, persons well-dressed, it is London in miniature.

(Celia Fiennes, 1698)

It is still visibly growing in wealth, people, business and buildings. It has an increasing trade, not only rivalling but outstripping Bristol in trade to the American colonies. They send ships to Norway, Hamburg, the Baltic, Flanders … like Londoners they are universal merchants.

(Daniel Defoe, 1724)

A small town 60 years ago, the slave trade to the Spanish colonies was the basis of its commercial greatness. A beautiful town.

(Alexis de Tocqueville, 1833)

EXTRACT B
Improved living standards

In noblemen's houses it is not rare to see rich tapestries, silverware and other plate. In the houses of knights, gentlemen and merchants you can see tapestries, pewter, brass, fine linen and costly cupboards with pewter. Many farmers also have beds with tapestries and silk hangings, tables with fine linen. Old men say that three things have altered most in their memory: the many chimneys on larger houses – in the old days there might have been only two or three in a town: the great improvement in beds – we used to lie on straw sacks or rough mats: the change from wooden vessels to pewter and from wooden spoons to silver or tin ones.

(*A Description of England*, William Harrison, 1577)

EXTRACT C
Upwardly mobile merchants, 1726

Trade in England makes gentlemen; for tradesmen's children, or their grandchildren, come to be as good gentlemen, MPs, judges, and noblemen as those of ancient families. As they grow wealthy they get coats of arms which they put on their coaches, furniture and new houses.

(Daniel Defoe, 1726)

EXTRACT D
London's water supply, 1599

Spring water is enclosed in stone cisterns in different parts of the town. It is let off into iron-bound buckets which men carry to houses and sell.

(*Travels in England*, Thomas Platter, 1599)

EXTRACT E
Leicester's water supply, 1690

They have a water house and a mill to turn the water into pipes to serve the town as it is in London. It comes on only once a day, so they save the water in deep cisterns; there are wells in some streets to draw water by handwheel for the use of the towns.

(*Journeys*, Celia Fiennes, 1685–98)

EXTRACT F
The diarist Samuel Pepys on the plague, 1665

30 April:	Great fear of the sickness in the City: houses already shut up.
7 June:	Saw houses in Drury Lane with red crosses on the doors.
10 June:	The plague is come into the City.
21 June:	I found almost all the town leaving, coaches full of people.
13 July:	About 700 dead of the plague this week.
27 July:	The weekly list of deaths, about 1,700 of the plague.
10 Aug:	About 3000 died of the plague this week. Wrote my Will.
31 Aug:	Every day sadder. Number of dead this week near 10,000.

Now test yourself

Knowledge and understanding

1 (a) Make a list of reasons why towns grew in England. (b) What reasons are common to the growth of many towns?
(c) How was the growth of some towns linked to the activities of individuals and companies that you read about (pages 56–7)?

2 How did the growth of towns (a) benefit some groups; (b) harm others?

Using the sources

1 (a) How do *extracts A and E* offer differing views of town life in the 17th century?
(b) How do you explain these differences?

2 Are the extracts and pictures in this topic useful to historians writing about town life in the 17th century? Why?

S COTLAND, 1500–1603

In 1503 Henry VIII's sister, Margaret, married James IV of Scotland (page 45, *picture 4*). But in 1512 Scotland sided with France and went to war against England. James was killed in the disaster of Flodden (1513). James V (1513–42) confirmed the alliance with France by marrying Mary of Guise (*picture 1*). In 1542 he led Scotland into war against England: he died two weeks after the defeat at Solway Moss. His daughter, Mary, now became Queen of Scots.

Henry VIII wanted to arrange a marriage between his 5-year-old son, Edward, and Mary, the 'baby Queen'. He hoped that this would end the threat from the North. However, in 1547 he sent an army to try to force the Scots to accept his proposal. The Scots sent the 5-year-old Mary to France, leaving her mother, Mary of Guise, to rule in her place. Ten years later, the Queen of Scots married the French King's eldest son and she became Queen of France. After the death of England's Mary I (1558), Mary, Queen of Scots, argued that she had a better claim to the English crown than did Elizabeth. Her coat of arms included the badges of three countries – Scotland, France and England (page 48, *picture 3*).

Mary of Guise was opposed by Protestant Reformers and by nobles hoping for a share in Church lands. In 1559 Knox (*picture 3*) became the Protestants' leader. Elizabeth I helped them in the fight against 'French Mary Guise' who was forced to sign the Treaty of Edinburgh (1560): the French had to leave and a Parliament was called. That Reformation Parliament (1560) abolished the Catholic religion and papal power in Scotland and outlined plans for a Scottish Church.

Mary, Queen of Scots, came from France (1561), now the widow of King Francis II of France. Her private practice of Catholicism angered Knox, and her two marriages lost her the support of most Scots. The first was to her cousin, Henry Darnley, who grew jealous of her secretary, Rizzio. He planned Rizzio's death (1566) only to be murdered himself in 1568. Mary then married the Earl of Bothwell, her lover and the person suspected of arranging Darnley's death. Her Catholicism and this marriage led Scottish nobles to rise against her. She was defeated, but escaped from prison to flee to England.

Elizabeth I condemned the Scottish rebels (*extract A*), but kept Mary under house arrest. She was the centre for Catholic plots against Elizabeth, especially after the Pope had excommunicated 'good Queen Bess' in 1570. Parliament clashed with Elizabeth over her moderate treatment of Mary, but it was in Elizabeth's own interests to keep Mary alive: the Armada attacked England only after her death.

Mary's son, James VI, ruled Scotland in his own right after 1587. He was involved in the argument about what sort of Church Scotland should have. Was it to be:

(a) Presbyterian, governed by delegates elected by local churches? or

(b) Episcopalian, governed by bishops?

Knox's supporters wanted the more democratic form, Presbyterian. James managed to keep some powers for the bishops, but not as much as English bishops had in their Church.

1. Mary of Guise.

2. Mary, Queen of Scots.

3. John Knox at the court of Mary.

When Elizabeth died (1603), Robert Cecil, her chief Minister, sent for James and brought this great-great-grandson of Henry VII to the throne as James I of England, Wales and Ireland. One of his first meetings was with various religious leaders in 1604 (*extract C*). That meeting contained the seeds of future problems for later Stuart monarchs.

4. James I of England.

EXTRACT A
Elizabeth I and the Divine Right of the Queen of Scots

'They had no authority by the law of God or man to dethrone their Queen, and to act as superiors over their Sovereign, no matter what they think of her.'

(Quoted in *Freedom's Own Island*, A.S. Bryant, 1986)

EXTRACT B
A French warning about the Queen of Scots, 1586

If you proceed to the extreme with the Queen of Scots, those connected with her in blood and friendship will take the same course (against you). If you show your goodness to her, all princes will watch over your preservation. Our King promises to hinder in every way all attempts made against you, as a sincere friend and brother. You will be more secure if she lives than if you kill her, as you know better than any other person.

(French envoy to Elizabeth I, December 1586)

EXTRACT C
James and the English Puritans, 1604

Dr Reynolds, for the extremists, referred to the synod, where a bishop, with his presbytery, determined all points. At this His Majesty stirred, thinking they proposed a Scottish presbytery. He said: 'I will tell you a tale. After Edward VI's religion was overthrown by Mary here in England, we in Scotland felt the effect of it. Master Knox wrote to the Queen telling her that she was Supreme Head of the Church and asked her to suppress the Popish bishops who oppose reform. By her authority the Popish bishops were suppressed. Then Knox and his followers felt strong enough to undertake the Reformation themselves. They made small account of the Queen's power as they made this further Reformation.' Then he said: 'My lords bishops, these men think they cannot win against you except by appealing to my supremacy. But, if once you were out and they were in, I know what would become of my supremacy. As I have said before, "No bishop, no King." I will make these men conform themselves, or I will harry them out of my kingdom.'

(An account of the Hampton Court Conference, 14 January 1604, by William Barlow, later Bishop of Rochester, and then of Lincoln)

Now test yourself

Knowledge and understanding

1 Make two lists to show the (a) long-term reasons; (b) short-term reasons why Mary, Queen of Scots, was a threat to Elizabeth.
2 What were the effects of the conflict between Mary, Queen of Scots, and Elizabeth on (a) Mary herself; (b) the Spanish; (c) James VI.

Using the sources

1 How can we use *extract C* to help us understand (a) James I's attitudes towards the Puritans; (b) the attitudes of many Scottish religious leaders towards the Catholics; (c) the attitude of the author of the extract?
2 Look at the pictures. Are they useful to historians who wish to know more about the characters of Mary of Guise, Mary, Queen of Scots, and John Knox? Give reasons for your answer.
3 Is *extract A* (a) a statement of fact; (b) opinion; (c) a mixture of both fact and opinion? Give reasons for your answer.

CROWN AND PARLIAMENT, 1603–42

In this period, two kings quarrelled with Parliament. The issues involved were:

❶ **Royal claims to Divine Right** (*extract A*). Elizabeth I had also made this claim (page 46, *extracts A–D*). But in 1601 she had the wisdom to give way to Parliament's anger.

❷ **Religion.** James I's defence of the bishops (page 63, *extract C*) angered the Puritans. More people were alarmed by Charles I's Catholic marriage and the 'Romish' policies of Archbishop Laud (*extract C*).

❸ **Wars and taxation.**
1625: MPs refused Charles the money to fight his unsuccessful war against Spain. He then forced the collection of illegal taxes and made many enemies.
1627: An attack on France was badly organized, led to 4000 deaths and the disgrace of Charles' favourite, Buckingham (*extract B*).
1628: Charles called a Parliament to get money for his war. Pym (*picture 1*) and Hampden (*picture 2*) attacked his war policy and illegal taxation. Coke (*picture 3*) drew up the Petition of Rights, listing Charles's errors. Because he needed money, Charles accepted the petition.
1629: MPs voted Charles the taxes he asked for, but for only one year, because he rejected their criticism of Laud (*extract C*). He, in turn, rejected their offer of a year's taxes as limiting his freedom, and he dissolved Parliament.

❹ **Ship money.** This was an old tax once paid by coastal towns for coastal defences. Charles imposed it throughout the country. Many wouldn't pay (*picture 2*).

❺ **Scotland.** The Scots were angry at Charles's cancellation of the grants of Church land made since 1540 and Laud's attempts to bring the Scottish Church into line with the Anglican Church. The introduction of a new Prayer Book led to rioting (*picture 4*), the formation of a National Committee and the signing of a National Covenant for the defence of 'the true religion'. In November 1638 a Scottish General Assembly deposed all bishops and banned the new Prayer Book. Charles invaded Scotland and began 'The Bishops' Wars'. He was forced to make peace and to

1. John Pym.

2. A list of those residents of Great Kimble, Buckinghamshire refusing to pay ship money. Hampden's name is at the top of the list.

3. Edward Coke: led the opposition to Charles I.

4. An angry scene when a clergyman tried to read the new Prayer Book in Scotland: from a 17th-century print.

call an English Parliament. He brought his friend, Wentworth, from Ireland (page 67, *extract D*) to lead a new attack on Scotland. But Parliament refused him the money he needed for this. Instead, it criticized his policies and his choice of advisers. He dismissed Parliament, but was forced to recall it when a Scottish army invaded England and occupied Newcastle.

6 **Wentworth.** The new Parliament included many Puritans. Wentworth wanted Charles to arrest Parliament's leaders. He hesitated and the Commons persuaded the House of Lords to try Wentworth (Lord Stafford). When he was found guilty of misconduct, Charles weakly accepted the decision and signed his adviser's death warrant on 9 May.

7 **Ireland.** A fresh Irish rebellion forced Charles to ask for money for a new army. Instead Parliament drew up a list of grievances (page 67, *extract E*).

8 **'The birds had flown'.** In January 1642 Charles went to arrest the five leading anti-royal MPs (*picture 5*). They escaped. Charles then left London – to which he would return as a prisoner awaiting trial (pages 68–9).

5. Charles I attempting to arrest his leading opponents – but they had fled.

EXTRACT A
James I's idea of Divine Right, 1610

The state of monarchy is the supremest thing on earth. Kings are God's lieutenants. They exercise a manner of divine power on earth. To dispute what God may do is blasphemy: so it is sedition for subjects to dispute what a King may do.

(James I to the Commons, 1610)

EXTRACT B
Parliament versus Buckingham and Charles I, 1626

Eliot moved that, as we intended to supply his Majesty with money, we should also give him advice. He asked for a declaration to the King of the danger in which the kingdom stood by the decay of religion, the insufficiency of his generals, the weakness of his councils, the

deaths of his men, the decay of trade, the loss of shipping, the many and powerful enemies, the few and poor friends abroad. Coke protested that the cause of these miseries was Buckingham, which led to acclamation by the House.

(Thomas Alured, 1626)

EXTRACT C
The High Anglicanism of Archbishop Laud

Laud departed from the Reformation and drew near to Rome. His theology was far from that of the Calvinists. His love for ceremonies, for holy days and sacred places, his dislike of the marriage of clergy, the zeal with which he asserted the claims of the clergy, made him hated by Puritans.

(*History of England*, T.B. Macaulay, 1849)

Now test yourself

Knowledge and understanding

1 Having read the text and the extracts, make three columns and put as many causes of the conflict between Charles I and Parliament as you can under these three headings: (a) causes going back before 1629; (b) causes which grew 1629–40; (c) causes which appeared after 1640.

2 Using the lists you have made, mark the causes either (a) political; (b) economic; (c) social. Explain your answer in each case.

Using the sources

1 Read *extracts A and B*. How do these extracts give differing views of the powers of king and Parliament?

2 How valuable is *extract C* for historians trying to discover more about Laud's policies? (Macaulay was biased in favour of the parliamentary argument.)

3 How useful are *pictures 2 and 5* as evidence of the opposition to the monarchy? Explain your answer.

IRELAND – CONTINUALLY RESTLESS

With Anglo-Irish nobles controlling some areas and Celtic chiefs even more, royal power in Ireland was limited to the Dublin Pale (*extract A* and page 41, *picture 7*). The Irish supported Simnel (*extract B*) and later another 'pretender', Warbeck in their attempts to take the throne.

Henry VIII closed the monasteries and schools as part of his Reformation. A Catholic rising ended in 1537 with the execution of five Earls at Tyburn. Henry tried to bribe Celtic chiefs with titles: O'Neil became Earl of Tyrone. But nationalism and Catholicism were stronger than such worldly considerations. Mary I planted English settlers in King's County (Leix) and Queen's County (Offaly), failing to see that, to the Irish, these were merely 'colonizers'.

Elizabeth I feared that Spain would use Ireland as a base for attacks on England. She planted areas of Ireland: Raleigh and other favourites became major landowning 'colonizers'. In 1595, Hugh O'Neil (Earl of Tyrone) had Spanish help in his rebellion. After his defeat of the English at Yellow Ford (1597) Elizabeth sent Essex to Ireland as Lord Lieutenant (*picture 1*). He failed to beat Tyrone, whose army (*picture 2* and *extract C*) used the terrain wisely and forced Essex to sign a truce. An angry Elizabeth recalled Essex whose foolish ambition led him to challenge Elizabeth. She had him executed.

James I signed a truce with Tyrone and Tyrconnel who were made viceroys to rule on his behalf. However, they led another rising (1607). When this failed they fled and James gave their Ulster estates to English and Scottish settlers.

Charles I sent his favourite, Thomas Wentworth, to rule Ireland. His ruthless and 'thorough' rule (*extract D*) united Ulster Puritans and Irish Catholics. It was the Catholics who rose in 1641 (*extracts F–G*) when Charles was involved in his Scottish Wars (page 64). Parliament refused him the money he needed for this, but issued its Grand Remonstrance (*extract E*) taking England to the brink of civil war.

1. The Earl of Essex.

Bias in people's views

The most recent research shows that about 4000 Protestants were killed by Catholic rebels in October 1641 and that as many Catholics were also killed by Protestants. The historian R.E. Foster wrote: 'The numbers killed in the "massacre" were inflated to fantastic levels' (*Modern Ireland: 1600–1972*, 1988).

2. Marching through Ireland.

EXTRACT A
England controls only the Pale, 1574

Continued revolts against the English planted here forced them into certain shires in Leinster open to receive help from England, a Pale from which they dared not peep.

(Walter Devereux, Earl of Essex, Earl Marshall of Ireland)

EXTRACT B
The Irish use Lambert Simnel, 1487

… Simnel called a meeting of Irish nobles whom he understood were opposed to Henry VII. He told them he was the son of the Duke of Clarence. This story was believed by the nobles who named him King Edward VI.

(*History of England*, Polydore Vergil, 1534)

EXTRACT C
An English view of the Irish soldiers, 1603

Their cavalry do not use saddles, stirrups, boots or spurs, so they can nimbly jump off their horses. They carry heavy spears and swords. They have no armour except a helmet. They use hit and run attacks … fly off, knowing we dare not follow them into the bog. Their real strength are their foot soldiers.

(*The Glory of England*, Thomas Gainsford, 1618)

EXTRACT D
Wentworth and the Church, 1633

You fear the Church is bound by Common Law. No such considerations shall direct me until I see my master's power set above Coke and his Year Books, and I am not assured that the same resolution governs your lordship. Let us then, in the name of God, go cheerfully and boldly. And thus you have my Thorough and Thorough.

(From a letter to Archbishop Laud, quoted in *Illustrated History of England*, G.M. Trevelyan, 1926)

EXTRACT E
The Grand Remonstrance, November 1641

183. Our intention is to reduce that power which the bishops have taken.
185. We desire a general synod of the most learned divines of this country with some from abroad, to consider all things necessary for the Church, the results of their consultation to receive the authority of Parliament.
197. That His Majesty be petitioned to employ such ministers as Parliament has confidence in, without which we cannot give him supplies for his own estate nor assistance for the Protestant party abroad.

(*History of the Great Rebellion*, Earl of Clarendon, c 1670)

WHAT HAPPENED AT THE START OF THE 1641 REVOLT?

EXTRACT F
How does he know?

The outbreak of the rebellion in 1641 had been marked by the massacre or death by starvation of about 12,000 Scottish or English planters. This was not part of a deliberate plan. Many Catholic priests intervened to save planters' lives.

(*A Short History of Ireland*, John Ranelagh, 1983)

EXTRACT G
And what is his bias?

In 1641 the Roman Catholic Church decided to exterminate Protestants in Ulster and there took place one of the most bloody massacres in Irish history. It was led by the priests, and the rivers ran red with Protestant blood. The River Bann was so choked with Protestant bodies, that Catholics could walk dry shod across the river.

(Ian Paisley, Democratic Unionist MP, September 1969)

Now test yourself

Knowledge and understanding

1 Explain (a) why the English wanted to conquer Ireland; (b) the short-term effects and (c) long-term effects of the English attempt to conquer Ireland.
2 List and explain the reasons why the English found it difficult to conquer Ireland. (Look at *extracts A–C*.)

Using the sources

1 Read *extracts F–G*. Are these sources equally reliable as evidence for what happened in the 1641 Protestant revolt? Explain your answer.
2 Read *extract E*. Now read page 49, *extracts A–E*. (a) Compare the views of the powers of the king, Parliament and the Church in *extract E* here with those given on page 41. (b) What is the significance of these differences?

THE CIVIL WARS

The first war began when Charles left London after failing to arrest the five leading MPs (pages 64–5). He went to the north hoping to find more supporters as he moved further away from London. In August 1642 he raised his standard at Nottingham and asked his people to follow him. Parliament began to raise an army in London.

The Civil Wars did not involve most ordinary people unless they joined one of the armies. Most people in the south and east of England supported Parliament; the north and the west (except for Plymouth) supported the king. Most of his supporters were noblemen and their followers; they were good horsemen (and were called Cavaliers). They were trained in using weapons so that they won most of the early battles. Parliament's support came from townspeople, small farmers and merchants. They were called Roundheads. Few of them had horses, so they fought on foot and, at the start, were at a disadvantage. However, as they gained control of more of the country, they could pay and equip troops, while Parliament's control of the navy made it difficult for the king to get supplies from France.

1. Parliamentarian troops destroying ornaments in a church: from a Royalist print

Oliver Cromwell was Parliament's best general. After early defeats by the Cavaliers, Cromwell trained a 'New Model Army': he insisted on discipline, training and the preaching of the idea that God supported their Puritan faith (*picture 1*). Cromwell's troops won important victories at Marston Moor and Naseby which persuaded the Scots to side with Parliament in 1643. In 1646 the Scots captured the king and sold him to Parliament.

In 1647 while the king was a prisoner, Cromwell offered him the Heads of Proposals to end the war. Parliament was to have control of the army for 10 years, before handing it back to the king, who would allow people freedom of worship. Charles rejected this offer, escaped from prison and made a deal with the Scots who wanted to have a weak king rather than a strong Cromwell in power in England. Cromwell defeated the Scots at Preston (1648) and the king was re-arrested.

In December 1648 Cromwell cleared the Commons of all MPs sympathetic to Charles and demanded that he be put on trial in January 1649. He was accused of many crimes (*extract C* and *picture 2*), but refused to defend himself in front of what he saw as an 'illegal court' (*extract D*). He was found guilty and executed (*extract E* and *picture 3*). England now became a republic led by Cromwell (pages 70–71).

2. Charles I on trial.

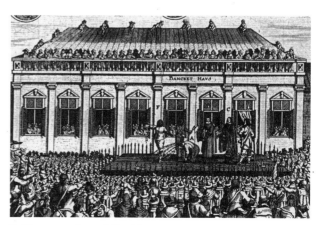

3. The execution of the king.

EXTRACT A
Two gentlemen on different sides in the war

My affections to you are so unchangeable, that war itself cannot violate my friendship to you. But I must be true to the cause I serve. God, the searcher of my soul, knows with what a sad sense I go to this service, and how I detest this war: but I look on it as God's work. May He send peace in his good time. We are both upon this stage, and must act the parts assigned to us in this tragedy. Let us do it in a way of honour and without personal animosities.

(Adapted from a letter by Sir William Walter, to his friend, the Royalist General, Sir Ralph Hopton)

EXTRACT B
Farmers suffer from both sides

I had eleven horses taken away by the King's soldiers, four of them worth £40. Going to market with a load of corn, Parliamentary soldiers met with my men and took away my whole team of horses. The King's soldiers accuse me of being Roundhead: Parliament's soldiers accuse me of paying my rent at Worcester, which is in Royalist hands.

(Adapted from a statement by a Midland farmer, quoted in *The Making of the United Kingdom*, Maltman and Dawson, 1992)

EXTRACT C
The accusations against Charles I, 1649

'Charles Stuart, King of England, who was entrusted to govern according to the laws of the land, had a wicked design to create an unlimited and tyrannical power, to rule according to his will, and to overthrow the rights and liberties of the people. He traitorously waged war against Parliament and the people. He renewed the war in 1648. He is thus responsible for all the treasons, murders, rapings, burnings, damage and desolation caused during those wars. He is therefore, a tyrant, a traitor, and a murderer, and an enemy to the Commonwealth of England.'

(Quoted in *British Monarchy*, J. Cannon and R. Griffiths, 1988)

EXTRACT D
Charles denies the court's right to try him, January 1649

I wish to know by what power I am called hither. I would know by what lawful authority. Remember I am your King, your lawful King, and what sins you bring upon your heads, and the judgement of God on this land, think well on it. I say, think well on it, before you go from one sin to a greater one. I have a trust given me by God, by old and lawful descent. I will not betray it to answer to a new and unlawful authority.

(Charles I to his judges)

EXTRACT E
An eyewitness at Charles I's execution

I stood amongst the crowd in the street before Whitehall gate where the scaffold was erected and saw what was done, but was not so near as to hear anything. The blow I saw given, and can truly say, with a sad heart: at the instant whereof, I remember well, there was such a groan by the thousands, as I never heard before and desire I may never hear again. There was one troop of soldiers sent immediately marching to scatter and disperse the people, so that I had difficulty to escape home without hurt.

(*Diaries*, Philip Henry, edited in 1882)

Now test yourself

Knowledge and understanding

1 Show how Charles I was brought to the scaffold by (a) Cromwell's generalship; (b) Cromwell's ruthlessness as a politician; (c) Charles's stupidity; (d) Parliament; (e) the army.

2 How far did (a) changes in the countryside (pages 54–5); (b) the development of a strong merchant class (pages 56–7); (c) the growth of towns (pages 60–61) provide long-term reasons for Parliament's success?

Using the sources

1 Read *extracts A and B*. How do they compare with one another as evidence of the effects of the Civil War? Explain your answer.

2 Read *extracts C and D*. How does *extract D* offer a different view of the power of the King from that given in *extract C*?

3 Look at *extract E* and *picture 3*. Are they equally useful as evidence for historians writing about the execution? Explain your answer.

CROMWELL'S RULE

England now had to find answers to two questions:

❶ Who had the lawful right to rule? Some wanted the king's son, Prince Charles, to be crowned as Charles II. Others thought that Parliament should rule. But in 1646 Cromwell had dismissed all MPs who had supported the king. The remaining MPs in 'the Rump Parliament' hardly had the right to rule.

❷ Who had the power to govern? Clearly only the army had – but it had no right to govern. This was a confused situation.

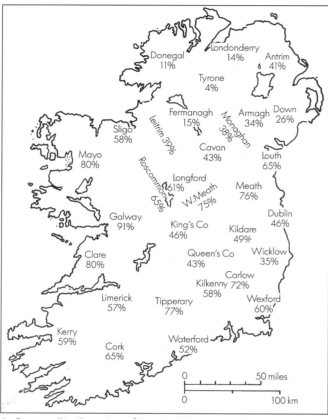

1. Cromwell's allocation of land, 1650 (*extract B*).

Cromwell was made President of the Council of State set up to govern while answers were sought to the two questions. First he crushed the Irish rebels led by the Earl of Ormonde, by cruelty (*extract A*) and by a harsh land settlement (*picture 1*). He then returned to attack the Scottish rebels (*picture 2* and *extract C*) and by 1653 had imposed his rule on Scotland. He then turned to England:

(a) He used the army to dismiss the Rump Parliament (*picture 3*).

(b) He allowed the independent Churches to elect a Parliament which spent its time arguing about the form of a future government. So the army wrote *An Instrument of Government*. This named Cromwell as Lord Protector for life and called for fresh elections. A group of extremists thought that everyone had the right to vote: these 'Levellers' were crushed by the army.

(c) The new Parliament criticized Cromwell's decision to allow people (except Catholics) to worship as they wished. So he dismissed Parliament and imposed taxes without its consent. He sacked judges who ruled against him in the courts and named five Major-Generals to govern the country. They imposed a Puritan-like system of rule. In 1656, because of a war with Spain, Cromwell called a Parliament to discuss taxation. Some MPs wanted Cromwell to take the title 'king' (*extract D*) while the powerful group of army officers were against this idea (*extract E*). Cromwell decided to dismiss Parliament and to use the army to help him collect taxes. He died in 1658.

2. Cartoon showing the Scottish rebels holding Charles II's nose to the grindstone.

Contemporaries were divided in their views on Cromwell. His soldiers and the Puritans admired him; Cavaliers hated him. Even some of his former friends thought that his success spoiled and changed him. Richard Baxter was one of them. He wrote: 'Pride made him selfish and greedy.'

3. Cromwell dismissing the Rump Parliament.

EXTRACT A
Cromwell on the massacre at Drogheda, September 1649

The enemy were about 3000 strong in the town. They made a stout resistance. Nearly 1000 of our men entered, but the enemy forced them out. God gave a new courage to our men: they entered again and beat the enemy from their defences. They had made three fortifications to left and right of where we entered, out of which they were forced to leave. We refused them quarter. I believe we put to the sword the whole number of defendants. I do not think 30 of them escaped. Those that did are in safe custody waiting to be sent to the Barbadoes. I am persuaded this is the righteous judgement of God upon these barbarous wretches who dipped their hands in innocent blood.

(Letter, 16 September 1649)

EXTRACT B
Cromwell's Irish land settlement

This, by far the worst part of Cromwell's work within the British islands, outlived him largely in the form he gave it. It completed the transfer of the soil from Irish to British owners, which had begun under the Tudors and pushed forward under the Stuarts. The object was threefold: to pay off in Irish land the soldiers who had fought and the capitalists who had provided the money for the conquest; secondly, to render the English hold upon Ireland secure against a rebellion like that of 1641; and lastly, to stamp out Catholicism. The first two objects were attained.

(*Illustrated History of England*, G.R. Trevelyan, 1926)

EXTRACT C
Cromwell on the Battle of Dunbar, 3 September 1650

The enemy's numbers were great – about 6000 horse and 16,000 foot at least: ours, about 7,500 foot and 3,500 horse. We resolved to put our business into this position: that six regiments of horse and a half of foot should march in the van … Colonel Monk to command the foot. The horse beat back all opposition, charging through the enemy's horse and foot; who were made by the Lord of Hosts as stubble to their swords. It became a total rout – about 3000 slain.

(Letter to Speaker of Parliament, 4 September 1650)

EXTRACT D
Cromwell as king, 1657?

I am commanded by Parliament to present this Petition to your Highness. The first part of the body of government is the head. Parliament liked not the name [Lord Protector]. They desire to give it the name 'king' and hope that your Highness will take that name. The name and office of king is better known and more suitable to the laws and constitutions of [Britain] than that of protector.

(Sir Thomas Widdrington's speech to Cromwell, 1657)

EXTRACT E
Cromwell's soldiers warn against 'kingship', 1657

… a number in Parliament have voted kingship for you with a small group against it, including most of the army officers. I beg your Highness to consider what you are doing. I have gone along with you since 1642. The experiences you have had of the power of God, should make you shrink from this threatening change.

(From a letter by William Bradford, a former soldier, to Cromwell, 1657)

Now test yourself

Knowledge and understanding

1 Explain how Cromwell showed his ruthlessness in dealing with (a) the Irish; (b) the Scots; (c) Parliament.
2 Look again at pages 68–9. What do you learn about the effects of the civil war in (a) the short term; (b) the long term?

Using the sources

1 Look at *extracts A–E* and *picture 1*. Are these sources equally useful as evidence for historians writing about the character of Oliver Cromwell? Give reasons for your answer.
2 Read *extract B*. (a) How does the author interpret the aims and the success of Cromwell's Irish policies? (b) Do you agree with Trevelyan's interpretation of Cromwell's policy and success? Why?
3 Read *extract C*. (a) How useful is this account to historians examining Cromwell's military methods in Scotland? (b) Do you think that this source is likely to be reliable as a record of Cromwell's conquest of Scotland?

CROWN AND PARLIAMENT, 1660–88

In May 1660 English politicians invited the exiled Charles II to return as king. By the Treaty of Breda, he was allowed (a) to decide when elections were to be held and when Parliament was to meet (b) to choose his ministers. He, in turn, had to agree (a) to pardon his enemies (b) to allow freedom of worship (c) not to restore land to former Royalists. Charles broke his promises (*extract A*). The 1662 'Cavalier' Parliament let him execute those who had signed his father's death warrant and to dig up and burn the bodies of Cromwell, Ireton and Bradshaw. His chief minister, Clarendon, pushed through the anti-Puritan Act of Uniformity (*extract B*). The Clarendon Code banned Puritans from places on local councils, the universities, and the army and navy. People who attended non-Anglican churches were fined or imprisoned.

By the Declaration of Indulgence (1672) Charles abolished all anti-Catholic laws. In the Treaty of Dover, Louis XIV of France gave him £170,000 a year as a reward for his Catholic policies and to help pay for England's part in the war against the Protestant Dutch. However, in 1673 Parliament refused to give Charles the taxes he needed to pay for that war until he withdrew his Act of Indulgence and accepted Parliament's anti-Catholic Test Act (*extract C*).

The Earl of Shaftesbury led the anti-Royalists, and London merchants gave the money to bring out the London mob in anti-Catholic riots. Shaftesbury's followers were nicknamed 'Whigs' and they called the Royalist Catholics 'Tories'. The Commons approved Shaftesbury's Exclusion Bill (*extract D*) but it was rejected in the Lords. In 1683 Shaftesbury's plan to murder the king at Rye House was foiled and the plotters executed (*picture 1*). Shaftesbury lost popularity and James II's accession to the throne was welcomed by Tories and many Whigs.

Once Monmouth's rebellion had failed, James seemed safe and Parliament gave him the money to maintain a full-time army, something it had refused Charles II. However, James tried to govern without Parliament and adopted a set of Catholic policies: (a) he appointed Catholics to important posts in government and army (b) he abolished anti-Catholic laws and got the courts to agree to this (*extract E*) (c) he issued a Declaration of Indulgence in 1685 (d) in 1688 he arrested seven bishops who refused to have the Declaration read in their churches. The courts freed them (*picture 2*), a sign that his Catholic policies were illegal and unpopular.

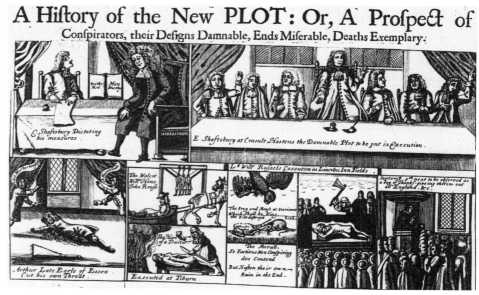

1. The Rye House Plot, 1683. Some of Charles's opponents, desperate after their defeat in 1681, turned to conspiracy. A half-hearted plan to assassinate Charles and his brother on their way back from Newmarket at the Rye House, Hertfordshire, was discovered in 1683. The frog and the mouse in the picture are meant to be Monmouth and William of Orange; the kite (bird) destroyed both of them.

Fears that James's new-born son would ensure a Catholic succession led Tory and Whig politicians to unite in inviting William of Orange to take the throne. He was James's nephew and married to his daughter, Mary (page 74). James II's navy, led by Catholics, was kept in London by unfavourable winds: James' chief general, Churchill, left him to side with William. James fled the country, and William and Mary were crowned as joint monarchs.

2. The seven bishops are released.

EXTRACT A
Charles II a clever deceiver, says a bishop of Salisbury

He charmed all who came near him, till they found how little they could depend on fair promises. He seemed to have no sense of religion but disguised his Popery to the last. He thought a King checked by a Parliament was only a King in name.

(*A History of His Own Time*, Geoffrey Burnett, 1643–1711)

EXTRACT B
Betraying Breda: The Act of Uniformity, 1662

All clergy shall be bound to use the Book of Common Prayer, and shall before the Feast of St Bartholomew, before his congregation declare his consent to the use of all things in that Book.

EXTRACT C
Parliament becomes anti-Catholic, 1673

The holder of any civil or military office must take the Sacrament of the Eucharist according to the rites of the Church of England, and make a declaration against the Catholic doctrine of the Mass.

(Test Act, 1673)

EXTRACT D
Parliament tries to keep James, Duke of York, off the throne, 1679

The Duke of York being a Papist, and the hope of his coming to the throne, having given the greatest encouragement to present conspiracies, a Bill be brought in to prevent the Duke from inheriting the Crown.

(Exclusion Bill, 1679)

EXTRACT E
The courts accept James II's dispensing powers, 1686

There is no law that cannot be dispensed by the lawgiver. We declare that the King may dispense any law, that this is not a trust given to the King by the people, but is the sovereign power of the Kings of England which never yet was taken from them, nor can be.

(Chief Justice Herbert, 1686)

Now test yourself

Knowledge and understanding

1 Show how Charles II passed laws which angered (a) Puritans; (b) Catholics.
2 Why was Charles II forced to pass such laws and what were the effects of his religious policies?
3 Is there enough evidence in the text and extracts to say that 'James II deserved to lose his throne because he did not learn from the mistakes made by James I and Charles I and II'? Explain your answer.

Using the sources

1 How useful are *extracts A, C and D* to historians trying to judge the depth of anti-Catholic feeling among many sections of the English people?
2 How reliable is *extract E* in helping us to judge how popular James II's view of kingship was in England? Give reasons for your answer.

CROWN AND PARLIAMENT, 1688–1750

William of Orange, a firm Protestant, was leading the Dutch War against Catholic Louix XIV. He wanted English aid and so he accepted the idea of a joint monarchy. His wife, Mary, James II's daughter, provided Parliament with the excuse that it was replacing one Stuart with another.

The Bill of Rights (February 1689), imposed by Parliament, made sure that William and Mary would be unable to rule without its consent. It said:

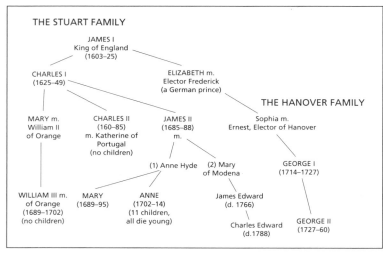

1. From Stuarts to Hanoverians, 1603–1760.

❶ Monarchs could not suspend or abolish laws unless Parliament agreed.

❷ Taxes could not be imposed without Parliament's consent.

❸ There was to be no full-time army during peace time.

❹ Protestants were allowed to have armaments in their homes.

❺ Elections were to be free from royal interference.

❻ Parliament was to meet 'frequently' and had to meet at least once a year to vote the money needed by the monarchs.

❼ MPs were to have freedom of speech and debate.

Parliament's powers were further increased by (a) the Mutiny Act (1689) which limited the Crown's power over the army in wartime (b) the Triennial Act (1694) which said that elections had to be held every three years (c) the Act of Settlement (*extract A*): on William's death (Mary having died in 1694), the Crown was to go to Princess Anne, James II's second daughter. If she died childless, the Crown was then to go to the family of Sophia of Hanover, James I's granddaughter (*picture 1*).

Monarchs had certain powers – they could choose their Cabinets (*extracts B and C*), but they could govern only with the approval of Parliament. Queen Anne (1702–14) chose both Whigs and Tories for her ministers, as William had done (*extract B*). She knew that the Tories wanted to bring James II's son to the throne. Indeed, when she died, they invited him to become king. He would not give up his Catholicism so George of Hanover became king. He spoke little English and rarely went to Cabinet meetings: ministers had to choose a chairman, or first (Prime) Minister. George feared that the Tories might bring a Stuart from exile so he named only Whigs as his ministers.

George II might have tried to take personal charge of government. His wife knew that they were safer with the Whigs (*extract C*). So from 1714 to at least 1760, the Whigs were in power, popular because (a) they avoided war and allowed trade to grow (b) they lowered import and export duties which lowered prices (c) they lowered taxes, especially land taxes, which pleased the Tory landowners. Walpole

2. Robert Walpole.

(*picture 2*), Prime Minister from 1721 to 1740, knew how to use the government's power to buy the support of many MPs (*extract D*). Under this 'corrupt' system England had the first Industrial Revolution.

Continuity and change

During this period the monarchy became less powerful. The power of Parliament grew. These changes continued the trends begun under the Tudors (pages 48–9) and the early Stuart kings (pages 64–5 and 68–9).

EXTRACT A
The Act of Settlement, 1701

That whoever shall come to the Crown shall join communion with the Church of England. That if the Crown come to anyone not a native of England, this nation be not bound to engage in war for the defence of any territories which do not belong to the Crown. That no one coming to the Crown shall leave the country without the consent of Parliament. That no one born out of these kingdoms shall be a Member of Parliament, or have any office, civil or military, from the Crown.

EXTRACT B
Which party can William III trust?

The Tories, friends to the Crown's power, are so friendly to the Jacobites that they cannot be trusted during the war. The Whigs, who support you in the war, will do all they can to lessen your power.

(Godolphin, Chancellor of the Exchequer, to the King, 1693)

EXTRACT C
George II (1727–60), Prime Minister, and Cabinet

Queen Caroline changed George II's first plan. He meant to have his ministers as mere clerks, not to give advice but to take orders. He meant to listen to all sides. The Queen persuaded him that he should have only one minister, and that it was essential that Walpole be that one. The King's behaviour to Walpole changed; instead of hating him, he employed him, and took every opportunity to declare him his first, or rather his only, minister. He was content to bargain for his two main interests – Hanover and money.

(*Memoirs of the Reign of George II*, Lord Hervey, edited in 1884)

EXTRACT D
Every man has his price: the king can buy MPs, 1690

Two hundred MPs gain from friendship with the Government – getting jobs, commissions in the Forces, contracts for supplying the Forces and so on. Think of the votes that this number have in the House, which they are ready to attend, more eager to destroy our constitution than the rest are to preserve it. They do not represent the country, but themselves; they always keep together, vote always the same way as if they were no longer free agents but so many engines turned by a mechanic motion.

(A pamphlet published in 1690)

Now test yourself

Knowledge and understanding

1 Under William and Mary the powers of the monarchy were limited by a growth in Parliament's power. Comment on how those developments were brought about by (a) the Bill of Rights; (b) laws about the army and about elections; (c) laws about the succession to the throne.

2 Which groups (a) gained; (b) lost during the reigns of Queen Anne, George I and George II?

Using the sources

1 Do you agree that the 'revolution' which brought William and Mary and their successors to the throne was a 'Glorious Revolution'? Give the arguments for and against this description of events.

2 How does *extract A* help us to understand (a) the power of Parliament in 1701; (b) the failure of the Catholic Stuarts to regain the throne in 1714 and 1745 (pages 72–3)?

3 Is *extract C* a reliable guide to historians writing about George II, Queen Caroline and Walpole? Give reasons for your answer.

THE UNION WITH SCOTLAND

Protestant nobles in the Scottish lowlands welcomed the new monarchs in 1688. Catholic highlanders rebelled in favour of James II (James VII of Scotland). Led by Viscount Claverhouse ('Bonnie Dundee'), they defeated the English at Killiecrankie (1689). But Dundee was killed; without him, the clans scattered and Scotland settled to be ruled by James's daughter and her Dutch husband.

In 1691 the monarchs decided that highland chiefs had to take an oath of loyalty. When Macdonald of Glencoe was late in taking the oath, Campbell of Glenlyon was sent to punish him (*extract A*). All highlanders were outraged. Lowlanders, too, came to hate William because of the Darien scheme (1695). Scots had raised huge sums of money to send colonists to the Darien Isthmus near Panama, hoping to get the sort of profits made by colonists elsewhere. However, the Spaniards, already in Panama, drove the Scots away and William supported the Spaniards, his allies in the war against France.

1. The Act of Union being presented to Queen Anne.

Scotland's hostility was shown by the Scottish Parliament's refusal to pass the Act of Settlement (page 75, *extract A*). It went on to pass the Act of Security (1704) which said that Scotland would restore the Stuarts unless the English helped Scottish trade to develop. In reply, the English passed the Aliens Act (1705): all Scots were to be treated as 'foreigners' and there would be no trade between the two countries until Scotland accepted the Act of Settlement. Politicians in both countries knew that this hostility ought to end: Scotland was too poor to fight England and was becoming poorer; England, on the other hand, feared a Franco-Scottish alliance. So, after much negotiating, the Act of Union was passed by both Parliaments in 1707 (*picture 1*). It said that:

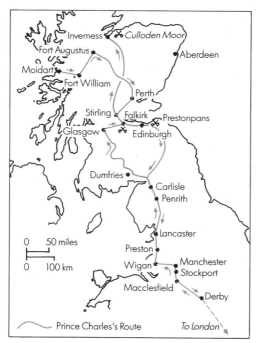

2. Bonnie Prince Charlie's campaign, 1745.

1️⃣ The Scottish Parliament was to be abolished: Scotland would elect 45 MPs to the Westminster House of Commons and 16 nobles to sit in the Lords.

2️⃣ Scotland accepted the Act of Settlement but was allowed to have its own Church and separate legal system.

3️⃣ Scottish merchants were to trade freely with England and its colonies.

Highlanders disliked the Act of Union. When Queen Anne died in 1714, the Earl of Mar raised the Stuart standard at Perth and named James Edward Stuart as James III. Mar and the Jacobites hoped to get French help: but Louix XIV had just died and his infant son was in the hands of a regent who was afraid to go to war. Nor did James inspire the highlanders. After the indecisive battle of Sherriffmuir, Mar and James left to live in France.

In 1745 James's son, Prince Charles Edward, took advantage of the war going on between England and France to start a revolt in Scotland. The highlanders proclaimed him king at Perth and, as the map shows (*picture 2*) he conquered Scotland, invaded England, won several victories and got as far as Derby. But the Scots were discouraged by the lack of support in England and, after several disputes between clan chiefs, they retreated to Scotland.

During the winter of 1745–6, George II's son, the Duke of Cumberland, led an English army to Scotland. On 15 April he found the highlanders' army at Culloden Moor near Inverness. Better armed and fed, and with the benefit of surprise, his forces slaughtered the clansmen and their families. Other rebel chiefs were captured and either executed or sent to imprisonment in America. All the highlanders' homes were destroyed, their cattle and horses taken away and their land given to 'loyal' chiefs. Clan chiefs were deprived of their traditional powers, and laws were passed banning the wearing of the kilt and the playing of bagpipes. Charles escaped to France. Many Scots remembered 'the bold chevalier' who had gone 'over the sea to Skye' and they wondered 'will ye no come back again'? He never did.

EXTRACT A
The Massacre at Glencoe, February 1692

Glenlyon, one of the (Campbell) Earl of Argyle's regiment, with Lieutenant Lindsay and six score soldiers returned to Glencoe, were billeted and had kind entertainment, living familiarly with the people. But on 13 February about four or five in the morning, Lindsay with a party of soldiers came to Glencoe's house, called in a friendly manner, and got in; they shot his father dead as he was rising from his bed; the mother having got up and put on her clothes, the soldiers stripped her naked and drew the rings from her fingers with their teeth. At Inneriggen, where Glenlyon was quartered, soldiers took nine other men, bound them hand and foot and killed them one by one. The slaughter was made by Glenlyon and his soldiers after they had lived peaceably with the Glencoe men about 13 days; the number slain was about 25 and after the slaughter the soldiers did burn the houses, barns and goods, and carried away horse, cattle and sheep above 1000.

(Commission into the Slaughter of the Men of Glencoe, 1695)

EXTRACT B
Scottish opposition to the proposed Union, 1706

For the English, the Union will make no change. They will keep the same Parliament, taxes, laws and courts. But the Scots will have to pay the English debts, now and in the future. Scotland will lose the right to manage its own affairs. For the Scots, the Union will be a complete surrender.

(Lord Belhaven to the Scottish Parliament, 1706)

EXTRACT C
One view of the Union, written by an Englishman in 1874

For Scotland, the Union brought nothing but good. The farmers of the lowlands learned new skills. Glasgow, which had been just a fishing port, grew into a mighty city. Peace changed the wild men of the highlands into peaceful herdsmen. The only thing the Scots lost was their old hatred of England.

(*A Short History of the English People*, J.R. Green, 1874)

Now test yourself

Knowledge and understanding

1 Show how the following groups reacted to English attempts to conquer them:
(a) Catholic highlanders, 1688–9; (b) the followers of Bonnie Prince Charles, 1745–6.
2 List and explain (a) the reasons for the English defeat of the Scots; (b) the effects on Scotland of the English victory.

Using the sources

1 Read *extract A*. Is this reliable evidence for historians writing about (a) the ruthlessness of William's forces; (b) the nature of highland society; (c) the reasons for the defeat of the highlanders by the English and their allies?
2 Read *extracts B and C*. (a) What differences are there between the extracts? (b) Do these differences make the sources invalid as evidence?

UNHAPPY IRELAND

James II appointed Catholics as judges, officers in the army and as ministers in an Irish government headed by the Catholic Tyrconnel, which refused to accept William and Mary in 1688 (*extract A*). In March 1689 James II landed at Kinsale with a French army, hoping to use Ireland as a base for the conquest of England and Scotland. The French hoped to make Ireland an ally in the war against Protestant William. The Catholic-Irish and Anglo-Irish nobles looked forward to their independence from English rule, although the Ulster Protestants feared rule by a Catholic government.

In May 1689 the Catholic-controlled Dublin Parliament (a) cancelled land settlements made by English kings (b) declared its independence from the English Parliament (c) named 2000 Protestants as 'traitors', so increasing Protestant fears.

Between April and June 1689, Tyrconnel's army, aided by the French, besieged Derry (*extract B*). After 105 days the Protestants there welcomed the London fleet which broke the boom and relieved the city. In August 1689 William's army went to fight Tyrconnel. In June 1690 William led his forces to victory over James's army at the Battle of the Boyne (*extract C*) and James fled.

The English then set about strengthening their grip on Ireland in several ways:

1. The Irish Parliament in session.

❶ **Political** – the Irish Parliament was allowed to exist, but the Westminster Act (1719) said that its decisions were not legal until confirmed by the English Parliament, while every law passed in Westminster would apply in Ireland (*picture 1*).

❷ **Penal Laws** were passed to punish Catholics, five-sixths of the population.
Political: along with Presbyterians, they were deprived of the vote.
Social: Catholics were forbidden to (a) stand in elections (b) become army officers (c) become civil servants (d) be town councillors (e) send their children to school (e) wear a sword (the mark of a gentleman) (f) own a horse worth more than £5 – any horse had to be sold to a Protestant who offered £5 for it.
Religious: bishops, nuns and monks were banned; priests had to register with local authorities who tried to stop churches being built (*picture 2*); Catholics had to pay one-tenth of their income to the local Anglican church.
Land: (a) Catholic landowners had to leave their land to be divided between all their children; in time, no Catholic would own any sizeable estate (*picture 3*) (b) Catholic tenants had to accept the harsh terms offered by Protestant landowners (*extract D*).

❸ Protestants as well as Catholics suffered from laws which (a) banned the development of any industry which might challenge an English one: the Irish could not have a woollen industry (b) prevented Irish merchants from trading freely with England, its colonies or the rest of the world.

It is not surprising that, later in the 18th century, Ireland became the centre of more anti-English unrest.

2. Going to Mass in a chapel on wheels.

EXTRACT A
An Irishman explains Irish support for James II

How can the Irish be deemed rebels to the Prince of Orange when they support James II against the said Prince, created king by the people of England? Was not James II the lawful king of the three kingdoms, and as such did he not reign for four years? Why then should the Irish disown him, their lawful sovereign, for the rest of his life? But you'll say that England, the principal kingdom of the monarchy, ought to be followed by Ireland in accepting or rejecting the kings of that monarchy. We answer thus: the behaviour of England is no rule to Ireland, a distinct realm, having different laws and a Parliament of her own.

(Adapted from a narrative of the war in Ireland, by a supporter of James II)

EXTRACT B
The siege of Londonderry, 1689

Dublin: June 12. There are fewer than 5000 in the King's camp at Derry, a great many have run away. We hear that some English ships are in the Lough of Derry: a boom of trees is across the river to stop any help arriving. I believe in a while they will be short of clothes, drink and coal. Many Catholics are angry about the French, for the natives are suspicious of them. Putting French officers in place of Irish ones caused great discontent, many soldiers ran away because of it.

(Letter of Intelligence, Somers Tracts, Vol. II)

EXTRACT C
James II runs away, July 1690

The attempt to starve out Derry, the last important Protestant stronghold, failed. In August (1689) the Huguenot general Schomberg landed in Ulster and in the following summer (1690) was joined by William himself. James advanced to the Boyne, 30 miles north of Dublin, to give battle. On 1 July the Catholics were defeated. James himself fled in haste: 'I do now resolve to shift for myself,' he told courtiers, and he was at Duncannon, on board ship for France, before William entered Dublin.

(*Illustrated History of the British Monarchy*, J. Cannon and R. Griffiths, 1988)

EXTRACT D
The land problem

The terms on which the Irish peasant rented the land were harsh and deprived him of any incentive and security. When his lease expired any improvement he had made in his holding became the property of the landlord. Then the majority were 'tenants at will', that is 'the will' of the landlord. He could turn them out whenever he chose.

(*The Great Hunger*, Cecil Woodham Smith, 1962)

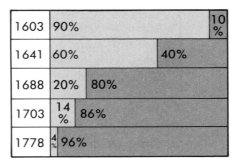

3. Transfer of ownership of land 1603–1778.

Now test yourself

Knowledge and understanding

1 (a) Using pages 64–5, 66–7 and 70–71 make a list of long-term causes for the growth of Anglo-Irish hostility. (b) Next to each cause, say whether it was social, political, religious, economic or caused by individuals.

2 List and explain the (a) short-term reasons for the Battle of the Boyne; (b) the (i) short-term and (ii) long-term effects of William's conquest of Ireland.

Using the sources

1 How do you think the evidence in *pictures 1 and 2* and *extracts A and D* were interpreted by (a) Irish Catholics; (b) Irish Protestants; (c) English politicians?

2 How are *extracts B and C* useful in explaining (a) why the Catholics lost to William; (b) the character of James II?

3 Do you think the evidence in this topic shows that the English found the conquest of Ireland more or less difficult than their conquest of Scotland? Give reasons for your answer.

The French Revolution and the Napoleonic era (study unit 5)

FRENCH SOCIETY, 1780–89

On pages 12–13 we looked at the medieval feudal system. In 1789 France was still, in many ways, a feudal society – government, writers and people talked and wrote about the three estates, over which the king was an absolute monarch. He chose his ministers to form a government. With them he decided policies – on war, taxation and so on. It was generally agreed that 'he was appointed by God' (pages 64–5), which gave him the right to rule over everyone.

However, many people had been influenced by the opinions of writers such as Rousseau and Voltaire, and wanted France to have a more democratic form of government (*extracts A and B*).

❶ **The First Estate** was the Church, which collected fees and tithes from the people (*picture 1*). Bishops and other higher clergy (usually the sons of noble families) had huge incomes, although the ordinary parish priest might be little better off than a skilled worker.

Many people criticized the luxurious lives led by the higher clergy and of the sums of money they took from the poor.

❷ **The Second Estate** consisted of the landowners, almost all of whom were nobles. Some were very rich and had large amounts of land. They got the top jobs in government and made sure that their class paid very little in taxation. Other nobles, with less land or with heavy debts because of high living, were less well-off. They could not afford the huge chateaux (castles) in which the very rich lived.

Both rich and poorer nobles were allowed to force their peasants to pay them feudal dues (as had been the case in medieval England – pages 12–13). They also imposed local taxes on the peasants (*picture 1*) and kept for themselves the fines they imposed on any peasant they found guilty of a crime – in trials which took place in the nobles' houses, with the nobles as judge, prosecutor and jury.

FAUT ESPERER Q'EU SE JEU LA FINIRA BENTOT

The peasant, carrying (by various taxes) the burden of maintaining both the feudal lords and the already rich Church. This cartoon of 1789 was captioned 'One hopes this will end soon'.

❸ **The Third Estate** had, at one time, been made up mostly of peasants. By the 1780s France had gone through many of the changes which had taken place in England since medieval times. It had taken colonies and developed a large overseas trade, as had England (pages 56–9). This had led to the growth of commercial towns where rich merchants (pages 60–61), bankers, shipowners, lawyers and manufacturers lived along with an increasing number of well-paid skilled craftsmen, shopkeepers and small traders.

It was still true that the bulk of this Estate consisted of the peasants who lived on nobles' estates, although there were a growing number of urban workers (who were as poor as the peasants).

The rich members of this Estate ('the middle class') – merchants, bankers and so on, were the ones who were most influenced by critics such as Rousseau and Voltaire. They formed political clubs where they debated such things as liberty and equality. They also produced or read an increasing number of newspapers, journals, pamphlets and plays which criticized the existing social, economic and political system.

We shall see that it was this more educated class which was responsible for the changes that were to take place during the French Revolution while the peasants had their own ideas about the changes that ought to take place.

What do we mean by the French Revolution?

Your dictionary will tell you that one meaning of 'revolution' is 'an uprising by the people to change the kind of government they have'. It may give examples of revolutions such as the one in England in 1688 (pages 72–3), the American Revolution of 1775–6 (pages 58–9) and the French Revolution of 1789 etc. The 'etc' in the dictionary is put there because the French Revolution went through many stages, as we shall see in this unit. We will also see that 'revolution' meant different things to different groups, for example, the peasants wanted the end of feudalism (pages 80–84), 'liberals' wanted a constitution, which they got by September 1791. There were also extremists who wanted a republic (pages 88–90), but then fought one another for power in that republic (pages 92–3). We will see that the Revolution became increasingly violent as those who wanted more change overthrew those who had thought they had won their 'revolution'. It has been said that 'revolutions devour the children who begin them and take part in them'.

EXTRACT A
The people should have power, 1775

Man is born free. No man has any natural authority over others; force does not give anyone that right. The power to make laws belongs to the people and only to the people.

(A pamphlet, banned by the French government in 1775, commenting on *The Social Contract* (1762), Jean Jacques Rousseau (1712–78))

EXTRACT B
One effect of the American Revolution, 1782

The freedom for which I am going to fight inspires me, and I would like my own country to enjoy such a liberty that would fit in with our monarchy, our position and our customs.

(The Comte de Ségur, writing as he was setting out to fight in America, 1782)

EXTRACT C
An Englishman's view of the peasants, 1787–90

I was joined by a poor woman who complained of the times. Her husband had only a morsel of land, one cow and a poor horse. But they had to pay 20 kg of wheat and three chickens as feudal dues to one lord, and 60 kg of oats, one chicken and five pence to another, along with very heavy taxes to the king's tax collectors: 'The taxes and the feudal dues are crushing us.'

(*Travels in France*, Arthur Young, 1792)

EXTRACT D
Yearly incomes compared: from various sources referring to 1785

Archbishop of Paris	50,000 livres
Marquis de Mainvillette	20,000 livres
Prince de Conti	14,000 livres
A Paris parish priest	10,000 livres
A typical village priest	750 livres
A master carpenter	200 livres

(The livre was replaced by the franc in 1795. You could exchange about 4 livres for £1 in the 1780s.)

Now test yourself

Knowledge and understanding

1 List and explain the reasons why many people in France were critical of (a) the king; (b) the Church; (c) the nobles.
2 Explain why the middle class had become an important part of French society.

Using the sources

1 Are *extracts A and B* equally useful for historians writing about the desire for change in French society? Explain your answer.
2 Study *extracts C and D* and *picture 1*. Do these sources explain why poor people in France resented the rich? Explain your answer.

THE FIRST STAGE OF THE FRENCH REVOLUTION, 1787–9

The king's problem 1787–8

By 1787 the French government was bankrupt, as the figures show:

Income: 560 million livres
Spending: 630 million livres
Total debt: 4000 million livres

France had spent a great deal of money fighting wars against Britain. Unlike Britain, it had nothing to show for it, whereas Britain had gained an empire. Some French people accused the Court, especially Queen Marie Antoinette, of spending too much money. Other people said that the tax system was corrupt: private companies collected the taxes – and did not hand over all that they collected.

In 1787 the King asked the nobility to help him reform the system of government and taxation. He wanted them to agree to pay some taxes. Since 'turkeys don't vote in favour of Christmas', it is not surprising that they refused to do so.

The harvest problem, 1787–9

As in medieval England, most people in France worked in, and depended on, agriculture. In the three years, 1787–9, terrible weather – heavy rain, hard winters, too hot summers – led to three very poor harvests.

This meant that farmers and peasants had smaller incomes while food prices rose sharply. Their lower incomes meant that they had less to spend on other goods while urban workers (many unemployed because of lower demand for their goods) had to pay higher prices for their food.

The king and the Estates-General

In August 1788 the desperate king decided to call the Estates-General – a gathering of representatives from all three Estates. This had last happened in 1614.

- The king hoped the Estates-General would approve new taxes.
- The nobles (along with the clergy) hoped they would control its affairs so that they could get concessions from the king.
- The middle classes hoped to create an English-style democracy.
- The peasants hoped for solutions to their problems (*extract B*). When their representatives were being elected, the people were asked to draw up lists of their complaints and hopes (in French, *cahiers de doléances*).

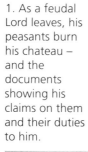

1. As a feudal Lord leaves, his peasants burn his chateau – and the documents showing his claims on them and their duties to him.

The king's mistakes, May–June 1789

- He summoned the three Estates to meet at his palace at Versailles (and not in Paris) where he had a body of troops. Some saw this as an attempt to frighten the representatives.
- He did not present the Estates with any proposals for discussion, so that they were left free to think up their own ideas.
- He arranged for the three Estates to meet in three separate buildings, hoping that the nobility and clergy would always vote against any proposals from the Third Estate, which would be outvoted 2–1.

The National Assembly, June 1789

The representatives gathered at Versailles on 4 May 1789 and spent six weeks arguing with the king over the Third Estate's demand that there should be one House of Representatives. He refused to agree.

On 19 June the representatives of the Third Estate were joined by some radical nobles (such as Mirabeau) and many radical clergy (such as Abbé

Sièyes) and declared that together they formed a National Assembly which would draw up a constitution showing how France was to be governed.

On 20 June the members of this (illegal) Assembly met in the royal tennis court at Versailles to swear an oath that they would not leave until the king met their demands. He gave way and agreed to the setting up of a one-chamber National Assembly.

The first step in a violent revolution

- The Paris mob, hungry because of poor harvests, and impatient with the weeks of argument about an Assembly, took the law into its own hands. On 14 July 1789 the mob rioted, attacked the state prison in Paris, the Bastille, freed its seven prisoners and stole guns and ammunition.

- Throughout France, the peasants, too, had become impatient. They took part in a widespread, but unorganized, series of attacks on the chateaux and palaces of their feudal lords (picture 1 and *extract C*).

EXTRACT A
From the collection of *cahiers* taken to the Estates-General, 1789

O rich citizens be so good as to leave for a time your chateaux and palaces and be so good as to glance at those unfortunates whose muscles are only occupied in working for you. What do you see in our villages? A few weakened men, faces withered by poverty and shame, their wives having too many children, each child wearing rags...

... All the peasants in our neighbourhood – Brittany – are making ready to refuse the church tax-gatherers and state that nothing will be taken without bloodshed.

EXTRACT B
A modern view of the calling of the Estates-General

The King wanted to hear the voice of his people in order to right all wrongs. What a surprising development. The King was all-powerful: therefore, the people thought, the wrongs must be about to end. The peasants chewed over their suffering with growing bitterness now that they had been invited to speak. They dredged up from the depths of their minds their memories of past sufferings.

(The modern French historian, Georges Lefèbvre, *La Revolution Francaise*, 1951)

EXTRACT C
Arthur Young, an eye-witness, July 1789

The whole country is in the greatest agitation. Many chateaux have been burned and others plundered. The lords hunted down like beasts. Their feudal documents burned. Their property destroyed.

(*Travels in France*, Arthur Young, 1792)

Now test yourself

Knowledge and understanding

1 List the following causes of the French government's problems in order of their importance, explaining your choice:
(a) foreign wars; (b) the Court; (c) tax system; (d) the harvest.
2 Read the text and *extracts A and B*. Do you agree that the king made a mistake when he called the Estates-General? Explain your answer fully referring to (a) the demands of the Three Estates; (b) the events of May–June; (c) riots in Paris and the countryside.

Using the sources

1 How reliable is *extract C* for historians writing about the start of the French Revolution? Explain your answer fully.
2 Look at *picture 1*. How can this be used to explain why there was a revolution in France?

THE REVOLUTION, AUGUST 1789–SEPTEMBER 1791

The representatives who made up the majority in the National Assembly were the middle-class members of the Third Estate (lawyers, journalists, academics, authors and so on) and radical clergy and nobility. All of them had been influenced by the ideas of Rousseau and Voltaire (page 81, *extract A*) and by the ideas they had picked up in their links with the American revolutionaries (page 81, *extract B*). They hoped to create a more equal, free and just society to replace the unfair society in which they had lived. The peasants may have wanted simply an end to feudalism (page 83, *extract C* and *picture 2*); the middle classes wanted to build a new state. They did so in a series of laws:

4 August 1789. The Assembly passed a law which abolished all feudal privileges (no more feudal dues and powers, no more justice based on the lords' chateaux) and unjust taxation (no more church tithes, no more private companies keeping part of the taxation).

12–26 August 1789. After a long debate, the Assembly issued *The Declaration of the Rights of Man* (*extract*). However, there was nothing in this about:

- The rights of women. A gathering of middle-class women complained (September 1791) of the need for a declaration of the rights of women.
- The position of slaves in France and the French empire. Too many of the wealthy landowners with influence in the Assembly had too many slaves for them to want 'the rights of slaves to be free'. In April 1791 the Assembly rejected a motion by the leader of an extremist left-wing group, Robespierre, who campaigned for the abolition of slavery.
- Who was going to impose those rights in a society. In our own time, the United Nations (pages 164–5) has issued high sounding declarations on human rights – but what has been done about giving those rights to the poor of Africa or Latin America?

August–September 1789. The Assembly, with the approval of the king, appointed new middle-class officials – elected by the people – to take charge of local government in place of the former agents of the king (intendants)

The new Constitution, 1789–91 (*picture 1*)

In 1791 there were to be elections for a new Assembly (or Parliament) which would pass laws as it saw fit and as the times demanded. This Assembly would be elected every two years by men (not women) who paid a certain level of taxation – about two-thirds of the adult male population gained the vote: these were to be called 'active' citizens.

- The king was to be called 'the King of the French' and not, as before, 'King of France'.
- The king would be allowed to delay the passing of any law for three years.
- 83 new 'departments' were created to become the centres of a new system of local government.
- Almost all officials were to be elected by 'active' citizens – judges, deputies (MPs), tax collectors and priests (see below).
- Economic reforms included the abolition of the import/export taxes previously paid on goods crossing the 'borders' between departments inside France; a national system of weights and measures; taxes to be based on people's ability to pay; a new currency (the assignat) was issued, with confiscated Church lands as its backing (instead of gold, as in Britain).

tôt tôt tôt
batter chaud
tôt tôt tôt
bon Courage
il faut avoir coeur à l'ouvrage.

1. A cartoon published in 1789. The members of the Three Estates are working together to hammer out a new way of life and of government for France.

Church reforms

- Church lands were nationalized. Income from the sale of some of these was used to pay off government debt.
- Marriages (which previously took place only in church) had to be celebrated as civil ceremonies in front of state officials; divorce was introduced.
- The old dioceses were abolished and 83 new ones created, each covering the area of one of the 83 new departments of local government.
- Priests were to be elected by the local people and were to receive a state salary.
- Priests had to take an oath of loyalty to the state, which many people saw as an attack on the power of the bishops and, especially, of the Pope.
- The Church tax (or tithe) was abolished.

EXTRACT
The Declaration of the Rights of Man, 12–27 August 1789

The representatives of the French people, as a National Assembly, holding that ignorance, neglect or contempt of the rights of man are the sole cause of public misfortune and corrupt governments, have resolved to list, in a solemn declaration, the natural, inalienable and sacred rights of man, so that this declaration, being constantly presented to all the members of the social body, may continually remind them of their rights and duties; that the acts of the law-making and executive powers may always be compared with the aims of every political institution and so be more respected; that the grievances of citizens, founded henceforth on simple and incontestable principles, shall always tend to the maintenance of the constitution and the happiness of all (12 August 1789).

Men are born equal and remain free and equal in rights which are liberty, property, security and resistance to oppression. Liberty is being able to do whatever does not harm others.

The law should express the will of the people. All citizens have a right to take part personally, or through their representatives, in the making of the law. Every citizen can talk, write and publish freely, unless this liberty is abused in a way which breaks the law (27 August 1789).

(Decree of the National Assembly, 1789)

Now test yourself

Knowledge and understanding

1 Outline (a) the ideas which inspired the middle-class members of the National Assembly; (b) the changes brought about by the Assembly, August to September 1789; (c) the reasons why some people objected to the work of the Assembly.
2 Explain how the changes in the Constitution affected (a) the king; (b) local government; (c) the economy; (d) the Church.
3 Which of these changes was the most important? Why?

Using the sources

1 Do you agree that the *extract* fully explains the changes that came about as a result of the election of the National Assembly? Explain your answer, noting the changes not mentioned in the extract.
2 Do you agree that the *picture* is an accurate guide to how the changes to French life and government were brought about? Explain your answer.

THE KING AND THE REVOLUTION, 1789–91

What sort of man was Louis XVI? Louis came to the throne in 1774. Like his father and grandfather (Louis XIV) he believed that he was God's servant and that this gave him, and him alone, the power to make laws and rule his country. But, unlike Louis XIV, he did not have the character to fit the 'job'. He was very much a family man, happy to be with his wife and children. Even during the dispute with the Three Estates in May–June 1789 (pages 82–3) he was more concerned with the fate of his son who was dying of tuberculosis than he was with the political crisis.

Louis was dominated by his strong-willed wife, Marie Antoinette, the sister of the Emperor of Austria. It was unfortunate for Louis that she was the subject of many rumours – about supposed love affairs, about her lavish spending on clothes and jewels and about the way she interfered in Louis's attempts to govern the country.

Louis and the events of 1789–91

It is possible that Louis never really understood the widespread demand for reform that swept France in 1788–9. Certainly he had no ideas to put to the Three Estates when they met in May–June 1789. Nor did he have much idea of what to do when the representatives took things into their own hands and decided to set up a National Assembly (pages 82–3).

Later, in 1792 Louis was to claim that he had freely given up some of his power for the good of the people and claimed that he deserved the title of 'restorer of French liberty'. He was also to claim credit for his actions, or lack of them, when the Paris mob came to Versailles on 5–6 October 1789, attacked his palace, captured him and his family and imprisoned them in the Tuileries in Paris. He could have ordered his guards to fire on the mob, but refused to do so. Was this the action of an absolute monarch? Or of a weak man? Or of a democratically minded king?

He claimed, rightly, that he played the role of an English-style constitutional monarch in 1789–91, signing the decrees of the Assembly so that they became law (pages 84–5), perhaps after holding things up, as the new laws allowed him to do. In September 1791, when the new constitution was finally proclaimed, Louis took an oath of loyalty to it, claiming later that this proved his good will. Did it? Or was it the action of 'the prisoner in the Tuileries' who knew that he really had no choice?

1. The king trying to face both ways tells the revolutionary politician (left) that he supports the changes being made, while he tells the priest that he is opposed to the Civil Constitution of the clergy.

The behaviour of the king, 1789–91

Many nobles fled the country once the peasants attacked their chateaux (page 82, *picture 2*). Louis sent money to these *emigrés* who went to live in the courts of neighbouring absolute monarchs.

He agreed with his wife when she wrote to the Austrian Ambassador in France saying that they had to try to leave France, and that they hoped their absolute monarch friends would invade France, put down the Revolution and put back Louis on his absolute throne. Louis himself wrote to the kings of Prussia, Spain and Sweden and to the emperors of Austria and Russia suggesting a meeting of all monarchs so that they could form an armed alliance to put down the Revolution.

2. The king and his family being brought back to Paris: the cartoonist wanted to show them as farm animals being brought back – to market to slaughter?

The flight to Varennes, 21–5 June 1791

During the night of 20–21 June, Louis and his family, in disguise and carrying false papers of identity, left the Tuileries Palace in Paris, and fled towards the Austrian Netherlands (modern Netherlands–Belgium). There, he hoped, he would rally the *emigrés* nobles, get the support of the Austrians and return with an army to defeat the revolutionaries.

Unfortunately for Louis, he was recognized along the route and at Varennes a mob prevented the coach from proceeding: some of his advisers wanted to shoot their way through the crowd, but Louis refused to allow this. And so, captured on 22 June, he was brought back to Paris (25 June) (*picture 2*). Here the members of the Assembly, unable maybe to think of their country without a king, allowed him to retake his constitutional position so that on 3 September he was asked to approve the new Constitution (pages 84–5) and to take an oath of loyalty to it – both of which he did. What would the other absolute monarchs in Europe do now?

EXTRACT
Can France trust this king – or need him?

The nation can never feel safe with a man who organizes a secret escape and obtains a false passport. He then travels towards a frontier covered with traitors and deserters, and plans to return to our country with an army capable of imposing his own tyrannical laws.

What kind of job must that be in government which requires neither experience nor ability, that is filled by chance, the chance of birth, e.g. by an idiot, madman or tyrant? The 30 million livres which it costs to support a king in brutal luxury presents us with an easy method of reducing taxes.

(Tom Paine, author of *The Rights of Man* (1791) who had fled to France to support the Revolution. This article was written in July 1791)

Now test yourself

Knowledge and understanding

1 Why did the personalities of both (a) Louis XVI and (b) Marie Antoinette help to bring about the downfall of the French monarchy?
2 Do you agree that the evidence in the text, *extract* and *pictures* shows that Louis XVI was a weak king? Explain your answer fully.

Using the sources

1 Does the author of the *extract* give a fair account of Louis XVI's personality and policies? Explain your answer.
2 How can historians use *both pictures* to explain the difficulties which Louis XVI faced?

E UROPE AND THE REVOLUTION, 1789–92

In the last topic, we saw that, after his return to 'prison' in the Tuileries, Louis XVI accepted the new Constitution. In fact, neither he, nor Marie Antoinette, nor the other autocratic rulers of Europe really accepted this downgrading of a monarch.

The 749 members of the National Assembly also realized that France faced a threat of invasion by other despots (absolute rulers) in Europe looking to restore the monarch to power and freedom. There were three main groups in the Assembly:

- **The Girondins** (so called because they came from the Gironde region around Bordeaux) were the largest. But many of them were too idealistic and wanted a war against the despots (*extracts A and B*).
- **The Jacobins** (so called because they held party meetings in a former convent of St Jacques, were a smaller but highly disciplined group – and were to prove to be the more ruthless. They saw war as a threat to the Revolution (*extract C*).
- **The Feuillants** (so called because of the title of a book its members published) included some royalists and some who had split from the extremist Jacobin group. Many of them wanted a war because, like the king, they expected a French defeat and a restoration of the monarchy (*extract D*).

In April 1792 the Girondist government declared war on Austria and its troops enjoyed some successes when they invaded the Netherlands. This led the Assembly to pass the Edict of Fraternity (*extract E*) which promised to help lower classes everywhere to overthrow their despotic rulers.

Soon, however, the war started to go badly wrong:

- Most former officers had been nobles, and two-thirds of them had fled after the burning of chateaux in 1789 (page 82, *picture 1*).
- The remaining officers had little sympathy with the ideals of the Girondists and some, including the Girondist leader, Dumouriez, went over to the enemy.
- Hastily promoted officers had no experience.

As defeat followed defeat so the economic conditions worsened:

- Too many young men had been taken to fight so that not all the harvest was gathered. This led to food shortages and rising prices – and anger.
- The new paper money (assignats, see page 84) was another cause of rising prices; the government printed too much to pay the armies and military suppliers.

Many people, and more significantly, the Paris mob feared that a successful invading army would take revenge on Paris (*extract F*).

On 10 August the Paris mob, inspired by Danton, rose, attacked the Tuileries and imprisoned the royal family. The Assembly, driven by Girondist idealism and under pressure from the mob, announced that the king was no longer king and that, after a decree of 21 September 1792, France was a Republic.

INTÉRIEUR DU TRIBUNAL RÉVOLUTIONNAIRE.

1. A contemporary drawing of a revolutionary tribunal at work– the accused are being pointed at (and already condemned?) as they come through the door into the courtroom.

The invaders crept nearer Paris and the mob got angrier. Looking for other 'traitors' – nobles and clergy who had supported the king, critics of some part of the Revolutionary settlement – the mob imprisoned hundreds of people (August) who were dragged from jails (September) to be put on trial before 'citizen judges' and then executed. About 1,400 people were killed in Paris in these September massacres.

In the same month as the massacres, elections to the National Assembly took place. Although all adult males could now vote, only about six in every hundred did so – the majority were sick of politics and politicians. By a decree of the outgoing Assembly, none of its members was allowed to stand for re-election. So in September 1792 came 749 inexperienced members to the National Convention.

EXTRACT A
A Girondist leader, Brissot, wanted a war in December 1791

A people which has just won its liberty after ten centuries of slavery needs a war to bring about its consolidation. War is actually a national benefit. The moment has come for a new crusade, a crusade for liberty the world over.

(A speech made in December 1791 by Jacques Pierre Brissot)

EXTRACT B
Another Girondist, Pierre Vergniaud, calls for the glory of war, 3 January 1792

The despots, with fifteen years of pride in their feudal souls, now demand in every land the gold and soldiers to reconquer France. You have renounced conquests, but you have not promised to suffer such insolence. You have shaken off the yoke of your despots, but this was surely not to allow you to bend the knee to some foreign tyrants and to submit your new system to the corrupt politics of their governments. So, led by the sublime passions beneath the tricolor flag that you planted on the ruins of the Bastille, what enemy would dare attack you: come, punish the tyrants. Glory awaits you. Once kings wanted the title of Roman citizens: now make them envy the title of Citizens of France.

(Vergniaud in the Assembly, 3 January 1792)

EXTRACT C
Robespierre, a Jacobin leader, opposes war, January 1792

France is in no state to fight a war. We have to put our own country in order before we try to take liberty to others in other countries. No one welcomes armed missionaries. A war will play into the hands of the King and lead to a military dictatorship.

(Robespierre in the Assembly, 3 January 1792)

EXTRACT D
The king welcomes the idea of a war

A war in Europe would greatly improve my situation. My poor country is in such a state that she could not resist even a partial campaign.

(Letter written by Louis XVI to his representative in Austria, December 1791)

EXTRACT E
The Edict of Fraternity, 19 November 1792

The National Convention [formerly the Assembly] declares in the name of the French nation that it will help all peoples who wish to recover their freedom, and promises that it will protect those citizens who have been oppressed.

(Decree of the Convention, 19 November 1792)

EXTRACT F
Manifesto issued by the invading forces led by the Duke of Brunswick, July 1792

Paris and all its inhabitants are called on to submit instantly to the King, to set him at full liberty, and to give him and all other royal persons that respect which are due by the laws of nature and of nations to sovereigns – on pain of losing their heads, following military trials, all the members of the National Assembly and others whom it may concern. Their Imperial and Royal Majesties allied together declare that if the Tuileries be attacked, if any violence be offered to the royal family, if they are not immediately set at liberty, that they will impose avenging punishments on those who deserve it and will expose Paris to total destruction.

(The 'Brunswick' Manifesto, 28 July 1792)

Now test yourself

Knowledge and understanding

1. In what ways did the following groups of people disagree with one another about how France should be ruled after the Revolution: (a) Girondins; (b) Jacobins; (c) Feuillants?
2. Put the following effects of the war with Austria in order of importance, explaining your choice: (a) bad harvests; (b) inflation; (c) the fall of the king; (d) the deaths of the 'traitors'; (e) election of the National Assembly.

Using the sources

1. (a) How do the writers of *extracts A–E* compare in their attitudes towards war? Explain these differences. (b) Which of these sources does the author of *extract F* support? Explain your answer.
2. Do you agree that the *picture* is a reliable source for historians writing about the effects of the Revolution? Explain your answer.

BRITAIN AND THE FRENCH REVOLUTION AT WAR, 1793–7

Once the Republic had been decreed, the Convention put the king on trial. The jury was the Convention itself, urged on by the Paris mob inside and outside the hall. Louis was accused of plotting against the Revolution, opposing the Constitution which he had signed and trying to flee the country. He was found guilty and condemned to be executed.

After his execution on 21 January 1793 (*picture 1*), he was quickly buried in a mass grave along with victims of the massacres which terrified French life in what became known as 'The Terror' (1793–4) when thousands died.

Pitt and the war, February 1793

Asking the British Parliament to approve the declaration of war, Pitt referred to the execution and to the Terror (*extract A*). But he also made much of the French decision to open the River Scheldt and the port of Antwerp to foreign trade – which was forbidden by many treaties (*extract B*). He feared that London's trade and British shipping interests would be harmed if this went ahead.

He hoped for a short war in which Britain would use:

- **Subsidies.** Pitt knew that the British army was too small to fight a European war. He relied on Austria and its allies to do the fighting. Britain would give them money (gold) to buy material and pay soldiers (page 96, *picture 1*).
- **Colonial wars.** Pitt planned to attack French colonies in the West Indies.
- **The navy.** He planned to use the navy to blockade French ports (and cut France off from foreign trade) and to help the army to attack the French coast and French colonies.

The first coalition, 1793–7

In 1793 Pitt arranged a coalition against France – Spain, Holland, Austria, Prussia, England and Sardinia (SHAPES) joined Russia in an alliance. However, it was a weak one: Britain wanted to gain colonies; Russia, Prussia and Austria were more willing to fight one another over Poland than to fight France. Their armies were badly led and moved very slowly across the vast distances which, for example, separated Russia from France.

The French, on the other hand, found a number of inspiring leaders: Carnot organized supplies and involved millions in this work; Danton inspired the people with his speeches, coining the phrase *L'audace, l'audace, et toujours l'audace'* ('boldness, boldness, always boldness'). The armies fought enthusiastically to defend their country against foreign invasion, as Americans had fought to gain their independence.

1. Part of a poster which was published in London in January 1793.

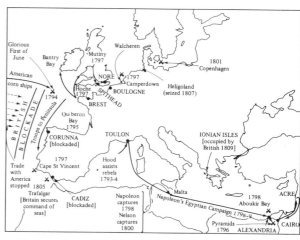

2. The naval wars 1798–1805

Britain and the first coalition

1793: Toulon was a naval base in southern France where royalists rose in rebellion. Britain sent a fleet and troops to help them. Led by a young officer, Napoleon Bonaparte, the French drove the British off in 1795.

1794: In attacks on the French West Indies (1794–8), 100,000 soldiers and sailors died, mainly from yellow fever. Few islands were captured – at a heavy cost.

1794: On 'the Glorious First of June' a British fleet fought a battle with French ships near Brest (*picture 2*) during which French ships, carrying corn, got past the British blockade and reached French ports – a hollow victory for Britain.

1795: Britain took the Dutch colony of the Cape of Good Hope – a useful link with routes to India.

1795: Prussia, concerned about Poland, made peace with France; so did Sardinia in 1796 and Austria in 1797 after being defeated at the Battle of Rivoli.

1796: Spain and Holland declared war on Britain, but the navy saved the country: Jervis, with Nelson as his second-in-command, defeated the Spaniards at Cape St Vincent, and Duncan defeated the Dutch at Camperdown.

EXTRACT A
Pitt on the execution of Louis XVI

I now submit to the House some observations on the many important subjects which arise out of the present situation. The attention of the House should first be directed to that calamitous event [the execution], that dreadful outrage against religion, justice and humanity which has created general indignation and abhorrence in every part of this island and every civilized country.

(William Pitt in the House of Commons, 1 February 1793)

EXTRACT B
On the French proposal to open the River Scheldt to shipping, 1793

To insist on the opening of the Scheldt is an act in which the French had no right to interfere at all, unless she was the sovereign of the Low Countries, or claiming to be the mistress of Europe. France has no right to cancel the international laws relating to the Scheldt, unless she is claiming the right to set aside also all other treaties between the powers of Europe.

England will never agree that France has those rights. Many treaties show that the navigation of the Scheldt is the right of Holland.

Unless we wish to watch state after state being overturned by France, we must now declare our resolution to oppose the ambition and aggrandisement which aim at the destruction of England, of Europe and of the world.

(William Pitt in the House of Commons, 1 February 1793)

EXTRACT C
The naval mutiny – the Nore, June 1797

On 24 May I sailed for the Nore, having 122 new-raised men on board. Approaching Yarmouth Roads on the 19th, I saw 2 large ships, one frigate and a sloop all with red flags on their topmast heads, which I took as the signal of insurrection. Next morning I found the fleet in the utmost disorder. I was surrounded by armed vessels and told that if I did not hoist the red flag, the tender would be sunk. The contagion spread like wildfire among the volunteers.

(Lt James Watson's letter to Admiral Digby, June 1797)

Now test yourself

Knowledge and understanding

1 (a) Using the text, list and explain the short-term reasons for these events. (b) Do you think that Louis XVI's execution was inevitable? Explain your answer fully, referring to the problems facing France (pages 80–91).

2 Put the following factors which prevented Pitt from defeating the French in order of importance, explaining your choice: (a) lack of money; (b) quarrels among the allies; (c) French bravery; (d) naval mutinies.

Using the sources

1 Read *extracts A–C*. Do these sources provide reliable evidence about the impact of the French Revolution on Britain? Explain your answer fully.

2 How useful is *picture 2* for historians writing about the naval wars in which Britain fought? Explain your answer.

THE REVOLUTION FALLS APART, 1793–5

From September 1793 new and well-led French armies won a string of victories. By the start of 1794 France had occupied Belgium, was attacking Holland, and its armies had crossed the Rhine and were advancing into Austrian and Prussian territories.

This success owed much to the setting up of a Committee of Public Safety on 6 April 1793, on the advice of the Girondist government.

- Carnot and four others of the Committee ran the military side of the war. All men had to do military service and all women were involved in getting supplies to the army. Spies were sent to each regiment to make sure that officers and men were 'enthusiastic'. If not, they were arrested and shot.
- Danton kept the Paris mob happy. The 'Law of Forty Sous' provided a payment for those who went to public meetings arranged by the Committee.
- Robespierre was the Committee's main public speaker. He made sure that the Convention let the Committee get on with the task of saving France.

Domestic policy

The Terror went on at an increasing pace: nobles, failed generals and anyone thought to be lukewarm about the Republic were sent to the guillotine.

In a new calendar, Day 1 of Year 1 was fixed as the day on which the Republic was set up; months were given new names (hot month, frost month and so on); the year was divided into units of ten (*decads*); and there were ten days in the week. Napoleon scrapped this calendar in 1804.

Catholicism was attacked. On 5 October 1793 Christianity was 'abolished', thousands of churches closed and many priests, who refused to accept the Civil Constitution of the clergy (page 85), were executed. A new religion, with a 'God of Reason' was introduced on 10 March 1793, but was replaced in June 1794 when Robespierre announced the worship of 'The Supreme Being' with a ceremony in the desecrated Notre Dame Cathedral where he acted as High Priest.

Anti-Revolution

Opposition to the Paris-led changes came from:

- supporters of the Girondists around Bordeaux, who resented the way in which 'the tail (Paris) was wagging the dog (France)'.
- royalists who rebelled in Toulon (August 1793) and 'moderates' who rose in Marseilles (June 1793). Marseilles was brought under control in August 1793 and Toulon in December.
- the Vendée, the area around Nantes, where the peasants (who had hoped that the end of feudalism was the end of the Revolution) rose in defence of their Church and baby king (*extracts A and B*). Their armies fought many battles with Revolutionary armies: thousands died in a rising which lasted from March to December 1793.

Vendée
Major peasant counter revolution, March 1793. Serious threat until defeated in December at Savenay

Bordeaux
Centre of Girondin opposition to Jacobins in Paris

Lyon
Revolt against government, June–October

Toulon
Royalist rebellion, August–December

Marseille
Moderates take control in June as part of Federalist revolt. Recaptured in August.

Key
Open revolt against radical Paris government

Unrest and opposition to the Revolution

Threat to Revolution from émigré nobles and foreign armies

1. The Revolution under threat.

'Revolutions devour their children'

10 July 1793: A new Committee of Public Safety was set up. Danton was dropped and Robespierre became the dominant person.

March 1794: With Danton's support (and control of the mob) Robespierre organized the execution of one section of the Committee – the Hébertists – and of their hundreds of supporters.

April 1794: Robespierre accused Danton of being lukewarm and organized his execution along with many of his supporters.

July 1794: Robespierre, drunk with power, threatened the lives of every member of the Convention (*extract C*). He had gone too far. A small group led by Barras, won the support of the middle-class parts of Paris. They attacked the Town Hall where the 'dictator' was captured and led out to the guillotine. The Convention now took control. The Committee came under its orders, the Jacobin and other societies were closed down, the Terror became less frightening – some imprisoned Girondists were released.

In 1795 ('Year 3') a new Convention appointed a five-man Directorate to run the state from 26 October 1795.

On 3 October 1795 the Paris mob rose and attacked the Convention. Barras, as head of the Directorate, had a young officer, Napoleon Bonaparte, as his subordinate. His artillery fired on the mob which fled (before what Napoleon called 'a whiff of grapeshot'). In return, Napoleon was made commander of the home army – his first step on the road to power.

EXTRACT A
Rebels in the Vendean village of Doulins oppose compulsory service in the army, 1793

They have killed our king: chased away our priests; sold the goods of our church; eaten everything we have, and now they want to take away our bodies: no, they shall not have them.

(Quoted in *Citizens*, Simon Sharma, 1989. This book was published to mark the bicentenary of the fall of the Bastille.)

EXTRACT B
'An Address to the French' by the Council of the Vendée, May 1793

Heaven has declared for the holiest and most just of our causes. Ours is the sacred sign of the cross of Jesus Christ. We know the true wish of France: it is our own, namely to recover and preserve for ever our holy, apostolic and Roman Catholic religion. It is to have a King who will serve as father within and protector without. You accuse us of rebellion: but it is you who were the first to claim that insurrection was the most sacred of duties. You have introduced atheism in the place of religion, anarchy in the place of

laws, men who are tyrants in place of the King who was our father.

(Quoted in *Citizens*, Simon Sharma, 1989)

EXTRACT C
Robespierre threatens the members of the Convention, 26 July 1794)

He declared: 'The French Revolution is the first to be founded on the rights of humanity and the principle of justice. Other revolutions require only ambition; ours requires virtue.' He warned that a conspiracy was growing that threatened the Republic. He defended himself against accusations of dictatorship and tyranny and gradually let the deputies see a picture of those he had in mind by referring to 'monsters' who had 'plunged patriots into dungeons and carried terror into all ranks and conditions. These are the tyrants and oppressors. I know only two parties, that of good citizens and that of bad.' Although he named no names, it was obvious that he was threatening almost everyone there.

(Adapted from *Citizens*, Simon Sharma, 1989)

Now test yourself

Knowledge and understanding

1 Explain (a) how much the Committee of Public Safety changed France 1793–5; (b) which politicians were most responsible for these changes.
2 The following groups helped to bring about the fall of the Paris government. Choose the *three* most important, explaining your choice. (a) Bordeaux Girondists; (b) royalists (c) Vendée peasants; (d) Barras and his supporters; (e) the army; (f) Napoleon.

Using the sources

1 Study *extracts A and B* and *picture 1*. Do you agree that the map is more useful than the extracts for historians writing about the threats to the Revolution? Explain your answer fully.
2 Do you agree that the evidence in the text and *extract C* shows that 'the revolution devoured its children'? Explain your answer.

NAPOLEON – NOBLE TO EMPEROR, 1769–1804

Born to a minor Corsican noble family, Napoleon became an artillery officer in the French army in 1785. He was first noticed because of his defence of Toulon (*extract A*) where he won promotion to the rank of brigadier-general. Then Barras used him to defend the Convention in 1795 (page 92) when he became a general.

In 1796 Napoleon was given command of the French army which invaded Italy. He claimed that he came as a liberator (*extract B*). By 1798 he had taken the northern Kingdom of Sardinia (and Piedmont), defeated the Austrians and their Italian allies, and made a series of treaties, without seeking the approval of the government. He:

- took money from the Pope who had to give land to France
- made Lombardy and Genoa into French-style republics
- forced Austria to sign the Treaty of Campo Formio in which it gave up Belgium, the Rhine frontier and Lombardy and was forced to share the new Republic of Venice with France. It also had to hold a conference to decide the future of the 300 or so German states which it had once controlled.

Egypt, 1798

In May 1798, with a fleet of 400 ships, Napoleon led an army to Egypt, which he saw as the route to British India. On the way he took Malta. Nelson, commander of the British navy in the Mediterranean, chased after him, defeated his fleet at Aboukir Bay and left his army stranded. It was then defeated at the Battle of Acre by British troops. In 1800 Nelson re-took Malta.

The second coalition

Pitt organized a coalition between Britain, Austria, Russia and Turkey (BART), which drove the French from Italy, before it broke up when the allies quarrelled. In 1800 Russia joined Denmark and Sweden in an anti-British Armed Neutrality which aimed to stop British trade in the Baltic. In April 1801 Nelson destroyed the Danish fleet at Copenhagen (*extract C*).

Meanwhile Napoleon, having beaten the Austrians, forced them to sign the Treaty of Luneville (1801), which left Britain facing Napoleon on its own.

Pitt had resigned when George III refused to agree to give Catholics the right to vote (1801). His successor, Addington, signed the Treaty of Amiens, 1802, when:

- Britain handed back all captured colonial territories, except Trinidad (from Spain) and Ceylon (from Holland)
- Napoleon agreed to remove French troops from Rome, Naples and Egypt
- Britain handed back Malta to its former rulers, the Knights of St John.

1. An English cartoon showing Napoleon's seizure of power in 1799. The French artist, David, painted a more flattering picture of this event, with Napoleon being applauded by the politicians.

Napoleon becomes Emperor, 1804

In France the elections of 1797 brought many royalists to the Assemblies. Barras feared this turn of events. Napoleon sent troops to help Barras arrest the new deputies. Barras was now head of a dictatorial Directorate which was both corrupt and inefficient.

Meanwhile, France was suffering as a result of ten years of war and revolution – roads were not repaired, bandits roamed freely, schools had no teachers, hospitals had no nurses, and there were royalists uprisings in 14 of the 83 departments of the country.

In November 1799 Napoleon returned from Egypt. In Paris his loyal army helped him overthrow the Directorate and dismiss the Assemblies. He introduced a new Constitution and named himself First Consul of France (*picture 1*).

In 1802 Napoleon made an agreement with the Pope: Catholicism was accepted as the main religion of the French people; Catholic priests (appointed by Napoleon) would be paid a government salary. In 1802 Napoleon also created the Legion of Honour for people who had served France well.

In 1804, he announced that he was now emperor and, in an ceremony attended by the Pope, crowned himself. In a new Constitution Napoleon created two National Assemblies, although there were no elections after 1804.

EXTRACT A
The British fail at Toulon, 1795

We were deceived in our expectations; everything in Toulon was shown in the most favourable light – the valour, zeal and unanimity of the Allies, the strength and excellence of the British forces, the loyalty of the native, etc. But how different was the truth? The Allies all quarrelling, the British army (of a few hundred only) brave but headstrong; the inhabitants so disloyal that at every attack we made we had to take care that they did not lock us out of the city; the peasants totally supportive of the Revolution.

(*The Journal of Lady Holland*, 28 December 1795, edited by the Earl of Ilchester, 1908)

EXTRACT B
Napoleon's proclamation to the Italian peoples, 1796

Peoples of Italy, the French army comes to break your chains; the French people is the friend of all peoples; meet us with confidence. Your property, your religion, and your customs will be respected. We make war as generous enemies, and we have no quarrel except with the tyrants who enslave you.

EXTRACT C
Nelson at Copenhagen, 1801

The contest had, by 1 p.m. not gone in favour of either side. A shot through the mainmast knocked a few splinters about us as we [Nelson and Stewart] walked the quarterdeck. He said, 'It was warm work and may be our last day; but I would not be anywhere else for thousands.' After a moment he said, 'What is that signal on board the Commander's ship? Number 39? That means to leave off action. Damn me if I do.' He then said, 'You know I have only one eye' … and then putting his glass to his blind eye, he said, 'I really do not see the signal.'

(Colonel Stewart)

EXTRACT D
Napoleon, a 'conservative' heir to the Revolution

I can understand how it was that men worn out by the turmoil of the Revolution, and afraid of that liberty that had long been associated with death, looked for repose under the dominion of an able ruler on whom fortune was seemingly resolved to smile. I may confidently assert that those persons believed quite sincerely that Bonaparte, whether as consul or emperor, would exert his authority to oppose the intrigues of faction and would save us from the perils of anarchy.

None dared to utter the word 'republic', so deeply had the Terror stained the name; and the government of the Directory had perished in the contempt with which its chiefs were regarded.

At the moment when Bonaparte placed the imperial crown upon his head, there was not a king in Europe who did not believe that he wore his own crown more securely because of that event.

(*Memoirs*, Madame de Rémusat, 1820)

Now test yourself

Knowledge and understanding

1 Write a paragraph on the following aspects of Napoleon's career: (a) his political ideas; (b) rise to importance 1793–6; (c) how he came to be the most powerful man in France.

2 Do you agree that Napoleon's domestic policies succeeded in keeping the main gains of the French Revolution while strengthening the country? Explain your answer, referring to pages 82–7 and 102–3.

Using the sources

1 Study *extracts A, B and C*. Do you agree that they provide reliable evidence about the particular battles referred to by the writers? Explain your answer.

2 Study *picture 1* and *extract D*. (a) How do you explain the contrasting attitudes towards Napoleon? (b) Do these differences make these sources less or more useful for historians writing about Napoleon? Explain your answer.

B RITAIN AND THE NAPOLEONIC WARS, 1802–5

The Treaty of Amiens, 1802, (page 94) was see as only as a breathing space. Napoleon wanted to defeat Britain which, on the other hand, could not allow Napoleon to dominate Europe.

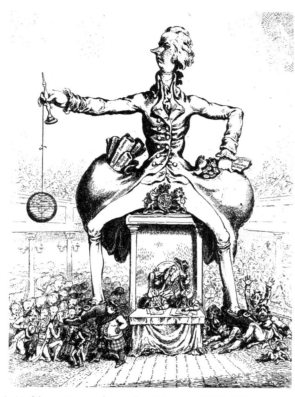

1. In this cartoon , drawn by Gillray in 1798, Pitt straddles Parliament like a colossus. His pockets are stuffed with 'resources for supporting the war', and he dangles the world on a string. Pitt's supporters kiss his right foot while his opponents are trampled with the left.

In 1803 he invaded and conquered northern Italy and invaded Switzerland. This led to the recall of Pitt (*picture 1*) to power (April 1804) and the formation of the third coalition – Britain, Austria and Russia. However,

- the Austrians suffered several defeats, ending with the one at Ulm which led to Napoleon's triumphal entry into the Austrian capital, Vienna (1805)
- the combined armies of Russia and Austria were defeated at Austelitz (1805), following which Napoleon redrew the map of Europe, creating a modern Holy Roman Empire, a united German Confederation and new kingdoms for his various relatives (*picture 2*).

Now there remained only Britain. Napoleon prepared an army and a fleet of invasion barges at Brest and other northern French ports (*extract A*). They waited for the arrival of the French fleet from Toulon and other Mediterranean ports. Nelson commanded a fleet which aimed to stop the French from leaving the Mediterranean.

However, the French escaped the blockade, and sailed to the West Indies to link up with another French and Spanish fleet. Nelson failed to catch the French on their way (*extract B*), but luckily caught up with the combined fleet when it put into Cadiz for a refit after sailing from the West Indies.

When the French and Spanish fleet left Cadiz, Nelson won the Battle of Trafalgar (*extract C*), which ensured that there would not be an invasion, and that while Napoleon was the master on land, Britain remained in control of the seas.

Helping the poor

By 1795 Britain was suffering from food shortages and rising prices. Men who were on low wages, mainly in rural areas, could not afford to feed their

2. Napoleon's Europe.

families (page 106, *pictures 1 and 4*). The magistrates at Speenhamland, near Newbury, Berkshire, decided to give money from the Poor Rates to working men so that they would be able be buy at least three gallon loaves a week if unmarried; they also gave a child's allowance (worth 30 pence a week per child) to help men with families. This saved many from starvation, but increased the Poor Rates.

EXTRACT A
Napoleon's preparations for invading England

Soldiers and sailors were eager to start for England, but the moment so ardently desired was put off. Every night they said, 'Tomorrow there will be a good wind and fog, and we shall start.'

At five o'clock in the morning signals were made, sailors were active and there was great joy, for the order to invade had been received. The soldiers marched, shouting, 'We are really going to start,' and they cheered.

The embarkation took place in silence and good order. Then, as the soldiers were about to say farewell to France, crying, *'Vive l'Empereur'*, a message came ordering the troops to disembark … the message announced that the Emperor would move his troops in another direction; the soldiers returned sadly to barracks.

(Adapted from *Memoirs*, L. Constant, 1830)

EXTRACT B
Nelson loses touch with the French fleet, July 1805

I am miserable at not having met the enemy's fleet and now cannot find them. I ought to have followed my own judgement, but, in the face of the advice from generals and admirals, I did not: I could not go North West when everyone said that the enemy had gone South. So where are the enemy? Gone northward? Making for the Mediterraneans? I long to hear that they have reached some port in Quiberon Bay.

(Adapted from Nelson's letters of 18 and 24 July 1805)

EXTRACT C
From an officer at Trafalgar, 1805

A victory, such as has never been achieved, took place yesterday in the course of five hours – but at such an expense. After performing wonders, Nelson was wounded by a French sniper and died three hours after. His decorations of many medals, and his bravery, was the cause of his death.

All were inspired by the idea of conquer or die: the enemy, too, were not less so. They are however, beaten, and I trust this will hasten peace.

Bonaparte forced them to sea. They had the flower of the Combined Fleet, but he has not yet learnt to cope with the English at sea. No history can record such a brilliant victory.

They were attacked in a way no one had ever thought of: Nelson led the way and was in the thickest of it. The last signal he made would immortalize any man – 'England expects every officer and man will do his utmost duty': the speed with which each ship acknowledged the signal showed how completely they shared his feelings. Would to God he had lived to see his prize, and the three Admirals he captured.

(Letter from Captain Blackwood to his wife, 20 October 1805)

Now test yourself

Knowledge and understanding

1 Using pages 94–7 make two lists showing (a) Napoleon's military and naval successes; (b) his naval and military failures up to 1805. Briefly explain your answers.
2 How did Napoleon's campaigns affect Britain?

Using the sources

1 Read *extracts B and C*. What use can we make of these sources when writing about the character and achievements of Horatio Nelson?
2 Study *extract A* and *picture 1*. How do these sources help to explain (a) the limits; (b) the extent of Napoleon's power? Explain your answer.

NAPOLEON'S ECONOMIC WAR AGAINST EUROPE

After Trafalgar, Napoleon tried to defeat Britain – 'a nation of shopkeepers' – by attacking its trade, the reason it had been able to stand up to him. He did this by:

- the Berlin Decree, 1806, which tried to cut Britain's trade with Europe (*extract A*),
- the Milan Decree, 1807, allowing France to seize neutral ships trading with Britain when they came out to sea again.

He forced his allies and the countries which he conquered to obey these decrees. British trade suffered: unemployment rose, profits fell. In 1811–12 there were food riots and outbreaks of machine-breaking by desperate men (page 119, *extract B*). Workers had to accept lower wages although food prices rose (page 106, *picture 4*). Britain replied to this 'economic warfare' by Orders in Council, 1807, which banned all trade with French ports – a ban enforced by the Royal Navy. Manufacturers made up some of the loss from European trade by finding new markets in Spain's former colonies in South America which had claimed their independence when France occupied Spain (see below).

Portugal and the Continental System, 1808–9

Portugal, long-time ally of Britain, refused to obey Napoleon: it had not been conquered, and felt free to defy him. This forced Napoleon to invade Spain (1808) to give him a route to Portugal. This angered the Spaniards, who were further enraged when he made his brother, Joseph, King of Spain.

Spaniards organised themselves into small groups (called *guerillas*) to attack the French as they struggled through the mountains. Napoleon said that 'Spain was a country where large armies would starve, while small armies would be beaten', (page 101, *extract A*). In June 1808 Arthur Wellesley (later Duke of Wellington) led British forces to help Portugal. In August he defeated the French at Vimiero, agreed with them that they would leave Portugal, but allowed them to keep their arms. This soft treatment led to his recall and replacement by Sir John Moore. Napoleon went to Spain where the Spaniards had forced Joseph to flee. In August 1808 he took Madrid and put Joseph back on the throne.

Moore decided to help the Spaniards, but when he heard of Napoleon's success, he went north to try to cut off Napoleon's army as it returned to France. He failed, and retreated to Corunna, where he died.

War with the USA, 1812

At first, the USA sympathized with France, which had helped them in their War of Independence (page 59). When, after 1808, Britain stopped neutral ships to see if they were carrying goods to or from France, Americans were angry and, finally, declared war on Britain (*extract C*).

Fighting took place mainly at sea and along the Canadian border. An American army invaded Canada and burnt down Yorktown (now Toronto). A British army invaded the USA, attacked the city of Washington, and set fire to some important buildings, including the President's home. To hide the burn marks, the house was painted white.

The war ended in December 1814 with the Treaty of Ghent, which failed to deal with Britain's claim to the right to search neutral ships.

1. English industry v. the Continental System.

Russia and the Continental System

In 1806 Napoleon defeated Prussia which had been allied to Russia. This defeat persuaded Tsar Alexander I to make peace with Napoleon. In the Treaty of Tilsit (1807) he agreed to join Napoleon in his fight against Britain. Meanwhile the Continental System remained in force. In 1808 only Portugal defied the ban on trade with Britain. But by 1809 the System was breaking down. British traders smuggled goods into Europe, where people were anxious to buy the output of industrialized Britain (*picture 1*). In March 1809 Napoleon was forced to issue licences, allowing even the French to trade with Britain.

Russia was less industrialized than France, so that its need for British goods was greater. In 1810 Tsar Alexander announced that he could no longer accept the ban on trade with Britain. Napoleon feared that other countries might copy this example of 'rebellion'. So in 1812 he invaded Russia. Austria and Prussia, his former enemies and once allies of Russia, sided with him.

EXTRACT A
Napoleon's Continental System, 1806

Berlin, 21 November 1806
We have decreed the following:
Article I – Britain is declared to be in a state of blockade.
Article II – All commerce with Britain is forbidden.
Article V – Trade in English goods is forbidden, and all goods coming from England or its colonies are declared a lawful prize.
Article VII – No vessel coming from England or its colonies, or which has visited them, shall be received into any European port.

(Berlin Decree, 1806)

EXTRACT B
Food riots, 1800

Bread will be sixpence the Quarter loaf if the People assemble at the Corn Market on Monday. Fellow countrymen, how long will ye suffer yourselves to be imposed on, and half starved by a set of mercenary slaves and Government hirelings? Can you still allow them to keep their wide monopolies, while your children cry for bread? No! let them exist for a day longer. We are the rulers: rise then from your lethargy. Be at the Corn Market on Monday.

(A placard, quoted in *The Dawn of the Nineteenth Century*, J. Ashton, 1906)

EXTRACT C
An attack on Pitt and his Tory successors, 1812

Is the trade with America of importance to this great, populous town? Is the war with America likely to destroy that trade? Now, I ask you whether you will be represented in Parliament by the men who have brought this great calamity about? I stand in this election against the followers of the man they call 'the immortal Pitt'. Immortal in the miseries of his country! Immortal in the loss of her liberties! Immortal in the wars which sprang from his cold ambition! Immortal in the heavy taxes and loads of debt the wars brought. Immortal in the triumphs of France and the ruin of our allies. I hope to leave as a memorial after I have laboured in your interest, 'An enemy of Pitt, a friend of peace and of the people'.

(Election speech by the Whig-Radical lawyer Henry Brougham, Liverpool, October 1812)

Now test yourself

Knowledge and understanding

1 Explain the effects that Napoleon's economic measures had on British (a) trade; (b) manufacturers; (c) workers.
2 List and explain (a) the reasons for Napoleon's invasion of Spain; (b) the effects on Britain of the war over Spain.

Using the sources

1 Study *extracts A and B* and *picture 1*. Do you agree that these sources are equally useful for historians writing about how the war with Napoleon affected Britain? Explain your answer.
2 *Read extract C*. Do you agree that the speaker was accurate in his comments about Pitt and the Tories? Explain your answer fully, referring to the information in the text about the wars.

THE DEFEAT OF NAPOLEON

After Moore's death (page 98), Wellesley returned to take command. He won battles at Oporto and Talavera (*picture 1*) where he was created Viscount Wellington of Talavera. Massena then came to command the French (*extract C*). Because his men were suffering (*extract A*), Wellington retreated to the lines of the Torres Vedras (*picture 1*), three lines of defence which the French could not overcome. Wellington's men were supplied by the navy, while Massena's men suffered more than the British had (*extract B*). This forced him to retire when he was chased by Wellington who won a series of battles in 1811 and 1812. After the victory at Salamanca, he occupied Valladolid and Madrid. He then went back to the frontier with Portugal to get ready for the spring of 1813. In that year he won a string of victories, pushing the French out of Spain altogether.

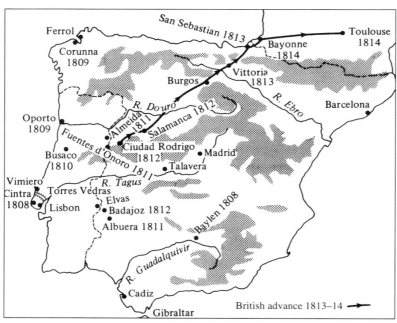

1. The Peninsular War, 1808–14.

Russia

Napoleon invaded Russia to punish his former ally for disregarding the Continental System. In the face of his 700,000 men, the Russians retreated, destroying crops, animals and buildings as they went so that the French found it hard to get the food they needed. Over 100,000 men died at the Battle of Borodino, which left Napoleon free to go on to Moscow (September 1812). Here he waited for Alexander to return and surrender. When this did not happen, and fearing the arrival of winter, Napoleon retreated on a march in which hundreds of thousands died, so that only 20,000 men survived.

The fourth coalition, 1813

Austria, Prussia, Russia and Sweden joined Britain in this last coalition. Allied forces defeated Napoleon at the Battle of the Nations at Leipzig (October 1813) and went on to occupy Paris (March 1814). With Wellington marching from the south also, Napoleon abdicated, leaving Louis XVIII to return to the throne, while Napoleon sailed into exile on the island of Elba.

The end

After ten months on Elba, Napoleon escaped, returned to Paris (the king fleeing) and gathered yet another army. In June 1815 Napoleon marched to the Netherlands, where he was outnumbered by allied forces: Blucher commanded the Prussians with Wellington commanding the British. On 18 June 1815 the enemies met at Waterloo where, after heavy fighting, Napoleon's army was put to flight. He returned to Paris, gave up the throne yet again and travelled to the coast where he surrendered to the commander of a British ship, the *Bellerophon*. When this reached Plymouth, Napoleon heard that the allies had decided to exile him to the lonely island of St Helena from where he would find it impossible to escape. He died there on 5 May 1821.

EXTRACT A
Hardship in Spain, 1809

To Viscount Castlereagh, Truxillo, 21 August 1809.

… the distress for want of provisions, and its effects, have at last obliged me to move towards the frontiers of Portugal in order to refresh my troops, Since the 22nd of last month, when the Spanish and British armies joined, the troops have not received ten days' bread; on some days they have received nothing; and for many days together only meat without salt; frequently flour instead of bread, and scarcely ever more than one-third, or at most, half of a ration. The cavalry and the horses of the army have not received, in the same time, three regular deliveries of forage…; and the horses have been kept alive by what they could pick up for themselves. The consequences of these privations has been the loss of many horses of the cavalry and artillery. We lost 100 of the cavalry last week; and we now want 1,000 to complete the six regiments of dragoons, besides about 700 that are sick, and will probably be fit for service only after a considerable period of rest and good food. The horses of the artillery are also much diminished and are scarcely able to draw the guns.

The sickness of the army, from the same cause, has increased considerably. Indeed, there are few, if any, officers or soldiers of the army who, although doing their duty, are not more or less affected by dysentry.

(*Dispatches of Field Marshall the Duke of Wellington*, edited by Lieut-Col. Gurwood, 1834)

EXTRACT B
French problems, 1810

Pero Negro, 3 November 1810
It is impossible to describe to your lordship the … distresses of the French armies in the Peninsula. All the troops are months in arrears of pay; they are in general very badly clothed; … their troops subsist solely upon plunder…; they receive no money, or scarcely any, from France; and they realize but little from their pecuniary contributions in Spain. This state of things has very much weakened, and in some instances destroyed, the discipline of the army; and all the intercepted letters [tell of] acts of … corruption, and misapplication of stores, etc., by all the persons attached to the army.

(*Despatches*, Wellington, 1837)

EXTRACT C
Wellington on his soldiers

Our army is composed of the scum of the earth … The English soldiers are fellows who have all enlisted for drink – that is plain fact.

(*Despatches*, Wellington, 1838)

EXTRACT D
A junior officer at Waterloo, 1815

The Emperor [Napoleon] was so much pressed by the Prussian advance on his right that he determined to make a last grand effort. His Artillery were ordered to concentrate their whole fire on the intended point of attack. That point was the rise of our position about half-way between Hougoumont and La Haye Sainte. The firing ceased, and as the smoke cleared away a most superb sight opened on us. A close column of Grenadiers … of la Moyenne Garde, about 6000 strong, led by Marshall Ney, were seen ascending the rise shouting *'Vive l'Empereur!'* They continued to advance till within fifty or sixty paces of our front, when the Brigade were ordered to stand up. Whether it was from the sudden … appearance of a Corps so near them or the tremendous heavy fire we threw into them, la Garde suddenly stopped. Those who from a distance could see the affair, tell us that the effect of our fire seemed to force the head of the Column bodily back.

(Captain Powell of the First Foot Guards, 1817)

Now test yourself

Knowledge and understanding

1 Do you think that the most important reason for Napoleon's defeat was (a) the military genius of Wellington or (b) the Russian campaign? Explain your answer fully.
2 Using pages 96–101 write an obituary of Napoleon Bonaparte in which you assess whether he was a 'great Frenchman'.

Using the sources

1 Study *extracts A and B*. What do these sources have in common as evidence about the Napoleonic Wars? (b) Are they equally reliable? Why?
2 Study *extracts C and D* and *picture 1*. (a) How fully do these sources explain why Wellington was able to defeat Napoleon? (b) Why are maps useful to historians writing about the wars? Explain your answer.

THE IMPORTANCE OF THE REVOLUTION AND NAPOLEON

During the nineteenth century, when politicians and writers mentioned the Revolution, everyone knew that they were not talking about events in Belgium (the 1830 Revolution) or Germany (the 1848 Revolution). The French Revolution was the Revolution during which the whole social and political system was rebuilt completely and on new foundations, when the Church was 'nationalized', a king's head cut off, and calls made for similar changes in other countries (page 89, *extract E*).

The major changes reviewed

- Feudalism was abolished, the nobles lost their powers, the peasants were given access to land – and the right to pay only their fair share of taxes.
- All adult men (not women) got the vote, even if Napoleon did not hold any elections.
- Marriage became a civil (state) ceremony and divorce was allowed.
- The Code Napoleon is still the basis of the French legal system with one set of laws for the whole country instead of different laws applying to different provinces as was the case before 1790. Those laws apply to all citizens, whatever their rank or income.
- The idea of 'revolution' (*picture 2*) became part of French thinking so that the French rose against unpopular rulers in 1830, 1848 and 1871.
- Once the Constitution and the legal, education and administration systems had been sorted out, the French also began the process of town planning – social and environmental considerations became more important in France from then onwards.

Some other effects of the period:

- The Revolutionary song, the *Marseillaise*, is still the national anthem (*extract D*).
- Napoleon's Legion of Honour continues to be France's highest award for service.
- The idea of the need for 'a strong leader' remains, and Napoleon III (1852), Marshal Pétain (1940) and General de Gaulle (1958) owe their positions to the success of Napoleon in 1799 and after.

1. Compare this cartoon with *picture 1*, page 80. Now the priest (with the scales of justice to show equality before the law) and the noble (with the sword to defend the country) carry the peasant. This cartoon appeared in 1790 after the abolition of feudalism and the setting up of a fairer system of taxation.

2. The Spirit of Revolution (the people respond to the call to arms of 1793) was carved in 1833 for the Arc de Triomphe – a lasting memorial to Napoleon's (and the Revolution's) successes.

The Revolution and the outside world

For many years after 1815, European rulers and politicians followed policies meant to prevent either the development of revolution in their own countries or the emergence of France as a major player in the international world.

If the Revolution had taken place in, say, Spain, the rest of the world might not have taken much notice. But, in the eighteenth century, France was one of, if not the, leading power in terms of size of population, ability of its writers, ambitions of its rulers and size of its economy. It is not surprising then that other people took notice of what happened in France and, in time, followed the French example with liberal and pro-democratic revolutions of their own. In Spain, for example, a pro-liberal and nationalist revolution took place in 1812 once Napoleon had been defeated there. Other Europeans followed the example of the Spanish liberals – Portugal, Germany (1848), Italy (1830 and 1848).

By the changes he made in the map of Europe (page 96, *picture 2*) Napoleon encouraged the growth of nationalism, particularly in Spain, Italy (page 95, *extract B*) and Germany, and, without having gone there, in the Balkans, where the Greeks (1821) and other peoples tried to gain their independence from rule by Turkey.

Effects in Britain

Because of the long wars, the British enjoyed even more rapid industrial growth because of the demand for munitions (and so for iron and coal) and for uniforms (and so for changes in textile production).

The Tories, who governed the country from 1784 through the wars, continued, after 1815, with the policy of repression and opposition to needed reforms of the electoral system (pages 114–15), social conditions (pages 112–3) and working conditions (pages 110–11).

EXTRACT A
The French Revolution – a world affair?

It is one of those events which belong to the whole human race.

(Friedrich von Gentz (1764–1832), writing in 1794)

It is understood everywhere that *the* event of these modern ages is the French Revolution. A huge explosion, bursting through all customs.

(The English philosopher, Thomas Carlyle (1795–1881), writing in 1837)

EXTRACT B
Napoleon – hero or villain?

'Dynamic leader' … 'unprincipled adventurer' … 'reformer' … 'the cause of tyranny, exploitation and bloodshed' … Each writer, and reader, makes his own Napoleon from the evidence available.

(D.G. Wright, 1984)

Examples of opposing opinions

The ideas of the Revolution and the character of the time produced Napoleon's power. But that power killed the ideas of the Revolution

(Tolstoy, Russian author, in 1860)

Kneel before the tomb of the great Napoleon.

(Queen Victoria in 1855)

Napoleon forgot that man cannot be God, that the nation is more than the individual, and that the law is above mankind: he forgot that war is not the highest aim, for peace is above war.

(Marshall Foch of France, 1921)

EXTRACT C
The Russian army affected by French liberalism rebels, 1825

We shed our blood against Napoleon. Now we are forced once again to accept feudalism. We freed Russia from the threat of Napoleon, and now we are ourselves victims of tyranny by our ruling class. Did we free Europe in order to be kept in chains ourselves?

(Bestuzhev, a leading member of the Decembrist movement, quoted in *Marc Raeff, The Decembrist Movement*, 1966)

EXTRACT D
The Marseillaise in Beijing, 1989

And as the students march, they sing the French Revolutionary song – now the anthem of the French Republic – the *Marseillaise*, first sung nearly two hundred years ago.

(From a BBC TV commentary on the uprising by Chinese students in Tianamen Square, 1989)

Now test yourself

Knowledge and understanding

Look at the list of effects of events in France 1789–1815 and explain which *three* were the most important: (a) the execution of the king; (b) abolition of feudalism; (c) the Code of Napoleon; (d) growth of nationalism and revolutionary ideas; (e) the wars fought to defeat Napoleon.

Using the sources

1 Study *extracts A–D* and *picture 2*. How can these sources be used to both (a) praise; (b) condemn the effects of the Revolutionary and Napoleonic eras? Explain your answer fully.

2 Study *picture 1* and compare it with *picture 1* on page 80. Do you agree that the differences between the pictures accurately show how France was changed by the Revolution? Explain your answer.

B ritain 1750–c.1900

M ORE PEOPLE AND NEW PLACES

Picture 1 shows that in 1700 the most populated areas were the south, south-west and East Anglia. Even there, the population was small. In 1700 Middlesex had the sort of population density found in modern Devon. Towns were small by modern standards (page 60) and most people lived in villages (page 54).

Picture 2 shows the distribution of the population in 1901. Now the most densely populated areas lie around the coalfields, sites of the Industrial Revolution (page 108). *Picture 3* is based on official censuses, the first of which took place in 1801. It shows that the proportion of people living in towns continued to grow. The following list gives the populations of some towns in thousands (the first figure shows the population in 1801, the figure in brackets gives the population in 1911): Leicester 17 (212); Blackburn 12 (129); Stoke-on-Trent 23 (215); Bradford 13 (290); Sheffield 46 (407); Manchester 70 (645); Liverpool 82 (704). Notice by how much these towns grew between 1801 and 1911.

The growth of these and other towns was a reflection of the overall growth of the population of England and Wales shown in census returns: 1801 – 11.5 million; 1831 – 17.8 million; 1861 – 24.5 million; 1901 – 42.1 million. Was the population growth due to an increase in the birth rate (*extract A*) or to a fall in the death rate (*extracts B and C*)? *Picture 4* shows a decline in the death rate. *Picture 5* shows how, towards the end of the century, the birth rate declined and middle-class families were smaller; the working class did not start to have smaller families until the 1930s.

Why did death rates fall (*picture 4*)?

In *extract B* you will find *five* reasons for this fall. Alongside these:

● Parliament passed many Acts which forced local councils to improve the environment – the 'better health conditions' in *extract B*. Some people called this socialism (page 131, *extract D*).

● 'Better health conditions' came from a cleaner environment. This included publicly owned water supplies to most homes, refuse collection and street cleansing, sewers and drains to most homes and streets. Disease had spread easily in a dirty environment (page 113, *extract E*).

● More people had more and better food (*extract C*; page 106, *pictures 1 and 2*; page 121, *extract D*; page 124, *picture 2*).

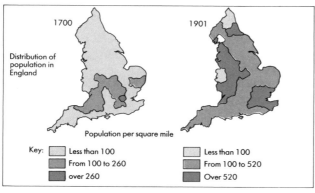

1. Population in England, 1700.

2. Population in England, 1901.

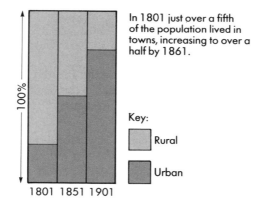

In 1801 just over a fifth of the population lived in towns, increasing to over a half by 1861.

Key:

■ Rural

■ Urban

1801 1851 1901

3. People living in town and country – in 1801 just over a fifth of the population lived in towns, increasing to over a half by 1861.

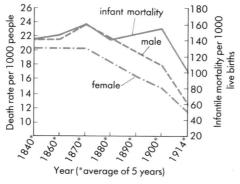

4. The declining death rate, 1840–1914.

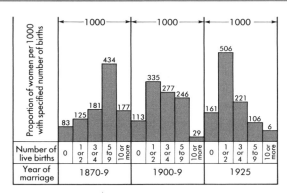

5. Changes in family size, 1870–1925.

EXTRACT A
Growing towns, 1774

The national wealth increased the demand for labour and raised wages which led to an increase in the birth rate. Why had the population of Birmingham increased from 23,000 in 1750 to 30,000 in 1770? Because there has been an increase in employment, more marriages and, because children are not a burden, more births. As soon as a child can use its hands it can maintain itself, and the parents, too, are fully employed.

(*Political Arithmetic*, Arthur Young, 1774)

EXTRACT B
The growth of London, 1800

Much of the growth in population is due to better health conditions, the improvement in medical knowledge, and the improved habits among the people who are cleaner, in homes and habits, than they used to be, partly because of cheaper clothing from our cotton factories, partly because of better knowledge about running the household.

(*Account of Persons Imprisoned for Debt in England and Wales*, Arthur Nield, 1800)

EXTRACT C
Growing national population, 1812

The country should be congratulated on the growth in population and on its ability to provide the people with food.

(Parliamentary debates, 1812)

EXTRACT D
The growth of Middlesbrough, 1811–1901

It is surprising when one sees the crowded Middlesbrough of today, to see that in 1831 the population was 154; then the railways were begun and in 1841 the population was 5,463. In 1850 ironstone was discovered in the Cleveland Hills within reach of the Durham coal fields, making Middlesbrough an ironmaking centre. The population grew from 18,892 (1861) to 39,284 (1871) and 91,302 (1901). And at the moment of writing, the census of 1911 gives the population as 104,787.

(*At the Works*, Lady (Florence) Bell, 1911)

EXTRACT E
Malthus on population growth, 1798

i The supply of food necessarily limits population.
ii If population is free from all checks, it will be increased in geometrical progression, i.e. 2, 4, 8, 16 and so on, but food supply will increase only in an arithmetic progression, i.e. 1, 2, 3, 4 and so on.
iii Three checks operate to keep population in line with food supply: these are moral restraint, vice and misery.

(Adapted from *An Essay on the Principle of Population*, T.R. Malthus, 1798)

Now test yourself

Knowledge and understanding

1 Use the text and *extracts A–E* to list and explain (a) the reasons for the rise in population 1705–1901; (b) the effects of this growth.
2 Use the text, *pictures 1 and 2* and *extracts* to write an account of 'the changing face of Britain'. You should show how changes in industry, agriculture and population were related to each other.

Using the sources

1 Read *extract B* and look at *pictures 1 and 2*. Do these sources support the views expressed in (a) *extract C* or (b) *extract E*? Why?
2 How accurate and valuable are *pictures 4 and 5* for historians trying to discover patterns of family size and mortality rates?

CHANGES IN FARMING, 1750–1846

Successful British farmers (page 55, *extract A*) produced enough food to feed the rising population (page 105, *extract C*). They continued to reduce their costs and to make their land more productive, sometimes because of falling prices (*picture 1*), although later to take advantage of rising prices and the export market (*picture 2*). In East Anglia and the Midlands most farming followed the medieval three-field system (*picture 3*). After 1750 most of this land was enclosed and strips exchanged to make compact farms. Sometimes this was done by a simple agreement between those concerned: sometimes it needed a private Act of Parliament (*extract A*).

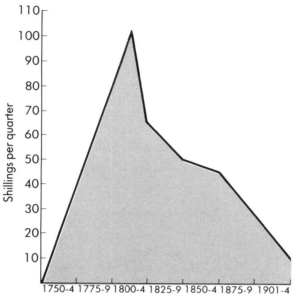

1. Wheat prices, 1750–1879.

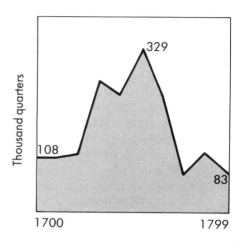

2. Wheat and flour exports, 1700–99.

General Acts passed in 1801 and after made things simpler. Some suffered by enclosure: tenants who could not prove a legal case for a tenancy got nothing; others could not pay for the fencing and sold out. The worst off were those who had tilled a few acres on the common; they lost everything (*extract B*). Many farmers gained, especially if they used the Norfolk system (*extract C*). Consumers gained from the extra supply of food, including fresh meat, once stockbreeders had shown how to produce larger animals which were fed through the winter on turnips and the new grasses.

Turnips, swedes and clover not only provided winter food for animals; they also fed the soil so that there was no need for a fallow year (page 20, *picture 2*). Stockbreeders, such as Robert Bakewell, bred healthier and heavier animals. In 1710 the average weight of cattle sold at Smithfield meat market was 144 kg (320 lbs); in 1795 it had more than doubled to 360 kg (800 lbs).

During the Napoleonic Wars prices rose sharply, and life was hard for the lower paid and unemployed (*picture 4*). After the wars, landowners in the unreformed Parliament (page 114) pushed through Corn Laws which banned wheat

4. Cartoon showing Pitt, as the butcher, and the starving poor.

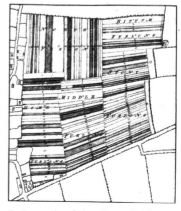

3. Records of the three-field system, Strettington, Sussex.

imports until British prices were very high. When the middle classes got their share
of political power they used it to repeal these laws (*extract D*). British farmers did
not suffer – at least, at first (pages 124–5).

EXTRACT A
An 'Inclosure' Act, 1766

February 3 1766: Mr Cholmley presented to the
House a Bill for inclosing and dividing the
commons and open fields … in Stillington. Read
for the first time.
February 10 1766: A Bill for inclosing …
Stillington was read a second time.
February 27 1766: Mr Cholmley reported from
the Committee to whom the Bill had been
committed. It had examined the Bill, found that
the Parties concerned had given their consent,
except a few who refused and some who were
not at home. No one appeared before the
Committee to object. Ordered: the Bill be
printed.
March 3 1766: A Bill for inclosing … Stillington
was read the Third Time. Resolved: That the Bill
do pass.

(Parliamentary Debates, 1766)

EXTRACT B
Losers from enclosure, 1799

Time was when these commons enabled a poor
man to support his family. Here he could put out
his cow and pony, feed his geese and pig.
Enclosures have deprived him of these
advantages. He now has only 14d per day to
keep himself, wife and five or six children when
bread is 3d per pound. Now the parish must
assist him. Poor rates rise to a terrible height.

(*Walking Tour*, Richard Warren, 1799)

EXTRACT C
New farming, Norfolk, 1771

… to give a review of the husbandry which
makes this country so famous. Great
improvements have been made by means of the
following:
First: by inclosing without the assistance of
Parliament.
Second: by the use of marl (powdered rock and
lime) and clay.
Third: rotation of crops: (i) turnips; (ii) barley;
(iii) clover; (iv) wheat.
Fourth: by the culture of turnips well hand-hoed.
Fifth: by the culture of clover and ray-grass.
Sixth: by the landlords granting long leases.
Seventh: by the country being divided into large
farms.

(*The Farmer's Tour*, Arthur Young, 1771)

EXTRACT D
**Against the Corn Laws and for free trade,
1833**

I am a manufacturer of clothing. Did you ever
hear any debates in the House to fix the price of
clothing in the market? When I went to
Normandy they said to me: 'Admit our corn and
then we'll import your clothing. We are millions,
willing to buy your clothes, and you have
millions of hungry mouths ready to take our
corn.' To pay for that corn we would have to
increase our exports which would increase the
demand for workers and clear the streets of the
two million unemployed that now exist.

(*Speeches*, Richard Cobden MP, edited in 1870)

Now test yourself

Knowledge and understanding

1 Show how 'progress' in agriculture
 (a) benefited some groups; (b) made life
 worse for others.
2 List the following factors affecting farmers
 in order of importance, explaining your
 choice of order: (a) war; (b) rising population
 (c) the Industrial Revolution; (d) Parliament;
 (e) farmers' education.

Using the sources

1 How could *extracts B and C* help the
 historian to give a balanced view of the
 effects of enclosure?
2 (a) What did Cobden (*extract D*) expect
 would happen to corn prices if the Corn
 Laws were repealed? (b) What light does
 picture 1 throw on his expectations?
3 Are cartoons such as *picture 4* more useful
 for historians writing about the Corn Laws
 than *extract D*? Why?

THE FIRST INDUSTRIAL REVOLUTION, 1760–1830

In the domestic system, merchants took raw material to the cottagers and paid them for the finished work (*extracts A and B, pictures 1 and 2*). This system could not meet the increased demand from colonial trade (pages 56 and 58) and the rising population (pages 104–5) so inventions were made to increase output (*picture 3*).

1. Hand spinning in the 18th century.

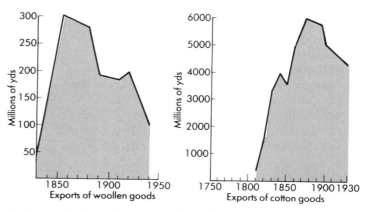

3. The graph shows the export of woollen and cotton goods from 1750 to the 1930s

2. A handloom weaver.

4. Hargreave's 'Spinning Jenny'.

The output of spinners was increased with the help of (a) the spinning jenny (1764) (*picture 4*) (b) Arkwright's water frame (1769) which had to be housed in a factory (c) the 'mule' (1779) (*picture 5*).

At first, handloom weavers gained from the increased supply of yarn (*picture 2* and *extract C*). They were ruined by the invention of the steam-driven and factory-based power loom (1785).

Iron and coal were linked by the Darbys of Coalbrookdale (*extract F*). Without their work, perhaps none of the other machines could have come about. This shows how one change can lead to other unintended changes.

The evolution of the steam engine

1689: Dr Thomas Savery invented a steam engine to pump water from Cornish tin mines. This had only an up-and-down motion.

1712: A blacksmith, Thomas Newcomen, made an improved version. By 1800 there were about 300 working engines, which used a great deal of coal.

1763: James Watt improved Newcomen's engine, making it more economical and more efficient. He was financed by a Birmingham factory owner, Mathew Boulton, whose foreman, William Murdock, helped Watt develop better engines. He was also helped by the skill of Wilkinson (*extract D*), who learned to make perfect cylinders while boring cannon for the armed forces.

1782: Watt, Boulton and Murdock built an engine which, with the help of a series of cogs and wheels, could produce rotary motion, so that it could drive all sorts of machines. This made cheap mass production possible.

5. Samuel Crompton's 'mule'.

EXTRACT A
The domestic system

The weaver's workshop was a rural cottage from which he could go to work in his garden if he wanted. The cotton was picked clean by his young children, carded and spun by the older girls and his wife. The yarn was woven by the weaver and his sons. He took in yarn from other spinsters: one weaver could keep three spinners at work.

(*The Philosophy of Manufacturers*, Andrew Ure, 1831)

EXTRACT B
Master clothiers cheat the domestic workers

We'll make the poor weaver work at a low rate,
We'll find fault where there is none, and so we will bate (pay less),
If trading goes dead, we will immediately show it,
But if it grows good, they will never know it,
By poor people's labour, we will fill up our purse,
Although we do get it with many a curse.

(*History of Wool and Woolcombing*, John Burnley, 1885)

EXTRACT C
The rise and fall of the handloom weaver

They brought home their work in top boots and ruffled shirts, carried a cane and took a coach. They used to walk about the streets with a five pound note in their hat bands … This prosperity did not last. The price for weaving a length of cloth fell to 29 shillings in 1797, and to 6 shillings in 1827. Weavers could not provide for their families although they worked all day.

(*The Life and Times of Samuel Crompton*, Gilbert French, 1860)

EXTRACT D
Wilkinson makes cylinders for Watt's engines, 1781

Only after many expensive experiments did Mr Wilkinson achieve perfection in casting and boring which satisfied us. Now we recommend his castings for all our engines.

(Letter from James Watts to a buyer, 1781)

EXTRACT E
The marvel of a cotton-spinning factory, 1835

We see a building with a 100 horse-power steam engine with the strength of 880 men, working 50,000 spindles and all the auxiliary machines. It needs only 750 workers to produce as much yarn as would have been spun by 200,000 men: one man now produces as much as 260 did in the old days.

(*History of Cotton*, Edward Baines, 1835)

EXTRACT F
The Darbys of Coalbrookdale use coal instead of charcoal

My husband's father tried to smelt iron with coal but it did not work. He then coked the coal into cinders, and this fuel worked. My husband was only six when his father died, but he had his genius and made many improvements. He succeeded in making bar iron from the pig iron using coal. Without these discoveries the iron trade would have died, because wood for charcoal had become very scarce.

(Letter from Mrs Abiah Darby quoted in *Iron and Steel*, Ashton, 1924)

6. The Soho Foundry, Manchester, 1814. The canal carried goods before the arrival of railways.

Now test yourself

Knowledge and understanding

1 Here are some factors which help explain changes in the textile industry. Write them down in order of importance and explain your choice: colonial demand; growing population; inventions in spinning, weaving and steam engines; war.
2 List six people who played important roles in the first Industrial Revolution. Which *one* do you think was most important? Why?

Using the sources

1 Which of the *extracts* and *pictures* are most valuable for historians writing about (a) textile production; (b) child and female workers; (c) the effects of the textile revolution on engineering and on canal transport?
2 Study *extract D* and the section on the evolution of the steam engine. Do you agree that James Watt was the most important of the steam engine inventors? Why?

FACTORY LIFE AND REFORM, 1780–1850

When the factory system was still new, many people wanted a return to the domestic system (*extract B*), in which cottagers chose when to start and end their day (page 108, *picture 1* and page 109, *extract A*). Factory owners had to force people to accept fixed times and to stay by their machines through the day. Children were easier to discipline so they were employed (*picture 1*).

1. Children working in a textile mill.

2. Children working in a brickyard, 1870.

The parish authorities who looked after the poor had always sent children to work for master craftsmen (*extract A*) and they continued to send them to factory owners. It was the fate of these pauper children which first roused the interest of reformers. In 1802 Robert Owen and Sir Robert Peel persuaded Parliament to pass an Act limiting the working day for these children to 12 hours. In 1812 Peel pushed through an Act which limited the working day for all children working in cotton mills: no child could be employed before the age of nine. But there was no one appointed to enforce these first Acts.

1830–32: Michael Sadler and Ashley Cooper (later Lord Shaftesbury) campaigned for factory reform. A Parliamentary commission heard from supporters of reform (*extracts B and D*), from opponents (*extract C*) and from good factory owners (*extract F*).

1833: the first effective Factory Act banned the employment of children under the age of nine and limited older children's working hours (*extract E*). It also appointed inspectors to enforce its conditions. However, it only applied to textile mills. Children still worked in coal mines (*extract G* and *picture 2*) until the Mines Act (1845), and in brickyards (*picture 2*) until education became compulsory in the 1880s.

In old age, a man remembered having to carry 40lb of clay on his head from the clay heap to where the bricks were made – for 13 hours a day nonstop and for sixpence a day. His biography, *George Smith of Coalville*, was published in 1896.

A 10-hour day campaign led by Shaftesbury forced Parliament to pass Acts in 1844, 1847 and 1850, when, at last, the working day for men and women was fixed at 10 hours, not including meal times. This was 70 years after Arkwright had opened the first spinning mill at Cromford. Reform is a slow process.

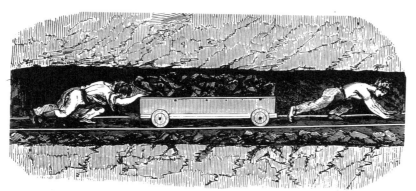

3. Children working in a coalmine.

EXTRACT A
Cruelty to child workers, 1738

It is normal to apprentice poor children to any master living outside the parish; if the child serves him for 40 days we are rid of him for ever. The master may be a tiger in cruelty, beat, abuse, strip naked, starve or do what he will to the poor lad.

(An Enquiry into the Increase of the Poor, 1738)

EXTRACT B
Parliament investigates the factory system, 1832

At what age are children employed? Never under five, but some are employed between five and six in woollen mills: they go to work between five and six am; in the summer they work until ten in the evening – as long as they can see.
How do they eat? They get breakfast as they can; they eat and work – generally water porridge, with a little treacle that they take when they get a minute.
Suppose our Bill forced owners to close down their mills? This would mean domestic work, the greatest blessing for England; the factory system is slavery.

(Report of the Committee on the Factory Bill, 1832)

EXTRACT C
Which side did the newspaper support?

Extreme hardship would be inflicted upon tens of thousands of families in Lancashire and Yorkshire by a law fixing the [working] hours at eight or even ten hours, and absolutely forbidding the employment of a child.

(*The Leeds Mercury*, December 1831)

EXTRACT D
Remembering being a child worker, 1832

After I had worked for a half a year, I could scarcely walk. In the morning my brother and sister used to take me under each arm and run with me, a good mile, to the mill. If we were five minutes late, the overlooker would take a strap and beat us till we were black and blue. I have seen my mother weep sometimes, but she would not tell me why she was weeping.

(Joseph Hebergan's evidence to the Committee on the Factory Bill, 1832)

EXTRACT E
The Factory Act, 1833

It shall not be lawful to employ in any factory as aforesaid any child who shall not have completed his or her ninth year; children aged between nine and eleven shall not work more than nine hours a day and 48 hours a week … to appoint four inspectors of factories where people under 18 years of age are employed. They shall have the power to make such rules as shall be necessary for the execution of this Act.

EXTRACT F
A reformed factory owner, 1845

From the working of my mills I have learned that as much cloth may be made at the same cost in 11 hours as in 12 hours. I propose to reduce hours to $10^{1}/_{2}$ without suffering any loss. I find the hands work with greater energy and spirit and are more cheerful and happy.

(Parliamentary Papers, 1845)

EXTRACT G
Child workers in coal mining, 1842

Children aged six or seven go down the pit at four in the morning and stay there for 11 or 23 hours a day. Their work is to open and shut the doors of the galleries when the trucks pass: for this the child sits by itself in a dark gallery for all those hours.

(Report on Mines, 1842)

Now test yourself

Knowledge and understanding

1 How did the Factory Reform Movement affect (a) children; (b) parents; (c) employers?
2 Factory inspectors, Robert Owen, Sir Robert Peel, Michael Sadler and Lord Shaftesbury all played important roles in the reform of working conditions. Who were the *three* most important? Explain your choice.

Using the sources

1 *Read extracts A–G*. How reliable would *each* of these sources be for historians trying to explain which groups (a) supported; (b) opposed factory reform, and their reasons for doing so?
2 Look at *pictures 1 and 2* and *extract G*. How do they provide a different interpretation of the Industrial Revolution than if we chose only *extracts C and F*?

THE STRUGGLE FOR PUBLIC HEALTH REFORM

Old, chartered boroughs had a local council (page 32). New industrial towns had no charter and no local government (*extracts A and B*). Even when there were councils, there were no laws about sanitary conditions. Everything, including the environment, was to be left to private enterprise. Private builders, working for profit, did build good housing for those who could afford to pay, but the majority of people were low-paid: their houses were small and lacking water, drainage and toilets.

The poor also had an inadequate diet (*extract C*) and they were often ill, saw their children die, and had a shorter life than the better off. Poor sanitary conditions in towns meant less chance of living to old age than the rural poor (*extract E*).

1. Poor people living in a cellar.

People and governments were slow to accept the need for new laws and for new administrative bodies (councils) to implement them. The first Public Health Act was passed in 1848 (*extract F*). It set up a General Board (the forerunner of the Ministry of Local Government) and allowed local ratepayers to elect a local Board of Health. Few towns wanted local Boards. So the Act allowed the General Board to force such elections – but only after a town had a very high death rate for seven years (*extract F*). Even this modest Act was opposed by influential groups (*extract G*), and people continued to drink dirty water and to live in poor quality housing in the world's richest country.

Why were many voters and politicians unwilling to support demands for social and environmental reform? Most of them supported the idea of Samuel Smiles that the poor should rely on self-help (page 131, *extract E*) and they believed in *laissez-faire* (French, meaning 'leave things alone').Because governments – national and local – also believed in *laissez-faire*, they were unwilling to interfere in the economic or social lives of the community. We can see this in:

● the demand for free trade: it was argued that tariffs (or government taxes) interfered with the free flow (leave things alone) of commerce (page 107, *extract D*)
● opposition to demands for factory reform (page 111, *extract C*)
● opposition to demands for social reform (*extract H*).

Supporters of *laissez-faire* claimed that reforms would lead to increased taxes which would leave businessmen with less money to invest in industry, and would create unemployment. By not passing laws which might have reformed society, governments allowed businessmen to have the money to invest, which led to more industrial development, greater profits and more employment. But at what cost?

We know, and governments of the time knew, from dozens of surveys and royal commissions (*extract D* is from one of the first) that millions of people lived in houses which had only two rooms – one up and one down, each about 2.75 metres wide and 3.5 metres long. In such houses, families with as many as 10 children lived – without running water or toilets (*extract B*).

EXTRACT A
Local government and the environment, 1818

Sheffield does not have a mayor and corporation. But in 1818 a private Act was passed 'for cleansing, lighting, policing and otherwise improving Sheffield'. Seven improvement commissioners were appointed to put this into effect and they bring offenders before the magistrates.

(*A New History*, Thomas Allen, 1831)

EXTRACT B
The environment where there is no local government, 1845

Merthyr is in a sad state of neglect. Because the poorer people, the majority of the population, throw all their refuse into the gutters in front of their houses, parts of the town are networks of filth. There is no local Act for drainage and cleansing. In some places, a toilet was common to 40 or 50 and even up to 100 and more.

(Health of Towns Commission Report, 1845)

EXTRACT C
Life among the poor, 1838

I visited 83 dwellings, all without furniture, old boxes for tables, stools or large stones for chairs, beds of straw, sometimes covered by torn pieces of carpet, sometimes with no covering. Food was oatmeal for breakfast; flour and water and skimmed milk for dinner; oatmeal and water again for those who had three meals a day. I saw children eating rotting vegetables in the market.

(*Tour in Manufacturing Districts of Lancashire*, William Cooke-Taylor, 1838)

EXTRACT D
Disease and the environment, 1842

Careful examination of the evidence leads to these chief conclusions:
1 that the various epidemics and diseases are caused by the damp, filth and crowded dwellings in which the majority of people live;
2 that where there is drainage, street cleaning, better ventilation and other improvements, the incidence of disease drops;
3 that lack of cleanliness is due to lack of good water supplies.

(Report on Sanitary Conditions, 1842)

EXTRACT E
Different ages of death for different classes, 1842

The average age of death	In Manchester	In Rutland
For professional people and gentry	38	52
For tradesmen and families	20	41
For craftsmen, labourers and families	17	38

(Report on Sanitary Conditions, 1842)

EXTRACT F
The first Public Health Act, 1848

IV That the General Board of Health in Whitehall shall control local Boards.
VIII That when one-tenth of the population of a town dies OR when the death rate (for seven years) has been more than 23 in 1000 inhabitants, the General Board shall send an Inspector to examine the sanitary conditions …

EXTRACT G
Opposition to the Public Health Act, 1852

A Briton's privilege of self-government is opposed to the communistic idea of government for one's neighbour. The Public Health Act is an attack on this holy principle. This Act and others have not done much mischief yet. But if Britons don't take care they will find their cesspools drained, their refuse carted away and that sacred principle of 'doing what they like with their own' trampled under foot by some poking inspector.

(*Punch*, 1852)

Now test yourself

Knowledge and understanding

1 Using the text and *extracts E and G*, describe the attitudes towards public health reform of (a) supporters; (b) opponents of reform.
2 From the text and *extracts A–E*, show how public health improved in some ways, but became worse for most people in the 19th century.

Using the sources

1 Read *extract F* and the text. Do you agree that the 1848 Public Health Act was a 'landmark in the history of public health law'? Why?
2 Study *picture 1*. Does it provide useful evidence in addition to the extracts of living conditions in the 19th century?

PARLIAMENTARY REFORM, 1832

Constituencies (*picture 1*) are the places represented by Members of Parliament (MPs) in the House of Commons. In 1832 each county had two MPs. Most boroughs chartered to elect MPs were in the south, where agriculture was the major industry (*extract A*). In some 'rotten' boroughs the local landowners simply named the two MPs. In other 'pocket' boroughs a patron (often the government – page 75, *extract D*) controlled the election of the two MPs.

Reformers wanted the new industrial towns to be represented (*extract C*), which would involve a redistribution of seats (*picture 3*).

The franchise, or right to vote, in county elections was simple: borough franchises were many and, to modern eyes, ridiculous (*extract B*). Imagine having a vote because you had a fireplace big enough to take a pot of a named size (a pot-walloper) or because your house was listed in an ancient charter (burgage-holder) or because it was liable to the ancient taxes of scot-and-lot. Reformers wanted a simple franchise, extended to the new classes (*extract D*).

Reformers set up local political unions (*extract D*). Their demonstrations sometimes led to violence (page 118) but finally convinced the Whig Party of the need for

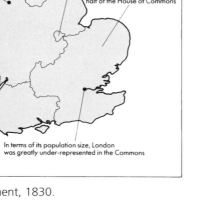

1. Representation in Parliament, 1830.

reform (*extract C*). The Whigs won the 1830 election, a year in which another French Revolution overthrew the Bourbons yet again. Some Whigs argued that Britain might suffer its own revolution if Parliament was not reformed (*extract E*).

1831–2: Two Bills were rejected by Parliament. When the Lords opposed a third Bill, the king agreed to create 100 new peers to push it through. The Lords let the Bill through and it became law on 7 June 1832.

In the constituencies, 56 small towns lost both MPs and 31 lost one of their two MPs; 21 seats went to smaller industrial towns and 22 larger towns got two MPs. Extra MPs were given to more populated counties, to Ireland and Scotland. The franchise for the boroughs was simple: any male occupier (owner or tenant) of a house valued (for rating purposes) at £10 a year got the vote. The county franchise was extended to tenants of some larger farms.

The results in the short term are illustrated by *extract F* and *picture 3*. In the future people would ask why the vote should not be given to occupiers of less valuable property or, indeed, to every adult male, or to women.

2. Whigs and the king driving the Tories from power.

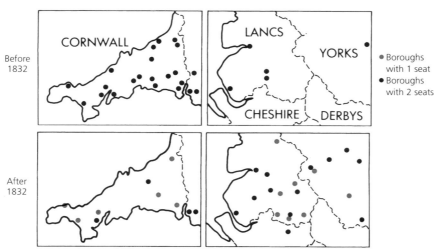

3. The distribution of seats in Cornwall and in the industrial North West before and after 1832.

EXTRACT A
Landowners are more important than other people, 1793

I suppose everyone would agree that the landed interest ought to have most weight in our affairs.

(The future Lord Liverpool, in the Commons, 6 May 1793)

EXTRACT B
The variety of qualifications for the franchise, 1793

In some places voting is limited to a select body of 30 or 40; in others it may be as much as 10,000. Burgage-holders, scot-and-lot men, pot-wallopers and freeholders, each has the vote in different boroughs. In some places the vote goes to the owner of a piece of land where no one has lived for years.

(Society of the Friends of the People, February 1793)

EXTRACT C
This is a new age, 1831

We don't live in the days of barons; we live in the days of Leeds, Bradford, Halifax and Huddersfield.

(Henry Brougham, a leading Whig MP)

EXTRACT D
Industrial wealth is as important as landowners' wealth, 1830

The interests of the aristocracy are well represented in Parliament. But the interests of Trade and Industry, the source of the nation's wealth and strength, are unrepresented.

(Birmingham Political Union, 1830)

EXTRACT E
Either reform or face revolution, March 1831

History is full of revolutions produced by causes similar to those now at work in England. A part of the people which had been unimportant, grows, and demands a place in the system. If granted, all is well. If refused, then comes the struggle between the young energy of one class and the ancient privilege of another. Such is the struggle which the middle classes are waging against the aristocracy and the owners of ruins who have powers still denied to cities.

(T.B. Macaulay, in the Commons, 2 March 1831)

EXTRACT F
Elections in Bath – before and after reform

October 1812 Our two MPs were re-elected by 10 aldermen and 20 councillors.
January 1833 Bath: population 38,063; number of £10 voters: 7,314.

(*The Bath Herald*, October 1812; *The Weekly Dispatch*, January 1833)

EXTRACT G
It did nothing for the working classes

It is safe to say that the Act did nothing for the working classes, in spite of their enthusiastic support for reform. It was the factory owners rather than the factory workers who benefited. Only about 400,000 new voters were added … the landed gentry had merely shared a little of its political power with the new industrial and commercial class.

(*Britain since 1700*, R.J. Cootes, 1968)

Now test yourself

Knowledge and understanding

1 How did the following factors lead to the passage of the Reform Act 1832: the Industrial Revolution; a growing middle class; political unions; Whig victory in the 1830 elections. Are there any other causes for the passage of the Act?
2 How did the 1832 Reform Act lead to changes in (a) the short term; (b) the long term?

Using the sources

1 How can we use the *extracts* to find arguments to support (a) the opponents of reform; (b) those who wanted reform?
2 How useful are *pictures 1 and 3* for showing how the Reform Act affected the electoral system? How should we check the accuracy of these sources?

CHARTISM

Working-class leaders who had campaigned for the 1832 Reform Act were angry with its terms (*extract A*). Many went on to lead the Chartist movement. Its aims were totally political (*picture 1*) although the Chartists really wanted solutions to workers' grievances (*extract A*) and were concerned with social issues (*extract C*), such as housing, unemployment (*extract B*), sanitary conditions and education. They knew that landowners had pushed through the Corn Laws which suited them and they watched the new middle-class voters working to get those Laws repealed (page 107, *extract D*). Chartists hoped that if the workers had the vote, Parliament would pass laws which would help them.

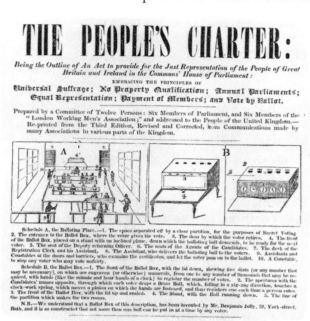

1. The Charter.

Unfortunately, the movement was divided. Feargus O'Connor, an Irish Protestant, believed in physical force. His newspaper, *The Northern Star*, called for an armed uprising, which alarmed Parliament as well as many workers (*extract D*), and could never have succeeded (*extract E*). William Lovett (1800–76), a cabinet-maker, led the Chartists who believed in moral force, arguing that Parliament could be persuaded into reform.

1836: Lovett founded the London Working Men's Association.

1837: Chartists submitted their first National Petition (*extract A*).

1838: Napier's army put down riots in Birmingham (*extract E*).

1839: During the continuing depression (*extract B*) 500 Chartist groups sent another petition to Parliament (*extract F*). John Frost led Welsh miners and ironworkers in an attempt to free the Chartist leader, Henry Vincent, from jail in Monmouth. Their clash with the army at Newport alarmed the government.

The year 1848 saw revolutions throughout Europe. Chartists held many demonstrations. Leaders of a mass meeting on Kennington Common planned to present a petition to Parliament (*picture 2*). The frightened government prepared to defend London (*extract G*). Heavy rain cut down the size of the crowd, and Wellington allowed the leaders to cross into London with their petition. This was shown to have many false signatures (*extract H*); some claim that Chartism was 'laughed to death'. Really it was killed by prosperity (page 120).

2. Cartoon showing the Charter being presented to Lord John Russell.

3. A contemporary drawing of the 1848 meeting on Kennington Common. Notice the well-dressed Chartists, the woman on the platform and a uniformed policeman (far right).

EXTRACT A
Disappointment with the 1832 Reform Act

It was the people's hope that a remedy for their grievances would be found in the 1832 Act. They have been bitterly let down. That Act merely transformed power from one domineering class to another.

(National Petition, 1837)

EXTRACT B
How economic depression affects people's lives, 1847

At no period have distress and privation prevailed more heavily on the working classes. The streets are crowded with paupers. A soup kitchen in Manchester gives out soup and bread daily.

(*The Times*, 17 February 1847)

EXTRACT C
'The knife and fork' question

How could every working man gain the right to a good coat on his back, a good dinner on his table, work that will keep him in good health and as much wages as will keep him in enjoyment of plenty?

(J.R. Stephens of the Anti-Poor Law movement)

EXTRACT D
Chartist divisions by William Lovett, 1845

The physical force agitation is harmful to the movement. Guns are not what are wanted, but education of the working people. O'Connor and Stephens [extract C] are splitting the movement. Violent words do not slay our enemies. O'Connor wants to take everything by storm and to pass the Charter into law in a year. The menace of armed opposition leads only to premature risings and our destruction.

EXTRACT E
A sympathiser, who leads the army against Chartists, 1838

People should have universal suffrage, the ballot, annual Parliaments and proper education. But by reason and Parliament. Physical force! Fools! We have the force, not they; they talk of their thousands of men. Who is to inspire them when I am dancing around them with cavalry?

(General Sir Charles Napier, 1838)

EXTRACT F
Presenting the Charter to the Commons, 1839

The petition started in Birmingham and is now presented to the House with 1,280,000 signatures, the result of 500 meetings. The men who signed it were angry that no effort had been made to relieve their suffering, whether they are handloom weavers or factory workers.

(T. Attwood, MP, in the Commons, 13 June 1839)

EXTRACT G
The Duke of Wellington appointed to guard London, April 1848

The Duke's preparations were large and complete. At the Thames bridges were bodies of mounted police and masses of special constables placed on either side. A strong force of military was kept ready.

(*Annual Register*, 1848)

EXTRACT H
Laughing the 1848 petition to defeat, April 1848

Many signatures are in the same handwriting. We also see the names of distinguished people, among them Her Majesty as Victoria Rex. Other names to be seen are the Duke of Wellington and Sir Robert Peel. Many names are obviously fictitious such as 'No Cheese', 'Pug Nose' …

(Spokesman in the Commons, 14 April 1848)

Now test yourself

Knowledge and understanding

1 Using the text and *extracts A–C*, explain the political, social and economic reasons why Chartism grew as a movement.
2 Using the text and *extracts D, E, G and H*, explain the reasons why Chartism failed in the short term.
3 Look at *picture 1*. Do you think Chartism succeeded in the long term?

Using the sources

1 How does *extract C* differ from *extract A* and *picture 1* in their views of Chartism?
2 Do you think that cartoons and pictures (*pictures 1–3*) are useful for historians writing about Chartism?

VIOLENT PROTESTS

Clashes between rioters and the army and police were common in this period. There was great unrest when the Napoleonic Wars ended (1815) (*extract A*); the author of *extract A* was present at the Peterloo Massacre (*picture 1*) in 1819.

The Luddites (*extract A*) were machine-wreckers. Croppers (*picture 2*) were replaced by steam-driven shearing machines (*picture 3*), as handloom weavers were by the power loom (page 109, *extract C*). Led by a mythical Ned Ludd, workers smashed machines (*extract B*), murdered their owners and destroyed factories.

Another mythical figure, Swing, led farm workers in attacks on new machinery (*extract C* and *picture 4*).

Between 1850 and 1870, 'the workshop of the world' provided more work for higher wages for more people. Skilled workers bought their homes (*picture 6*); their trade unions gave them their own 'welfare state' (*extract D*). However, with the trade depression after 1870, there was rising unemployment. Many felt that society offered no solution to their grievances (page 117, *extract A*) and they demonstrated in London and elsewhere (*extract E* and *picture 5*). Trade unions, too, became more militant and there were violent nationwide strikes.

1. The Peterloo Massacre.

5. Riots in Trafalgar Square, 1887.

4. A contemporary engraving of a rick burning in Kent, 1830 (*extract C*).

6. The comfortable interior of a miner's cottage, 1893.

3. The new shearing machine.

2. Croppers at work.

The making of a new sort of people, 1760–1880: five generations

1760–80: Children of domestic workers (page 108, *pictures 1 and 2*) went to live in towns and work in factories (page 108, *picture 2*), but were not true town dwellers.
1820: Their children, born in towns, were more ready to protest (*picture 1*).
1850: Their grandchildren formed strong trade unions (*extract D*).
1880: Their great-grandchildren were a more confident 'new breed' (*picture 5*).

EXTRACT A
The threat of an English revolution, 1815–16

A series of disturbances began with the Corn Law (1815) and continued until the end of 1816. Riots broke out in London when that Bill was being discussed and lasted for several days; at Bridport and Bideford there were riots over the high prices of bread; at Bury by the unemployed to destroy machinery; at Newcastle by miners; at Glasgow because of the soup kitchens; at Preston by unemployed weavers; at Nottingham by Luddites; at Merthyr on a drop in wages; at Birmingham by the unemployed …

(*Life of a Radical*, Samuel Bamford, 1859)

EXTRACT B
A Luddite letter, 1812

Sir, I was asked by my men to give you warning to pull down your detestable shearing frames. If you do not, I shall send 300 men to destroy them and we will burn down your building to ashes … murder you and burn all your housing. Signed by the General of the Army of Redressers, NED LUDD.

(Letter sent to a Huddersfield manufacturer, 1812)

EXTRACT C
Captain Swing and agricultural rioters, 1830

Sir, Your name is among the Black Hearts in the Black Book and this is to advise you and the like of you, to make your Will. You have been the Blackguard Enemies of the People. Ye have not done as ye ought. SWING.

(Handwritten letter from 'Captain Swing' to a Kent farmer, 1830)

EXTRACT D
Contented industrial workers, 1867

The object of this society is to provide mutual support for its members in case of sickness, accident, old age and on the death of members and their wives, for emigration, loss of tools by fire, water or theft, and for unemployed members. They pay one shilling and 3d a quarter.

(William Applegarth for the Amalgamated Society of Carpenters, 18 March 1867)

EXTRACT E
Unemployed rioters, 1887

At three o'clock the men from the East End made towards Trafalgar Square. When the procession reached the end of St Martin's Lane the police, mounted and on foot, charged, striking in all directions. At four o'clock the procession of men from South London reached the Westminster Bridge, and the police made for them: they freely used their weapons and the people, armed with iron bars, pokers, gas-pipes and even knives, resisted.

(*Reynolds' News*, 20 November 1887)

Now test yourself

Knowledge and understanding

1 Violent protests occurred for many reasons: economic, social, political. In three columns write down which protests were caused by each of these causes. Explain your choice.

2 Towards the end of the 19th century the reactions of prosperous workers (*extract D* and *picture 6*) differed from those of poorer workers (*extract E* and *picture 5*). Comment on the differences and explain them.

Using the sources

1 Are the *extracts* equally useful as evidence to show the extent of protest in the 19th century? Explain your answer.

2 Do you agree that the text and *extracts* show that Britain was a violent society? Why?

3 How do the *pictures* add to the evidence given by the *extracts*?

4 Study *extracts B, D and E* and *picture 6*.
(a) How do they show (i) differences; (ii) similarities of response to industrialization?
(b) Do such differences make these sources less useful? Why?

SKILLED WORKERS AND INDUSTRIAL CHANGE, 1780–1880

Some historians argue that workers suffered because of the Industrial Revolution. Others argue that they gained, and point to what happened to skilled workers in the 19th century. Such workers had formed trade unions in the 18th century (*extract A*) and had their own form of welfare state. During the time of the French Revolution, governments had seen them as dangerous and made them illegal in 1799 (*extract B*). Even after unions were legalized in 1824, governments, industrialists, magistrates and judges (*extract C*) tried to stop their formation.

1. Membership card of one of the model unions for skilled men.

However, with the collapse of Chartism (pages 116–17) skilled workers formed legal unions which gave them welfare benefits (page 119, *extract D*) and got them higher wages, so that they enjoyed an improving standard of living (*extract D* and *picture 2*).

This 'aristocracy of labour' demanded a share in the political system (*extracts E and F*). The 1867 Reform Act gave the vote to:

(a) every male householder in a borough constituency
(b) male lodgers paying £10 a year for unfurnished rooms.

This Act gave the vote to about 1,500,000 men. The Act also redistributed constituencies, so that 45 smaller boroughs lost representation and larger towns as well as more densely populated counties gained seats (*picture 4*).

The working classes used their new political power: there were laws favourable to trade unions (1871 and 1875), a Ballot Act (1872) which provided for secret voting, and the extension of the borough franchise to the counties (1885) which added 6,000,000 to the electoral registers and made a further redistribution of seats (*picture 4*). Some workers had benefited from the Industrial Revolution.

2. A skilled worker's home.

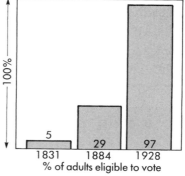

3. Those adults eligible to vote (in %).

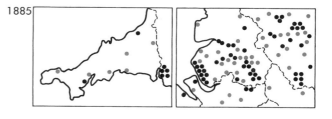

• One Borough member   • One County member

4. Distribution of seats in Cornwall and in the Industrial North West in 1867 and 1885 (see page 114, *picture 3*).

EXTRACT A
Early unions, 1794

Jonathan Sowton was asked about the clubs. He said: 'It is a contribution made by each woolcomber which enables the member to travel in search of work, and to have relief when he is sick and, when he dies, to be buried by the club.'

(*The House of Commons Journal*, 13 March 1794)

EXTRACT B
Wilberforce (the slavery reformer) calls for laws against unions, 1799

Mr Wilberforce said that all combinations of workmen ought to be made illegal. He regarded them as a general disease in our society. Mr Pitt said he would bring in a Bill to remedy the evil of combinations of workmen which has become too general.

(*Debrett*, Vols LIII–LIV, 17 June 1799)

EXTRACT C
The illegal punishment of trade unionists, Tolpuddle, 1834

I am not sentencing you for any crimes you have committed or that you were about to commit, but as an example to the working classes of this country.

(Judge Williams, Dorchester Assizes, 19 March 1834)

EXTRACT D
Rising living standards for some workers, 1830–80

The working classes have enjoyed an improvement in wages in the last 50 years of between 50 and 100 per cent. There has also been a fall in prices. The condition of the masses has improved vastly as shown by the fall in the death rate, the increased consumption of tea, sugar and the like, by the increase of savings bank deposits and other forms of saving. What has happened is a revolution: instead of millions on the brink of starvation we now have new millions of craftsmen and fairly well-paid labourers.

(*Essays in Finance*, Richard Giffen, 1887)

EXTRACT E
John Bright demands Parliamentary reform

The Tories are afraid of 5,000,000 men who are shut out by the present system of representation, but who could vote if they went to live in the Cape, Australia or Canada. I hold this to be dangerous. It was so in 1831–2, when there was the antagonism of the class that then had power to the just claims of the people.

(Birmingham Town Hall, 13 January 1865)

EXTRACT F
Gladstone proposes Parliamentary reform

There has not been a call on the self-improving powers of the workers which has not been fully answered. Thousands of them use the libraries at the Working Men's Free Libraries and Institutes throughout the country. There are 650,000 depositors in the Post Office Savings Bank which we started four years ago. Parliament has been trying to make the workers fit for the franchise. Can anything be more unwise and senseless than to refuse to recognize the increased fitness of the workers for the exercise of political power?

(Gladstone, House of Commons, 12 April 1866)

EXTRACT G
Against Parliamentary reform, 1867

The proposed extension of the franchise to many householders will lead to changes, the results of which we cannot predict. In Leeds, for example, there are now 8,300 electors. With household suffrage there will be about 35,000.

(Lord Carnarvon to the Duke of Richmond, 11 March 1867)

Now test yourself

Knowledge and understanding

1 How did skilled workers improve themselves (a) economically; (b) socially; (c) politically?
2 Why did unskilled workers find it difficult to improve their position?
3 What were the two most important changes that affected skilled workers in this period? Give reasons for your answer.

Using the sources

1 Read *extracts A–D*. How would the use of only *extracts B and C* give a different view of trade unions to that given by the use of only *extracts A and D*?
2 How useful are *pictures 2, 3 and 4 and extracts E, F and G* for historians writing about the attitudes of (a) supporters; (b) opponents of Parliamentary reform?
3 Do you think that the fact the *extracts* reveal differences of opinion reduces their value?

POVERTY AND POLITICS, 1880–1910

1. Dockers waiting for work.

2. Socialism shown as the Angel of the labourer.

Only half the workers enjoyed the changes noted by Giffen in 1887 (page 121, *extract D*). The Salvation Army (founded 1878) worked among the worst off (*extract A*) whose lives were described in Charles Booth's *Life and Labour of the People of London* (*extract B*). This showed that 31 per cent of the people lived below the line fixed at 'an income of between 18 and 21 shillings a week'. Seebohm Rowntree made his own survey of York where he was the main employer. He hoped to prove that Booth's findings did not apply outside London. To his horror 'we find it equalled in York' (page 131, *extract A*).

In 1889 the unskilled and low-paid labourers at London Docks (*extract D* and *picture 1*) won their strike for sixpence an hour. This led to the formation of other unions for unskilled workers (*extract F*). They could not afford fees for welfare benefits (page 119, *extract D*) nor could their wages pay for decent housing, clothes or food. They needed 'socialism' (*picture 2* and page 131, *extract D*). Several socialist societies were formed in the 1880s and Keir Hardie formed the Independent Labour Party (ILP) (*picture 3* and *extract F*) hoping to get the support of the trade union movement.

In 1900 the Labour Representation Committee (LRC) was formed by the socialist societies, the ILP and a few unions. Skilled unions only joined the LRC when the ability to strike was threatened by the Taff Vale Judgement (1901) which forced a union to pay £23,000 for damages done to the railway company by a strike. By 1904 two-thirds of all unions had joined the LRC which, independently of the Liberals (*picture 3*), grew rapidly (*extract G*).

3. Cartoon showing the refusal of the ILP to dance to the tune played by the Liberals.

4. Keir Hardie.

EXTRACT A
Life in Darkest England, 1890

The foul smell of our slums is as poisonous as that of Africa. A population eaten up by every social and physical illness, these are the people of Darkest England, 3,000,000 men, women and children, the Submerged Tenth.

(*In Darkest England, and the Way Out*, William Booth, founder of the Salvation Army, 1890)

EXTRACT B
Charles Booth visits the East End of London

In one room lived Mrs O'Brien and her two boys. The husband is in hospital, his wife in great poverty. Nothing in the room but a market basket upside down to serve as a table at which the children would kneel, and a bundle of rags in the corner to serve as a bed.

(*Life and Labour of the People of London*, 1889)

EXTRACT C
Ricketts and industrialization, 1889

In areas such as the Clyde district, almost every child was affected by rickets, a disease caused by poverty and malnutrition. A map of the disease's distribution in England was a map showing the density of the industrial population.

(*Medical Congress Report*, 1889)

EXTRACT D
Fighting for a job in the Docks, 1889

We are driven into a shed, iron-barred from end to end. Outside the bars a foreman walks about with the air of a dealer in a cattle market. He picks and chooses from the crowd of men, who, anxious to get work, trample each other underfoot as they fight for a day's work.

(*Memories*, B. Tillett, 1931)

EXTRACT E
Unskilled unions have no welfare benefits

I do not believe in sick pay, out-of-work pay and other pays. The thing to do is firstly to organize, then reduce hours of labour, and that will prevent illness and unemployment.

(Will Thorne, leader of the Gas Workers' Union, 1889, quoted in *My Life's Battles*, Will Thorne, 1925)

EXTRACT F
Unions to support Labour candidates?

Before the London Dock Strike, membership of unions was limited, by the high contributions demanded from members, to about 500,000. Since then, almost every worker can join a union, which increases the power of the trade union organization. Socialists have tried to set up societies. At a general election unions could put up 2000 voters for every member of a socialist society. Moreover they have the money. A penny a week from every member of a trade union would raise £300,000 and could easily provide £30,000 to support 50 Labour candidates at £600 each. Representation of the working classes at elections will depend on the unions and not on the socialist bodies.

(*Fortnightly Review*, George Bernard Shaw, 1 November 1893)

EXTRACT G
A growing Labour Party, 1910

Between the elections of 1900 and 1906, three victories were won: Shackleton was returned for Clitheroe: Crooks won at Woolwich, and I beat both the Tory and Liberal candidates at Barnard Castle. In 1906, 29 of our 50 candidates were successful. In January 1910 we ran 78 candidates and 40 won seats, and formed a separate and independent group.

(*The Aims of Labour*, A. Henderson, 1918)

Now test yourself

Knowledge and understanding

1 How did the following respond to the debate on poverty: (a) Charles Booth; (b) Seebohm Rowntree; (c) skilled workers unions; (d) leaders of the unskilled workers; (e) the Labour Party?
2 What were the *two* most important causes of poverty in this period? Explain your answer.

Using the sources

1 Read *extracts A–D* and *extract D* on page 121. How would the use of this last extract give a differing interpretation of British society to that given by the use of *only* the extracts in this topic?
2 How do *extracts F and G* and the final paragraph of the text explain why the Labour Party became stronger?
3 How reliable are the authors of these extracts for historians of the Labour Party?

FARMERS AND FOREIGNERS

The Corn Laws were repealed in 1846 (page 107, *extract D*). Many thought that home farmers would be ruined. Instead they enjoyed 30 good years because of:

❶ the continual growth of the urban population (pages 104–5) which needed food
❷ the growing demand from more prosperous townspeople
❸ the business sense of a new breed of landowners (*extract A*)
❹ the absence of foreign competition due to high transport costs
❺ farmers learning to make their land more productive by the use of natural and chemical fertilizers, and the use of new methods of drainage (*extract B*)
❻ the steam-driven machines for ploughing, reaping, mowing and threshing which increased output or lowered costs, or both
❼ the railways which carried the farm produce cheaply and quickly to market. Too many farmers failed to adopt the new methods (*extracts D and E*). They did not see that investment was, and is, the key to future success.

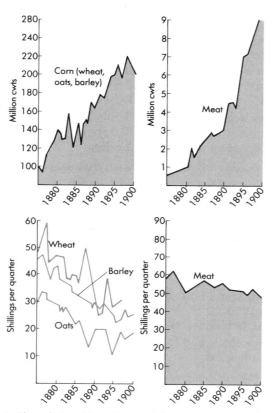

1. The relationship between rising imports and falling prices.

In 1873 everything changed. A series of bad harvests was combined with a flood of cheap foreign food (*extract F* and *picture 1*). Grain was imported cheaply from the USA and Canada, and meat came in refrigerated steamships from Argentina and New Zealand. There were two reasons for the slump in farming:

❶ The development of the railways in the USA and Canada allowed the carriage of wheat grown on rent-free land, where many machines were used from the start.
❷ The development of larger, lighter and more efficient steamships allowed the carriage of the imports at very low cost (*extract G*).

Not all farmers suffered. The falls in the prices of wheat, meat and potatoes allowed many people to buy more and varied food. Dairy, vegetable and fruit farmers benefited (*picture 2*). Townspeople also benefited from the sharp falls in food prices (*extract H*). Well-stocked shops (*picture 3*) competed for customers, another sign of the social progress that follows industrial change (page 121, *extract D*).

2. Farm workers loading fresh strawberries on to a London-bound train, 1906.

3. A well-stocked shop in Dudley around 1900.

EXTRACT A
New landowners and agricultural improvements, 1850

The best landlords are capitalists from the towns. They buy estates and manage them with the same attention to business principles as they used in town. They drain land thoroughly, erect good buildings, then let the land to good tenants. The rents are high but these farms can pay a good rent, much better than can a poor estate pay even a moderate rent.

(*Letters*, Sir James Caird, 1850)

EXTRACT B
The importance of drainage

Until land is free from stagnant water and made able of yielding its best to the efforts of the farmer, all other outlay is useless. Wherever it is applied it always pays off – land is more suitable for plants and animals and so much easier to work.

(*English Agriculture*, Sir James Caird, 1850–51)

EXTRACT C
The railways – the farmers' friend, 1868

During the last year the Great Eastern Line brought 306,000 sheep to London from the Eastern Counties, 41,900 pigs, 610,330 sacks of flour, 277,740 quarters of wheat …, malt, beer, potatoes, poultry, fruit and vegetables.

(*Quarterly Review*, October 1868)

EXTRACT D
Too much undrained land

Out of 20,000,000 acres needing drainage only 3,000,000 have been drained; of all kinds of improvement needed, only one-fifth has been done.

(Report, Select Committee of the House of Lords, 1873)

EXTRACT E
Too little machinery, 1873

Even the best new machines are not yet in general use. Some farmers haven't had a chance to see them, and most machine-makers live in the four Eastern counties where most machines are used.

(Report, Lords Select Committee, 1873)

EXTRACT F
The agricultural depression, 1882

The two important causes are bad seasons and foreign competition, made worse by the heavy loss of animals. Once, the farmer suffering from bad seasons would have benefited from the higher prices for the smaller crop. Now the foreign supply comes in at greatly reduced prices [*picture 1*].

(Royal Commission, 1882)

EXTRACT G
Railways, shipping and the farmer, 1882

The cost of building a steamship is much less than it was 10 years ago. The cost of working ships has fallen with the better engines – less coal is burned, fewer men are required, steam winches have replaced hard labour. Ships used to carry 2000 tons from America: now they carry 4000 tons and such ships are worked at much less than double the cost of the smaller ones. Transport costs fall. Every line of railway built in America brings another farming area to compete with ours. The cost of transport is very small. For practical purposes, Chicago is as near as London as is Aberdeen.

(Royal Commission, 1882)

EXTRACT H
Depression and human happiness, 1887

The last 10 years of depression have contributed more to solid progress and true happiness than the booms of the past.

(*Contemporary Review*, Alfred Marshall, March 1887 – see also page 121, *extract D*)

Now test yourself

Knowledge and understanding

1 (a) In what ways was the period 1850–1900 one of both (i) prosperity and (ii) decline for British farmers? (b) How were people who were not farmers affected by the prosperity and decline of agriculture?
2 How did technological changes (a) help the growth of some parts of British agriculture; (b) cause the decline of other parts?

Using the sources

1 (a) How far do *extracts A, B, D and G* and *picture 1* give a complete picture of (i) why agriculture prospered; (ii) why it ran into difficulties? (b) Why do these sources not give a full explanation?
2 Look at *pictures 2 and 3*. Are these reliable and useful sources to historians of British agriculture? Why?

S LOWER INDUSTRIAL GROWTH AND ECONOMIC DECLINE

In 1851 a 'Crystal Palace' was built in Hyde Park to house the Great Exhibition, which showed off Britain's industrial power. Britain produced most of the world's goods and also loaned money to foreigners to help them buy its railway lines and engines, and textile machinery (*extract A*). This increased output, employment and exports.

In 1900 the French organized the Paris Exhibition. British scientists saw that foreign industry had overtaken Britain's. Because of that, Britain's share of world trade had declined (*picture 1*).

What had happened? New inventions and new discoveries had led to the growth of new industries such as the chemical and electrical engineering industries. These relied less on physical power (as did coal and iron) and more on the work of scientists, trained workers and expensive machinery. Britain was slow to adopt these rapidly growing industries: it relied on the old and slow-growing ones. Others outstripped Britain in steel production (*picture 2*) while it relied on increasing textile exports to an expanding empire (pages 128–9).

Who was to blame? Some blamed foreign countries which used import duties to keep out British goods (*extract A*) while benefiting from Britain's free trade policy (*picture 3* and *extract F*). Some blamed industrialists (*extracts B and D*), others blamed governments and the educational system (*extract C*). More and more 'capitalists and industrialists' (*extract C*) were taught at public schools, where there was little interest in science. Most factory managers came from grammar schools where Latin was more important than science. In July 1916 Britain's lack of munitions was caused, mainly, by a shortage of trained chemical engineers. 'Four German firms have more chemists than all British industry,' said a former Secretary of State in the Lords on 12 July 1916.

Because of the decline, Britain had a smaller share of world trade (*picture 1*), exported less (*extract E*) and imported foreign goods (*extract F*). This led to increased unemployment, even for skilled workers, which helped drive them into the infant Labour Party (page 122). It also led to the call for an end to free trade (*extract G*). It was a long way from the free trade days of 1851.

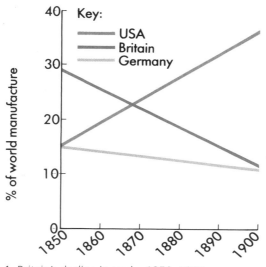

1. Britain's decline in trade, 1850–1900.

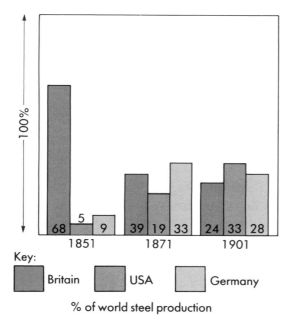

2. Steel production, 1851–1901.

CAUGHT NAPPING!

3. A cartoon showing Germany taking Britain's trade.

EXTRACT A
Foreign competitors and British trade, 1881

In 1851 England had a monopoly of the manufacturing industries of the world. She produced more than she used, other nations produced almost nothing. The world had to buy from her; they could not buy anywhere else. Now, France, America and Belgium have our machinery, our workmen and our capital. Each year they send us their goods which drive out our own, and every year they close their markets to our goods.

(*Nineteenth Century*, Edward Sullivan, 1881)

EXTRACT B
Industrial investment leads to lower prices, 1904

Automatic machinery is more used in America than here. Up-to-date factories have enabled Americans, paying the highest wages known in the world, to produce steel plates at a cost of three shillings per ton for labour and averaging 225 tons per shift. Our mills cannot do this.

(Tariff Commission, 1904)

EXTRACT C
The need for more education, 1903

One of the evil consequences of our educational failure is the slow progress we have made in the industries which are based on recent scientific discoveries. These depend on the appreciation, by capitalists and industrialists, of the way in which science promotes industrial development. We are also in need of general education: our competitors have reaped the benefit of their awareness of the value of knowledge as a basis for industrial prosperity.

(Sir J.W. Swan, 1903)

EXTRACT D
Who is to blame? 1918

The decline in British industries is due to workers who tried to limit output, to manufacturers and to Government. Employers have neglected new processes and inventions; they relied on cheap labour rather than on efficient organization.

(*The British Dominions Year Book*, 1918, Sir L. Money MP, 1918)

EXTRACT E
A slow-down in our foreign trade, 1903

Since 1872 our export trade has grown by £22 million, something like 7 per cent. Since 1872 our population has grown by 30 per cent. In that time USA exports have grown by £110 million and German exports by £56 million. Our export trade has been practically stagnant for 30 years.

(Joseph Chamberlain, 6 October 1903)

EXTRACT F
Importing foreign manufactured goods, 1896

Some of your own clothes were probably woven in Germany: more surely were some of your wife's clothes. Go through the house and the foreign mark will greet you everywhere – the piano, the mug on the dresser, your drainpipes, the paper wrappings for your book. You put those in the fire – with a poker forged in Germany.

(*'Made in Germany'*, The New Review, E.E. Williams, 1896)

EXTRACT G
The end of free trade? 1881

We propose a tariff of 10 per cent on all foreign goods to be used when bargaining with countries, from whom we import, to admit our goods as freely as we admit theirs.

(*Fair Trade*, William Farrer Ecroyd, 1881)

Now test yourself

Knowledge and understanding

The following have been blamed for Britain's industrial decline: industrialists; dependence on old industries; foreign imports; government; education system; failure to adopt new industries. (a) What were the three most important causes of Britain's industrial decline? (b) How did the decline affect the British people?

Using the sources

1 How completely do the extracts explain Britain's industrial decline?
2 Are *pictures 1–3* useful for historians trying to explain the decline in British industry?
3 Does any *one* of the extracts offer the best explanation for the decline? Explain your answer.

AN AFRICAN EMPIRE, 1880–1902

The Tory leader, Disraeli, called colonies 'millstones around our necks'. India, 'the jewel in the crown', was a vast country which had to be defended against possible attacks from Russia, and led to wars in Afghanistan. The sea routes to India had to be safeguarded, so that the British had to gain control of the Cape of Good Hope (South Africa) and, later, the Suez Canal, Aden and other coaling ports.

The USA had shown that, once colonies did not need Britain to defend them against possible attacks, they were liable to seek independence (page 59). In 1837 the Canadian colonies rose in a revolt which had to be put down, but later, they, too, gained their freedom.

Why then, by 1900, were the Tories for 'Queen and Empire' (*picture 3*) in Africa?

❶ Markets for British goods would provide employment (*extracts A and F*).
❷ Money would come from investment in colonial development (*extracts A–C and H*).
❸ Materials – colonies were a secure source of raw materials.
❹ Arrogance – the lawyer Dicey (*extract E*) spoke for many people of the time.

1. An engraving showing Britannia and her armies.

The making of a colony began with the work of trading companies, as it had in India (page 57, *extract C*). Companies were given charters (page 56, *picture 3*) giving them the sole right to trade in a certain area: Nigeria, Kenya, South Africa and so on. Company agents signed treaties with tribal chiefs, ensuring the company's rights (*extract D*). The government gave these charters, encouraged investors (*extract B*) and, when needed, fought to defend the companies (*picture 1* and *extract H*). And, if a company failed, the government annexed the area concerned: Uganda, Kenya and Nigeria were annexed in this way.

Chamberlain, Colonial Secretary, 1895–1903, encouraged expansion in Africa (*extracts A and B*). He also tried to unite the 'white colonies' (Australia, New Zealand, Canada and, after 1902, South Africa). He asked them to put a lower tariff on British goods than on other foreign goods: in return he proposed an import tariff on non-colonial food imports into Britain. Because this would push up prices (*picture 3* and *extract G*), the tariff campaign failed. Expansion of the empire created markets for old-fashioned goods: the export of capital meant a lack of investment in Britain in new industries (page 126, *picture 2*). Britain's decline continued.

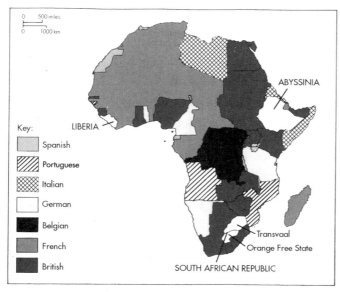

Key:
- Spanish
- Portuguese
- Italian
- German
- Belgian
- French
- British

ABYSSINIA
LIBERIA
Transvaal
Orange Free State
SOUTH AFRICAN REPUBLIC

0 500 miles
0 1000 km

2. The division of Africa.

3. Chamberlain speaking in Birmingham, 1904 (*extract G*).

EXTRACT A
Colonies as markets needed investment

Our colonies cannot be developed without our assistance. I will consider any case in which investment of British money may help to develop colonies. In such development I see a solution of our social problems: there is no way of securing more employment than by creating new markets and developing old ones.

(Joseph Chamberlain, speaking in 1895)

EXTRACT B
The need for investment, 1895

Our profit is in the prosperity of our people and in the development of new markets. This involves risk. But if we are not willing to invest our wealth in the colonies, then I see no future for them.

(Chamberlain, 1895)

EXTRACT C
How was the investment used?

About £100 million a year was invested abroad – South Africa, Egypt, colonies on the coasts of Africa, India, Australia … for railways, docks, water and gas works, and mining concerns.

(*The Export of Capital*, C.K. Hobson, 1914)

EXTRACT D
The acquisition of Rhodesia, 1889

A company has been formed to develop the Bechuanaland and countries to the north. Mr Rhodes of the Cape Colony, representing the holders of the concession from Lobengula, promises to cooperate. The example of the East Africa Company shows that such companies save the Government much expenditure. The company for Bechuanaland will render valuable help in South Africa.

(Colonial Office to the Foreign Office, 16 May 1889)

EXTRACT E
The price of imperialists, 1877

Englishmen are bound by a manifest identity to found empires and to make themselves the dominant race in countries in which they wander.

(*The Nineteenth Century*, Edward Dicey, 1877)

EXTRACT F
A British tariff, imperial unity and employment, 1903

Tariff reformers believe that a British tariff may secure a lowering of foreign tariffs and a fairer exchange of goods than we have now. More importantly, they might secure, by arrangements with our colonies, a great development of Imperialist trade, so adding greatly to the employment of our ever growing population.

(Chamberlain, 4 November 1903)

EXTRACT G
Chamberlain mocks the attack on his tariff campaign, 1904 (picture 4)

Liberals say that a tariff on imported wheat would make the loaf dearer, or, if the price stayed the same, smaller. Here, in one hand, is a 'free trade loaf' and, in the other, 'a tariff reform loaf'. Can you tell the small difference between them? Of course not.

(Birmingham, 1904)

EXTRACT H
Investment leads to government support

It is not too much to say that modern British foreign policy is mainly a struggle for profitable markets for investment. People who enjoy the income from this investment try to extend the fields for their investment and to safeguard their existing investments.

(*The Exports of Capital*, C.K. Hobson, 1914)

Now test yourself

Knowledge and understanding

1 Here is a list of factors which led to the growth of the British empire in Africa: need for new markets; raw materials; investors' pressures; British arrogance. Place them in order of importance and explain your choice.
2 Outline and explain the role of Britain towards Africa (a) when British interests were attacked; (b) when Chamberlain was Colonial Secretary.

Using the sources

1 Do *extracts A–E and H* show that 'colonies were millstones around our necks' or aids to British prosperity? Explain your answer.
2 Read *extracts F and G* and look at *picture 3*. (a) Do you think that Chamberlain's arguments were reliable? Why? (b) How can you check their reliability?
3 What does *picture 2* tell you about the way Britain controlled Africa in the 19th century?

RELIGIOUS CHANGE AND SOCIAL REFORM

Walpole and the Whigs (page 74) remembered how religion had led to Civil War (page 68) and the overthrow of James II (page 72). They appointed bishops who behaved more as politicians than religious leaders. Local clergy were left to do much as they liked: some became lazy and failed to look after their parishes. The Anglican Church also failed to meet the needs of the new industrial towns: in many there were no churches; in others, the parish was too big for the clergy.

1. A pawnbroker's shop.

John Wesley, an Anglican clergyman, and his friends were nicknamed 'Methodists' because of their methodical lifestyle (prayer, study and work). He went to the people to preach (in the open), to help them start schools and local churches where non-clerics (lay preachers) held services. At first some clergy led mobs to attack Wesley. By 1820 many Anglicans had come to imitate him and brought the Gospel (Evangel) to the masses. Some became active in social reform: Wilberforce led the anti-slavery movement; Shaftesbury worked for factory reform. Methodists saw that ordinary people could run a local church; some went on to run trade unions (pages 118 and 120) and saw skilled workmen become well-housed, well-dressed and 'respectable'.

However, the mass of the people were trapped in a cycle of poverty (*extract A*) and had poor housing and food, and a high death rate (page 113, *extracts A–E*). Some religious people thought that the poor ought to imitate the skilled workers by saving and providing for themselves (*extracts B, C and E*). They condemned 'Socialism' (*extract D*), and the poor had to wait before a start was made on the creation of a welfare state.

2. Mealtime at a workhouse in St Pancras, 1900.

EXTRACT A
The cycle of poverty, 1900

The labourer's life is marked by alternating periods of want and plenty:

1 In early childhood he probably will be in poverty.
2 When he and the other children earn money, they add to the father's wages to raise the family above the poverty line.
3 Then, when he is earning money and living at home, he will have more money than is needed for lodgings, food and clothes. This is his chance to save.
4 If he has saved enough to furnish a cottage, this prosperity may continue after marriage, until he has two or three children when poverty comes again.
5 This poverty lasts until the first child is 14 and begins to earn: if there are more than three children it will last longer.
6 While the children are earning and living at home, the man has prosperity.
7 He sinks back into poverty when his children have married and left home, and he himself is too old to work.

(*Poverty*, S. Rowntree, 1902)

EXTRACT B
The poor should save and so provide

The poor should meet the ORDINARY problems of life, relying not on charity but their own thrift and self-help. The worker knows that:

1 temporary sickness will sometimes visit his household;
2 times of slackness of work will occasionally come;
3 if he has a large family his resources will be taxed to the utmost;
4 old age will make him incapable of work.

All these are the ordinary problems of life. If the worker thinks they will be met by State aid he will make no effort to meet them himself.

(Annual Report of the Charity Organization Society, 1876)

EXTRACT C
An ageing Prime Minister and the need for workers' self-help, 1884

People think that the Government can do this and that and everything. If the Government does what a man ought to do for himself, it will do more harm to the man than good. The spirit of self-reliance should be developed among the masses of the people.

(William Gladstone, Edinburgh, September 1884)

EXTRACT D
Chamberlain, as a Radical Liberal, challenges Gladstone, 1885)

It is ridiculous for a political Rip Van Winkle to wake up and tell us that these reforms are to be excluded from the Liberal programme. We have to grapple with the misery of the people. I shall be told that this is Socialism. Of course it is. Most local government work is Socialism. The Education Act is Socialism and every Act by which we show care for the poor is Socialism. It is none the worse for that. Our aim is to remove the great inequality in social life.

(Joseph Chamberlain, Warrington, 8 September 1885)

EXTRACT E
Laissez-faire: **leave people alone, 1859**

Self-help is the root of all genuine growth in the individual. Whatever is done for men takes away the need of doing it for themselves. The most that institutions [e.g. governments] can do is to leave man free to improve his individual condition. No laws can make the idle work, the spendthrift save, or the drunk sober.

(*Self-Help*, Samuel Smiles, 1859)

Now test yourself

Knowledge and understanding

1 Why did many working-class people (a) abandon the Anglican Church; (b) become Methodists; (c) take up Socialism as a cause?
2 How did Anglican evangelicals, Methodists and socialists imitate each other?

Using the sources

1 Read *extracts A, B and E*. How reliable and different are their interpretations of the life of the poor?
2 (a) How do *extracts C and D* add to those interpretations? (b) Why do you think there were these differences of interpretation?
3 Do you agree that *pictures 1 and 2* are useful and reliable for historians writing about (a) the effects of poverty; (b) the reasons why people campaigned against poverty?

*T*he 20th-century world

1 914: AN INEVITABLE, PLANNED AND WELCOMED WAR

1. The Balkans in 1914.

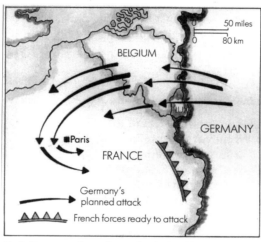

Germany's planned attack

French forces ready to attack

2. A German plan of attack, devised in 1905.

BRAVO, BELGIUM!

3. A British view of Germany's threat to Belgium, 1914.

In 1910 Europe was divided into two hostile 'armed camps'. Germany, Austria and Italy (the Triple Alliance) faced France and Russia (the Dual Alliance).

Germany was a large industrial power (page 126, *picture 2*), a threat to British industry and trade (pages 126–7, *pictures 1 and 3 and extracts E–G*). It was also seeking colonies so that, in Africa particularly, Germany was a threat to British power. That threat became clearer when, in 1906, Germany decided to build a navy as large as, or larger than, Britain's.

France wanted revenge for the humiliation suffered in the Franco-Prussian War (1870–71) when Germany had seized Alsace and Lorraine with their large ironfields. Traditionally hostile to Britain, France agreed to settle its differences (the *Entente Cordiale*, 1904) so as to gain an anti-German friend.

Until 1890, Germany, Austria and Russia were linked in the Three Emperors' League (*Dreikaiser Bund*), renewable every three years. A new German Kaiser refused to renew the agreement in 1890, having previously shown that he would support Austria against Russian ambitions in the Balkans (see below). This left Russia isolated and it turned to France as an ally (1894).

Austria and Russia both wanted to have an influence in the Balkans (*picture 1*) where by 1900, six Christian nations had won their independence from the Turkish empire. Austria was alarmed by the growth of Serbia, because millions of Serbs lived in the Austro-Hungarian empire and they wanted to break away so that they could unite with Serbia. Serb ambitions were supported by Russia, the largest Slav nation.

On 28 June 1914, the heir to the Austrian crown was murdered in Sarajevo, capital of Bosnia (*picture 1*), which the Serbs claimed was part of 'larger Serbia'. Austria declared war on Serbia (26 July) when it refused to allow Austria to send troops into Serbia to find the murderers. On 30 July Russia mobilized its army, showing its wish to defend Serbia. On 1 August Germany (Austria's ally) declared war on Russia and its ally, France.

Germany had planned a war against France (*picture 2*) by going through Belgium. On 2 August Britain asked Germany to honour the Treaty of Neutrality of Belgium (1839) (page 140, *picture 2*). When it refused, Britain declared war (4 August). German plans were ruined by (a) the need to take troops from France to fight in Russia (b) the British (*extract B*). Paris was never encircled (*picture 4*) and a second plan, to capture the Channel ports, also failed (*extract C*).

In Britain millions volunteered for the army (*extracts D–F*) in response to Kitchener's call (*picture 5*). Later, military service became compulsory. Some refused to serve: these conscientious objectors were harshly treated by the government and many people. Objectors and critics were both victims of propaganda (pages 140–41).

EXTRACT A
From the British Ambassador, Berlin, to the British Foreign Secretary, 6 August 1914

The German Chancellor (Prime Minister) was very angry. He said that the step taken by the British government was terrible, and only for a word – 'neutrality' – just for a scrap of paper, Britain was going to war against a kindred nation which only wanted to be friends with her.

EXTRACT B
The first Battle of Mons, August 1914

About 100,000 British soldiers had their first taste of battle at Mons. Here the Germans faced the rapid British rifle fire. It was so fast and so accurate that the Germans thought the British had thousands of machine guns. A German wrote, 'They were well dug in and hidden. They opened a murderous fire. Our casualties increased. Our rushes became shorter. Finally the whole advance stopped, but only after bloody losses.'

(*The Army*, P. Lane, 1978)

EXTRACT C
Ypres, November 1914. The Germans fail to reach the coast

The supreme memorial to the British regular Army.

(The military historian, B.H. Liddel-Hart)

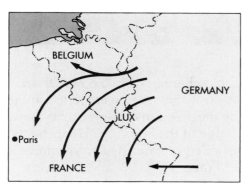

4. The revised German plan, 1914

5. A famous – and successful – recruiting poster.

EXTRACT D
From a young English soldier to his parents, July 1916

I could not pray for a finer death, and you my dear Mother and Dad, will know that I died doing my duty to my God, my Country and my King.

(Letter from E. James Engell of the 16th London Regiment)

EXTRACT E
A young recruit explains to his mother why he volunteered to fight

I have no wish to remain a civilian any longer. Although the idea of war is against my conscience, I feel that in a time of national crisis like this I have no right to my ideas if they are against the best and immediate needs of the state.

(Letter from Harold Parry to his mother as he left to join the King's Royal Rifles)

EXTRACT F
A young public schoolboy explains why he volunteered to fight

What really made me volunteer was less a feeling of patriotism than the wish to please my schoolmates. To have a conscientious objector at my school – even if I had wanted to be one – would have been unthinkable.

(G. Alan Thomas of the 6th Royal West Kent Regiment)

Now test yourself

Knowledge and understanding

1 Explain why war occurred in Europe in 1914.
2 How was Germany prevented from gaining the expected quick victory in 1914 by (a) Russian mobilization; (b) British resistance; (c) the Battle of Ypres?

Using the sources

1 How and why do *extracts D, E and F* give differing views of the war?
2 Do *pictures 2 and 4* and *extract C* fully explain why Germany failed to win a quick victory in 1914?
3 What does *picture 3* tell you about British attitudes towards (a) Germany; (b) Belgium in 1914?

TRENCH WARFARE, 1914–18

For many men, the war began and ended in trenches defended by barbed wire, machine guns and individual rifles. Even the best trenches (*extract A*) became mudholes because of rain and artillery bombardment (*extract B*), ordered by distant commanders who thought that 'one more attack would win the war'. The poet Rupert Brooke (*extract E*) had died in 1915 in the Dardenelles. Perhaps, if he had lived, he would have shared most soldiers' views about the madness of trench war and the idiocy of most generals. Wilfred Owen wrote *Apologia Pro Poemate Men* in which he gave thanks for servicemen's friendship but bitterly attacked civilians at home who had not shared their suffering (*extract G*).

1. The reality of the trenches.

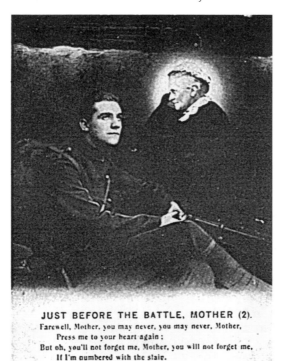

JUST BEFORE THE BATTLE, MOTHER (2).
Farewell, Mother, you may never, you may never, Mother,
Press me to your heart again;
But oh, you'll not forget me, Mother, you will not forget me,
If I'm numbered with the slain.

2. A typical postcard from the 1914–18 War.

Men were sent to charge across 'no man's land' between the rival trenches: they were killed in their thousands while the position of the trenches hardly altered. In the Battle of the Somme, 1916 (*extracts B and C*), the numbers killed or wounded were enormous. Britain (420,000) France (195,000) and Germany (400,000) were almost bled to death. By the end of the war, it seemed as if a whole generation of youth had died. The numbers killed were: Germany (1,950,000); Austria (1,050,000); Italy (533,000); USA (116,000); Russia (1,700,000); France (1,500,000); Britain (and the empire) (1,000,000).

To understand the seemingly weak foreign policies of Britain, France and the USA in the 1930s, it is important to understand why these countries were unwilling to risk yet another terrible war. Their politicians had either lived through the war or, in many cases, had fought in the trenches. Only dictators (pages 146–9) or ambitious soldiers, as in Japan (page 146), wanted another war.

EXTRACT A
Life in the trenches

A good trench was about six-foot deep, so that we could walk in safety from rifle-fire. In each bay of the trench we built fire-steps about two feet off the bottom. This allowed us to put our heads over the parapet. During the day we had an hour's sleep, on a wet and muddy fire-step, wet through to the skin. When anyone had to visit the company on our right he had to walk through thirty yards of waterlogged trench, chest deep in water in some places. The duckboard track was always being shelled. In some places over a hundred yards had been blown away. It was better to keep off the track, but then sometimes you had to walk through very heavy and deep mud.

(*Old Soldiers Never Die*, F. Richards, 1933)

EXTRACT B
The Somme, July 1916

'For a week about 300 guns poured shells on to the Germans. The noise seemed to throb in our veins even during the quiet of the night. Then, again, in the morning, the guns opened up. For a mile, our trenches belched out dense columns of green and orange smoke. It rose, curling and twisting, blotting everything from view. It seemed impossible that men could stand up to this terrible onslaught. The air was full of a vast and agonised violence, bursting into groans and screaming and pitiful whimperings …'

(Quoted in *The Army*, P. Lane, 1978)

EXTRACT C
A French officer's diary just before he died

Mankind is mad! It must be mad to do what it is doing. What slaughter! What scenes of horror and killing! Hell cannot be so terrible. Men are mad!

(Lt Alfred Joubaire, quoted in *Eye-Deep in Hell*, J. Ellis, 1976)

EXTRACT D

I know a simple soldier boy, Who grinned at life in empty joy
Slept soundly through the lonesome dark And whistled early with the lark.
In winter trenches, cowed and glum, With crumps of lice and lack of room,
He put a bullet through his brain. No one spoke of him again.

(*Suicide in the Trenches*, S. Sassoon, 1915)

EXTRACT E

Now, God be thanked. Who has matched us with His hour,
And caught our youth, and wakened us from sleeping.

(*Peace*, R. Brooke, 1915)

EXTRACT F

'Good morning; good morning,' the General said,
When we met him last week on our way to the line.
Now the soldiers he smiled at are most of 'em dead,
And we're cursing his staff for incompetent swine.
'He's a cheery old card,' grunted Harry to Jack
As they slogged up to Arras with rifle and pack …
But he did for them both with his plan of attack.

(*The Generals*, S. Sassoon, 1915)

EXTRACT G

Nevertheless, except you share with them in hell the sorrowful dark of hell,
Whose world is but the trembling of a flare, And heaven but as the Highway for a shell,
You shall not hear their mirth, You shall not come to think them well content
By any jest of mine. These men are worth Your tears. You are not worth their merriment.

(W. Owen, 1915)

Now test yourself

Knowledge and understanding

1 Use the text and extracts here and on pages 132–3 to explain (a) why trench warfare lasted so long; (b) the conditions endured by the soldiers; (c) why no one seemed able to improve them.
2 How was the war affected by technological changes resulting from the Industrial Revolution, studied earlier in this book?

Using the sources

1 Read *extracts C, D and F*. How do they give a different interpretation of the war from that given by *extract D* on page 133? Use *extracts A and B* to explain these differences.
2 How can *picture 1* and *extracts A–D* be used to explain what life was like in the trenches; (b) how soldiers reacted to the conditions?
3 How well do the sources and the text explain why politicians were unwilling to risk another war after 1918?

SUBMARINE WARFARE

Before 1914 Britain had been angered by the German building of a large navy. In spite of this, however, there were few large naval battles during the war. On 31 May 1916 the two fleets did meet at Jutland. After a day's fighting the German fleet withdrew. Jellicoe, the British Commander, did not chase it because he feared German minefields. The Germans claimed a victory: they had lost fewer ships than the British, a tribute to their gunpowder, armour and seamanship. The British claimed a victory because the Germans remained trapped in Kiel (*picture 1*).

The British navy was used to protect troops crossing to France and going to fight in the East and the Dardanelles. It was also used to blockade Germany to prevent goods being imported. In 1918 this blockade led to the demoralization of the German people. Short of food, clothing, heating and other necessities, they demanded an end to the war while their troops were still in retreat, but on French soil. The British navy had also to protect ships bringing goods to Britain, which relied heavily on imported food (page 124, *picture 2*). Both sides used mines and submarines against the enemy. In February 1915 the Germans announced an unrestricted campaign by which they threatened to sink all shipping around the British coast (*extract A*). This was called off in May 1916 after the USA had protested over the sinking of the passenger liner, the *Lusitania*, with the loss of American lives (*extract B*).

Submarines continued to attack British merchant shipping; the British lost many ships, lives and imports (*extract A*). Some people thought that this campaign would lead to a German victory. However, a change of government brought Lloyd George as Prime Minister and a more vigorous anti-submarine campaign (*extract A*). Because of the new convoy system, the Germans lost many submarines, while a system of food rationing lessened the demand for imports.

In February 1917 the Germans announced that they were restarting the unrestricted campaign. The German Foreign Secretary, Zimmermann, had warned his diplomats about this (*extract C*). His 'telegram' was published in the USA and led to a demand for American entry into the war. With the US declaration of war on Germany (April 1917) the Allies received the benefit of fresh troops and large supplies of munitions, plus added protection for Atlantic convoys.

In February 1917 the Russians overthrew the Tsar and set up a democratic government. This was overthrown by the Bolsheviks in October 1917. They signed the Treaty of Brest-Litovsk in March 1918 which ended Russia's part in the war. This released millions of German troops who were sent to make a 'final push' in France before US troops arrived. But their push failed and they were driven back towards Germany. There the people were suffering from food shortages because of the allied blockade. There were anti-government risings throughout Germany. The Kaiser fled to Holland and a new, 'liberal' government was set up to ask for an armistice (ceasefire). On 11 November 1918 the war came to an end.

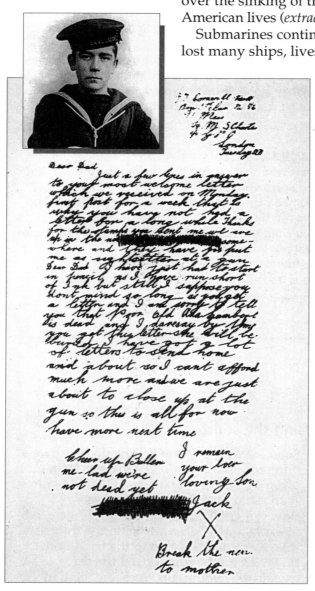

1. A young sailor who died at Jutland, and his last letter home.

EXTRACT A
Submarine warfare, 1916–18

At first they relied on cruisers and mines and other normal ways of attacking our merchant ships. When their last cruiser had been destroyed, the Germans used their 'little swordfish' which had already destroyed more of our ships in a month than their cruisers had sunk during a year. Then they built many more and much larger submarines. By the end of 1916 their submarines had sunk 738 of our ships, nearly one-fifth of all the ships we had had in 1914. No wonder we thought that we could not continue to fight for much longer. And I found that no one on our side had prepared any system for defeating the submarines.

Once the new government was formed in December 1916, the problem of the submarines was the first one we looked at. We considered several suggestions for dealing with the situation:
1 A system of convoys for merchant shipping in the danger zones;…
7 An increase in home supplies of food, timber and ore, and a reduction in consumption.

(*War Memoirs*, D. Lloyd George, 1933–6)

EXTRACT B
The sinking of the liner *Lusitania*, May 1915

The horror of the sinking of the *Lusitania* stirred the people more deeply than any other murderous acts committed by the Germans. The lives lost number over 1,400 and every one foully murdered. It makes clear the hideous policy of brutality which has placed the whole German race outside the pale. The Germans have shown that they are determined to wage war under conditions of cold-blooded murder. Never before has a whole race, many millions of people, been organized for wholesale murder and destruction.

(*The Times*, 10 May 1915)

EXTRACT C
The Zimmermann telegram, 16 January 1917

We intend to begin unrestricted submarine warfare on 1st February. We shall try to keep the USA neutral. If this fails we offer Mexico an alliance – to make war together … and with our help, Mexico to reconquer Texas, New Mexico and Arizona. The unrestricted use of submarines will force England to make peace within a few months.

(Zimmermann to German Ambassador, Washington, 1917)

EXTRACT D
The USA declares war against Germany, 2 April 1917

The new policy has swept every restriction away. Ships of every kind have been sunk without warning. I advise that Congress declares this to be nothing less than German war against the USA, and that Congress takes immediate steps to put the country in a state of defence and to use all its power to bring the end to the War.

(President Wilson to US Congress, April 1917)

2. Cartoon showing the Germans with their 'baby', the U-boat.

Now test yourself

Knowledge and understanding

1 Explain the varying effects of British control of the sea by commenting on (a) Jutland; (b) the blockade of Germany; (c) the convoy system; (d) the entry of the USA into the war.
2 Name the *three* most important effects of naval warfare on the outcome of the war. Explain your answer.

Using the sources

1 Is there enough evidence in this topic to explain why Germany failed to win the war at sea? Explain your answer.
2 What does *picture 2* tell you about British propaganda?
3 What does this propaganda tell you about (a) the attitude of the British government; (b) the attitudes of the people who looked at it at the time?
4 How useful is *picture 1* for historians writing about censorship and sailors' attitudes towards the war?

NEW ROLES FOR GOVERNMENT, WORKERS AND WOMEN, 1914–18

Control of labour

Britain's peace-time army was destroyed in 1914 (page 133, *extracts B and D*): millions of volunteers died in 1915–16 (page 133, *extracts D–F*). In May 1916 all unmarried men aged between 18 and 41 (and widowers with no dependants) had to sign a register making them liable for military service – 27 Liberal MPs voted against this interference with 'men's freedom'. This registration showed how unhealthy people were (*extract A*).

1. A 1915 propaganda poster.

Control of food

The submarine campaign made the government bring in the Corn Production Act (1917) which guaranteed farmers fair prices for their products. Many Liberals opposed this interference with market forces. They were more angered by the introduction of food rationing (1918), which ensured that everyone had the right to the same weekly ration of basic foods. In wartime many homes had higher incomes than in 1913, and many people were better fed as a result (*extract B*).

Workers' hopes

Unions gave up their right to strike, and let unskilled workers do the work usually done by skilled men. Three union leaders became government ministers in 1916, and many others joined committees formed to raise production levels. Unions hoped that, in peacetime, they would continue to have a share in decision making and that living standards would improve (*extract B*).

Votes for women

In 1913 Lloyd George had opposed Mrs Pankhurst and her campaign for votes for women. In 1914 she demanded 'the right to work': Lloyd George accepted this and millions of women joined the workforce. In 1918 a Parliamentary Reform Bill was amended to give women over the age of 30 the right to vote (along with all men aged 21 or over) (*extract D*).

2. The opening of a communal kitchen in 1918 – everyone was rationed to the same amount of food.

3. 'Votes for Women' – a 1918 Punch cartoon.

EXTRACT A
The unhealthy results of a century of industrialization

Of every nine men of military age in Great Britain, *three* were perfect, fit and healthy, *two* were of a poorer quality of health and strength because of some disability or some lack of development, *three* were unable to do any real physical work and could best be described as physical wrecks, and the remaining one was a permanent invalid with only a slight grasp on life.

(Government report on conscription, 1917)

EXTRACT B
The wartime improvement in working-class diet

We have found that in June the working classes as a whole were able to buy as much food as they had bought in 1913. Indeed, our figures show that the families of unskilled workers were slightly better off in 1918 than they had been in 1914. This finding is confirmed by reports from School Medical Officers. From London comes the report that the proportion of children in a poorly fed condition is less than half what it was in 1913.

Parents are now better able to give their children the better food they need. This can be seen from the figures of children who need to claim free meals from the education authorities. The figures for 1917 show that, compared with the figures for 1914, there has been a fall of about four-fifths in the numbers of 'necessitous children'.

(Government report on working-class diet, 1919)

EXTRACT C
Women and munition workers, 1915

On July 18 1915 there was the great Women's War Pageant. Thousands of women marched for miles along London streets. They brought me, as Minister of Munitions, a deputation which expressed their welcome of the National Register, and offered their services to help the country. Their leader, Mrs Pankhurst, also asked for wage conditions which would safeguard their standard of living and prevent them from being exploited by manufacturers. I gave a guarantee that they would have a fair minimum wage for time work, and that they would have the same rates as the men for any piece work. These conditions were strictly imposed by the Ministry throughout the war. This had a permanent effect on the status of women workers in this country.

(*War Memoirs*, D. Lloyd George, 1933–6)

EXTRACT D
An opponent describes how women first got the right to vote, 1918

Let me describe how gradually, but how inevitably we descended the slippery slope. First of all it was not proposed to include women (in the 1918 Reform Act). Then an important member of the House of Commons said that it was impossible to exclude from the franchise the brave men who had fought in the war. That argument was enthusiastically welcomed, and soldiers were admitted.

Then another MP said; 'If you are giving the vote to the brave soldiers, what about the brave munition workers?' That argument had to be accepted once you had accepted the argument about the 'brave soldiers'. Then a cunning MP said; 'What about the brave women munition workers?' And, once we had given in to the argument about men munition workers, it was impossible to resist the claims of the women.

(Lord Birkenhead, formerly F.E. Smith, MP, in the House of Lords, 1928)

Now test yourself

Knowledge and understanding

Using the text, *pictures 1 and 2* and *extracts A–D*, show how the war was a force for change in (a) the short term; (b) the long term. You might refer to (i) conscription; (ii) food supply; (iii) diets; (iv) the role of women; (v) trade union expectations.

Using the sources

1 How can *extract C* be used to show the importance of (a) women; (b) Lloyd George during the First World War?
2 What interpretation does *extract D* provide about the effects of the war on women's demand for the vote?
3 How useful are *pictures 1 and 3* as evidence of the different types of propaganda at this time?

POETRY, PROPAGANDA, POSTERS AND PRAYER

In 1917 a US Senator said, 'The first casualty when war comes is truth.' Look at *picture 1* and then read *extract A*. Someone was lying.

Another wartime 'casualty' was the patriotic idealism which inspired Rupert Brooke (*extract B* and page 135, *extract E*) and many other men.

The slaughters of 1914–16 (page 135, *extracts A–D*) killed that idealism. Even later volunteers seemed less 'patriotic' (page 133, *extracts E and F*). Sassoon, 'a patriotic volunteer', became critical of the war and of his leaders (page 135, *extracts D and F*). Owen was even more bitter (*extract C* and page 135, *extract G*).

Propaganda took various forms. Soldiers were supposed to be angered by the Kaiser's contempt for them (*picture 1*) and by his attack on 'little Belgium' (*picture 2* and page 132, *picture 3*). Popular songs influenced opinion (*extract D*).

Posters were used to attract volunteers (page 133, *picture 5*), to shame the less willing (page 138, *picture 1* and page 133, *extract F*), and to hide from relatives the true nature of trench warfare (*picture 3* and page 134, *picture 2*). Prayer for victory in 'the holy war' turned many against religion.

Picture 4 shows that, even in 1919, some people feared that the politicians could not prevent the outbreak of a future war. Why did they fail?

- Germany would want to break the treaty (pages 142–3, 144 and 148).
- The USA refused to join the League of Nations and retreated into 'isolationism', leaving Europe to solve its own problems.
- In Britain and France, most politicians and people were unwilling to do anything that might have led to war in the 1920s and 1930s. They had been 'converted' by the war poets, and horrified by the heavy losses in the Great War, which had been called 'The war to end all wars'.
- Most people in western Europe believed that Russian communism, with its leaders' talk of 'a world revolution' was a greater danger than Italian Fascism (page 146) or Hitler's Nazis (page 148). This led the British and French governments to a policy of appeasement – which meant letting Japan, Germany and Italy get away with aggression on other countries.

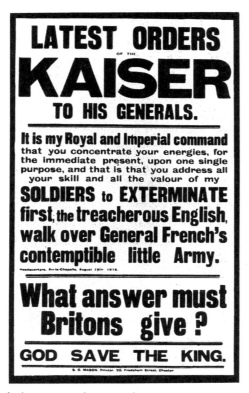

1. A propaganda poster from 1914.

2. An enlistment poster mentioned the 1839 treaty.

3. A totally misleading view of life at the front.

EXTRACT A
The German Kaiser's comment on the British poster (*picture 1*)

I never made such an order. On the contrary, I always stressed the high value of the British Army and warned against underestimating it.

(William II, Chancellor of Germany, 1914)

EXTRACT B
Brooke's welcome for a 'patriotic' death

If I should die, think only this of me:
That there's some corner of a foreign field
That is for ever England. There shall be
In that rich earth a richer dust concealed
A dust whom England bore, shaped, made aware,
Gave, once, her flowers to love, her ways to roam,
A body of England's, breathing English air,
Washed by the rivers, blest by suns of home.

(*The Soldier*, R. Brooke, 1915)

EXTRACT C
On the horror of fighting

If in some smothering dreams, you too could pace
Behind the waggon that we flung him in,
And watch the white eyes writhing in his face …
My friend, you would not tell with such high zest
To children ardent with some desperate glory,
Dulce et decorum est,
Pro patria mori.

(*Dulce et Decorum Est*, W. Owen, 1915)

EXTRACT D
Music-hall encouragement to volunteers

We don't want to lose you, But we think you ought to go,
For your King and your Country, Both need you so …

EXTRACT E
A nurse's attack on 'holy war'

I wish that people who write about 'a holy war' could see a case of mustard gas, the poor men burnt and blistered, with blind eyes and always fighting for breath, their throats closing and they know they will choke.

(*Eye-Deep in Hell*, J. Ellis, 1976)

EXTRACT F
On the horror of war

But War – as war is now and always was
A dirty loathsome, servile murder – job:
Men, lousy, sleepless, ulcerous, afraid,
Toiling their hearts out in the pulling slime …
Men stunned in brainlessness, and gibbering
Men driven to death and worse than death …
Cursing with their last breath, the living God
Because He made them, in His image, men.

(G. Frankau, 1917)

PEACE AND FUTURE CANNON FODDER

4. A cartoonist drew a crying child (the '1940 class' of military service) to predict a future war. The men in the drawing are (from right Wilson (USA), Clemenceau (France), Orlando (Italy) and Lloyd George (Britain). They had drawn up the Treaty of Versailles (pages 142–3).

Now test yourself

Knowledge and understanding

1 Read *extracts B and C*. Why do you think these two poets had differing attitudes towards the war? (See also page 135.)
2 What do the primary sources in this topic tell us about the effects of war on (a) patriotism; (b) propaganda; (c) the power of governments?
3 What were the long-term effects of the war on the leaders of the USA and Europe?

Using the sources

1 Do you think the extracts are biased (a) for or (b) against war and patriotism? Explain your answer.
2 How does *picture 3* differ from the truth about life in the trenches as shown on pages 134–5?
3 Is *picture 3* of any use to historians?

THE TREATY OF VERSAILLES, 1919

In 1919 four politicians met at Versailles, near Paris, to draw up a peace treaty for Germany to sign (page 141, *picture 4*). They were:

- Wilson, President of the USA. He wanted to be lenient towards Germany, to help Poland and a new country called Czechoslovakia to be strong, to ensure that France would be safe from another German attack, and to set up a League of Nations.
- Clemenceau, Prime Minister of France. He wanted to punish Germany for the heavy damage done in France and for the many who had died.
- Orlando of Italy wanted to gain territory for Italy.
- Lloyd George, Prime Minister of Britain, wanted a fair settlement and a lasting peace (*extracts A–C*). Pressure from British public opinion made him support Clemenceau's 'revenge' policy.

On 28 June 1919 two German delegates were invited to sign the treaty. They knew that, if they refused to do so, the allies would renew the war, which might well lead to a communist uprising in Germany. So they accepted what they later described as a 'diktat'. Almost all Germans hated the terms of the treaty, some of which are shown in *extract D*:

- They resented clause 231, the so-called 'German war guilt' clause.
- Soldiers and sailors resented clause 160 and clauses which limited the size of the German navy, and banned the building of submarines, planes and tanks.
- National pride was outraged by the giving of land to France, Belgium, Denmark, Poland and Czechoslovakia, particularly since such territories contained many Germans who wanted to be united with Germany.
- Clauses 232 and 233 led to a reparations bill of £6,600 million (about £300 billion in today's money). Germany could not afford to pay such a sum. To help it, the USA made huge loans to Germany which it was supposed to pass on to the allies as reparations. Following the Wall Street Crash of 1929 (page 144), these loans dried up and Germany stopped paying reparations.

Effects of the treaty

The treaty was hated by all Germans and, as we shall see, played a part in the rise of Hitler. Even in 1919, a cartoonist (page 141, *picture 4*) saw that the German desire for revenge would lead to a future war. Many English people supported the view of the writer Bernard Shaw: 'Since 1918 all the powers behaved badly to Germany. When Germany was defeated they

Key:
- Former territory of Imperial Russia
- Plebiscite areas
- Lost by Germany 1919
- Austria-Hungary until 1918
- Saar: League of Nations control 1919–1935
- Pre 1919 borders in black

1. Frontier changes in Europe after 1918.

sat on Germany and kept on sitting on her. Hitler snapped his fingers at the treaty – just as we would have done in the same position.' Even more important were the criticisms of the leading economist, John Maynard Keynes. He resigned from the delegation to the peace conference in 1919 and wrote *The Economic Consequences of the Peace*. His view that the treaty had been too harsh and that the reparations policy would harm world trade, influenced many politicians and leaders.

EXTRACT A
A just and lenient peace treaty?

We [British] seek no selfish and greedy aims; we have only one purpose – to obtain justice for others. We do not seek to destroy Germany or to diminish her boundaries: we do not seek to enlarge our Empire.

(D. Lloyd George, 5 January 1918)

EXTRACT B
Still looking for a lasting peace, early 1919

It is easy to patch up a peace which will last for thirty years. It is hard to draw up a peace which will not provoke a fresh struggle when those who have gone through the War are dead. You may strip Germany of her colonies, reduce her army to a mere police force and her navy to that of a fifth-rate Power; but if she feels she has been unjustly treated, she will find ways of getting revenge on her conquerors.

(D. Lloyd George in a memorandum)

EXTRACT C
German anger at the final treaty, 7 May 1919

Lloyd George went to Versailles to present the Peace terms to the Germans. I do not think David realized, before he went, what an exhausting event it would be. He came back quite exhausted with emotion. The Germans were arrogant and insolent. He says that it has made him more angry than any incident of the War, and if the Germans do not sign, he will have no mercy on them. He says for the first time he feels the same hatred for them that the French feel. I am glad they stirred him up so that he may keep stern with them: if they had been submissive he might have been sorry for them.

(Diary extract by Frances Stephenson, Lloyd George's secretary and, later, wife)

EXTRACT D
Extracts from the Treaty of Versailles, May 1919

42 Germany is forbidden to have any fortifications on either side of the left bank of the Rhine or on the right bank to the west of a line 50 km to the east of the Rhine.
43 In the area defined above, the assembly of armed forces of any kind is forbidden.
45 As compensation for the destruction of the coal mines in north France, Germany cedes to France the coal mines in the Saar Basin.
51 The territories ceded to Germany in 1871 are restored to France.
80 Germany will respect the independence of Austria.
119 Germany renounces, in favour of the Allied Powers, all her overseas possessions.
160 The German Army must not exceed 100,000 men including officers and men at depots. It shall be devoted exclusively to the maintenance of order within the frontiers.
231 The Allies confirm and Germany accepts the responsibility of Germany and her allies for causing all the loss and damage to which the Allies and their peoples have been subjected as a consequence of the war imposed on them by the aggression of Germany and her allies.
232 Germany will make compensation for all damage done to the civilian population of the Allies and to their property.
233 The amount of the above damages shall be fixed by an Allied commission.

Now test yourself

Knowledge and understanding

Explain (a) why Germany was harshly treated after the First World War; (b) the short-term and long-term effects of this harsh treatment. Refer to the economic, social and political effects of the treaty.

Using the sources

1 Explain how and why *extracts A and C* differ in their interpretation of Lloyd George's attitudes to how Germany should be treated in 1919?
2 Do you agree that *picture 1* is a useful source for historians writing about how Europe was changed after the First World War?
3 Do you agree that the allies were wrong to be harsh to Germany after the First World War? Give reasons for your answer.

THE COLLAPSE OF GERMAN DEMOCRACY

When the Kaiser fled in 1918, Germany became a Republic. The new government was blamed for accepting the humiliating Treaty of Versailles (page 142). It became more unpopular as it tried to deal with the problem of reparations. One solution seemed to be to print more money: this led to massive inflation (making money worth less). The price of a loaf of bread rose from 2 marks in 1921 to 470 billion marks in 1923. Millions of Germans saw their savings (in old marks) wiped out.

1. This Socialist Party poster reads 'Our Last Hope, Hitler'.

Things became even worse in 1923 when Germany stopped paying reparations. The French army marched into the Ruhr, seized the German coalfields – this led to more unemployment in Germany. It was then that Adolf Hitler first tried to win public support. He had become leader of the National Socialist (Nazi) Party. In 1923 he tried to seize power by an uprising. He was defeated, tried and imprisoned. In prison he wrote *Mein Kampf* (*My Struggle*) in which he outlined his political ideas.

In 1924 the USA made the first of a series of loans to help the German government restore the value of its money. Germany then had five years of prosperity, partly due to the US loans. The USA could afford such loans because, in the 1920s, the American economy was booming. However, in 1929, this boom came to an end. American banks tried to get back the loans they had made to businesses, which could not repay them so that many businesses went 'bust' (or bankrupt). Millions of Americans lost their jobs and savings. One result of the US depression was a sharp drop in the number of imports into the USA. This led to unemployment in the exporting countries, including Britain and Germany. Another result was that US banks stopped lending money to Germany and harsh times returned. With millions of Germans out of work, Hitler's Nazis became increasingly popular (*extract D*).

Hitler became Chancellor in a coalition government in March 1933 and was given the power of a dictator later that month. In May he abolished the trade unions and in July banned all other political parties – most Germans approved.

2. A Nazi rally, Nuremberg.

EXTRACT A
The Nazi anthem

Hold High the banner! Close the hard ranks serried!
SA (Stormtroopers) marches on with sturdy stride.
Comrades by Red Front and Reaction killed, are buried.
But march with us in image at our side.
Gang way! Gang way! Now for the Brown Battalions!
For the Storm Troopers clear roads o'er the land!
The Swastika gives hope to our entranced millions,
The day for freedom and bread's at hand …

(By Stormtrooper Horst Wessel, 1925)

EXTRACT B
Hitler on the use of propaganda – and lies, 1924

Most of the people have little intelligence, so propaganda must consist of a few points in a few simple words, repeated again and again until even the most stupid know them. In the big lies there is always a certain force of credibility. The masses easily fall victim for the big lie rather than the small one, because they themselves often use small lies but would be ashamed to try a big one. The huge lie always leaves traces behind even after it has been shown to be a lie.

(*Mein Kampf*, Adolf Hitler, 1924)

EXTRACT C
Using government power to help win the election in March 1933

February 3 1933. I talk about the start of the election campaign with the Leader. The struggle is an easy one now, since we are able to use all means of the State. Radio and Press are at our disposal. The Leader is to speak in all towns having their own broadcasting stations. We transmit the broadcast to the entire people and give listeners a clear idea of all that occurs at our meetings. I will introduce the Leader's speech and I shall try to give the hearers the magical atmosphere of our huge demonstrations.

(*My Part in Germany's Fight*, J. Goebbels, 1935)

EXTRACT D
Unemployment and the rise of the Nazis to power, 1919–33

	Seats in the Reichstag		Unemployment in millions
	Nazis	Communists	
May 1924	32	62	0.5
Dec 1924	14	45	0.5
1928	13	54	2.5
1930	107	77	4.0
July 1932	230	89	6.2
Nov 1932	196	120	6.0
Mar 1933	288	81	5.8

EXTRACT E
A cowed Reichstag gives Hitler total power, 24 March 1933

Hitler said that it would be against the spirit of national resurgence if he had to bargain with the Reichstag for every action. So he needed the Enabling Law. Its rejection would be taken as a sign of 'Now, gentlemen, you may choose peace or war'. Only 535 of the 747 deputies were present: others were in concentration camps. Due to the full weight of Nazi pressure and terror, the Enabling Law passed with a vote of 441 in favour. This marked the real seizure of control by the conspirators. The Reichstrat (Upper House) met immediately after and approved the Law without debate.

(Adapted from reports in *The Times*, March 1933)

Now test yourself

Knowledge and understanding

1 (a) Put the following factors which led to Hitler's rise to power in order of their importance: the Versailles Peace Treaty; Wall Street crash; Hitler's personality and policies.
(b) Explain your choice of order. Which other factors helped Hitler to rise to power?

Using the sources

1 Study *extracts A–E* and *pictures 1 and 2*. Are they equally useful for historians writing about the effects of Nazi propaganda and intimidation?
2 Make a timeline from 1918 to 1933 showing the key events in the history of Hitler's rise to power.
3 What do you think the opponents of the Nazis thought of Horst Wessel's description of the Nazi movement? Give reasons for your answer.

ITALIAN FASCISM, THE LEAGUE OF NATIONS AND ABYSSINIA

1. *Evening Standard* cartoon. Japan trampling on the League of Nations; Britain repairs its face.

2. A group of Blackshirts.

THE AWFUL WARNING.

France and England *(together ?)*. "WE DON'T WANT YOU TO FIGHT, BUT, BY JINGO, IF YOU DO, WE SHALL PROBABLY ISSUE A JOINT MEMORANDUM SUGGESTING A MILD DISAPPROVAL OF YOU."

4. *Punch* cartoon suggests Anglo-French 'mild disapproval'.

Italy had been united only in 1870 and its democracy was still young. In 1919 there was great discontent: ex-soldiers faced unemployment; nationalists were angry at Prime Minister Orlando's failure to gain much at Versailles (*extract B*); millions hoped for a Russian-style communist revolution. Mussolini, an ex-socialist, founded the Fascist Party in 1919. He was supported by industrialists (frightened of a Bolshevik revolution), by the unemployed (hoping for work, and willing to join his Blackshirts, *picture 2* and *extract C*) and ex-soldiers. In 1922 his threatened 'March on Rome' led the weak king to make him Prime Minister and he used his new powers to get himself made dictator. His aggressive foreign policy was meant to please Italians and distract attention from their poor conditions at home.

Such aggression was supposed to be dealt with and stopped by the League of Nations. However, Mussolini had seen that the League failed to halt Japan's seizure of Manchuria in 1931. It had ignored China's appeal for help against Japan, a member of the League Council and failed to act when Japan ignored the League's appeal for an end to the invasion (*picture 1*). Japan carried on with the invasion and left the League of Nations. Later, Japan tried to conquer mainland China (1937–45 (page 154, *picture 1*). Mussolini followed Japan's example with his invasion of Abyssinia (*picture 3*). This aggression should have been stopped by the League (*extract A*). But the main powers, France and Britain, were unwilling to act (*picture 4*). They were already more afraid of Hitler and they saw Mussolini as a possible anti-German ally. Mussolini realized how lucky he had been (*extract F*). Hitler realized that the League would never act, and so he, too, began an expansionist policy.

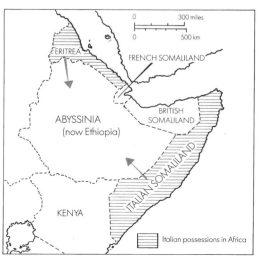

3. Invasion of Abyssinia.

EXTRACT A
The League of Nations promises action

Should any member of the League resort to war, all members undertake immediately to break off all trade relations. It shall be the duty of the Council of the League to recommend what effective military, naval or air force the Members of the League shall contribute to the armed forces to be used to protect the Covenants of the League [against aggressors].

(The Covenant of the League of Nations, Article 16, 1918)

EXTRACT B
Why Italians supported Mussolini, 1919

When I returned from the War I found the politicians had betrayed the soldiers, reducing Italy to a shameful peace. Many, even the most generous, tended to Communism. In my opinion, three-quarters of Italian youth would have become Bolsheviks: a revolution at any cost! Mussolini gave youth that programme which they searched for.

(*Recollections*, Air Marshal Balbo, 1932)

EXTRACT C
Mussolini's Blackshirts frighten many

If you met them in the daytime they would be humble and fawning. By night, and together, they were wicked and evil. They have always been at the disposal of anyone who gave orders, and always will be. But recruiting them into a special army, with special uniform and arms, is something peculiar to the last few years. Such are the Fascists. Their boldness had another explanation, too. Each of us would have been a match for three of them. But what chance did we have in their midst? There we were in the middle of the square. Everyone thought only of himself, of the best way of getting out of that square of armed men.

(*Fontamara*, I. Silone, 1965)

EXTRACT D
The League ready to act, October 1935?

When the Council met on 5 October 1935 I told them that since war had broken out we must act speedily: a Committee of six gathered a few minutes after the end of the Council's meeting. By the evening of 6 October the Fascist Government's action was condemned: 'The Committee concludes that the Italian government has restored to war in disregard of its obligations under the Covenant of the League.' The Assembly met on 9 October, and on 10 October 50 states had agreed to apply sanctions.

(*The Eden Memoirs*, A. Eden, 1962)

EXTRACT E
Too few sanctions

We have to admit that the purpose for which sanctions were imposed has not been realized. The League put sanctions on some goods only, because the incomplete membership of the League made it impossible to make all sanctions effective. Oil could not be made effective by League action alone. It has to be said that sanctions did not succeed.

(Foreign Secretary Eden in the Commons, 18 June 1936)

EXTRACT F
Mussolini admits that he was lucky

'If the League had extended economic sanctions to oil, I would have had to withdraw from Abyssinia within a week.'

(Quoted in *The Diaries of O. Harvey*, 1937–40)

Now test yourself

Knowledge and understanding

1 Explain why Mussolini gained the support of (a) the unemployed; (b) industrialists; (c) nationalists; (d) soldiers; (e) the young.
2 Why did the League of Nations fail to stop Mussolini's invasion of Abyssinia? What were the effects of this invasion?

Using the sources

1 Read *extracts A, D, E and F*. What do you learn from each of them about (a) the strength of Mussolini; (b) the strength of the League of Nations?
2 What do *pictures 1 and 4* tell us about (a) Italian and Japanese foreign policy; (b) attitudes in Britain towards these policies?
3 Look at *extract C* and *picture 2*. How reliable are these sources for historians writing a history of the Blackshirts?

HITLER'S EXPANSIONISM

Once in power Hitler ignored the terms of the Versailles Treaty (page 143, *extract D*): he built up the army, the navy and the air force and spent massive sums on rearmament (*extract B*). When Mussolini defied the League over Abyssinia (pages 146–7), Hitler 'invaded' the Rhineland and the League failed to act (*extract C* and *picture 2*). Like Mussolini in Abyssinia (page 147, *extract F*), Hitler knew that he could not have defied League action in 1936 (*extract D*). In 1938 he again broke the Treaty of Versailles when he invaded Austria (*picture 1*). Then, with the agreement of the British, French and Italians, he divided the state of Czechoslovakia (*picture 3* and *extract E*).

1. German expansion, by March 1939.

Hitler's foreign and domestic policies pleased most Germans:

- National pride was restored.
- Industrialists welcomed the profits from rearmament (*extract B*).
- Workers gained from rearmament and from government-sponsored projects, such as the building of a network of motorways.
- Children were taught Nazi-controlled history at school and, in their thousands, joined Nazi organizations, such as the League of Youth, which provided them with entertainment including holidays at summer camp.
- Almost everyone accepted the 'truth' as provided by the government-controlled radio and press (page 145, *extract D*).
- Opponents were rounded up and put in prison or concentration camps. Opposition political parties were banned.
- Few people were willing to speak out against Hitler's policies. A Lutheran pastor Martin Niemoller wrote: 'First they came for the Jews. I was silent. I was not a Jew. Then they came for the Communists. I was not a Communist. Then they came for the trade unionists. I was not a trade unionist. Then they came for me. There was no one left to speak for me.' He died in a concentration camp.

Appeasement

Appeasement describes the policy of Britain and France

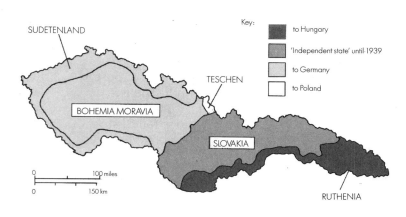

3. The destruction of Czechoslovakia.

THE GOOSE-STEP.
"GOOSEY GOOSEY GANDER,
WHITHER DOST THOU WANDER?"
"ONLY THROUGH THE RHINELAND—
PRAY EXCUSE MY BLUNDER!"

2. 'The Goose-Step', Punch cartoon, 1936.

in the 1930s. It means giving into the demands of a country so as to prevent war. Until 1939 most people in Britain supported this policy: 'Germany had been treated too harshly in 1919' (pages 142–3); 'We don't want another war'; 'Stalin's communism is a bigger danger than Hitler'. Today, we can see that appeasement encouraged Hitler, allowing Germany to become stronger, and ignored Hitler's plan (*extract A*), to conquer Europe.

EXTRACT A
Hitler condemns the Treaty of Versailles, 1924

What use could be made of the Treaty! Each one of the points could be branded in the minds and hearts of the Germans until 60 million find their souls aflame with rage and shame, and a torrent bursts forth as from a furnace, and a will of steel is forged from it, with the cry; 'We will have arms again'.

(*Mein Kampf*, Adolf Hitler, 1924)

EXTRACT B
Aggression will pay for German living standards, 1943

Our armaments have swallowed fantastic sums: either these debts will be put on the people in the shape of taxes, or they will be paid by the profits from the occupied territories.

(Hitler, speaking in 1943)

EXTRACT C
The Rhineland: a small case study, 1936

11 March 1936: The French know that the invasion of the demilitarized zone was against the advice of the German Generals; they feel that if we show firmness, we may discredit Hitler with his people. If we do nothing, the League will cease to have any meaning. But the country will not let us take action in what they see as a purely French interest.
12 March 1936: The French say that the Covenant has been broken and they ask us to fulfil our obligations under the Covenant and the Treaty of Locarno. The French are right. Hitler gambled. If we send an ultimatum to Germany she will climb down. What is the good of that? It

will mean communism in Germany, which is why the Russians are keen on it. So we have to swallow the humiliation.

(*Diaries and Letters*, Harold Nicholson, 1930–39)

EXTRACT D
Hitler on the Rhineland crisis, 1936

7 March 1936: In the train going to Munich this evening, Hitler said: 'We had no army worth mentioning; it would not even have had the strength to maintain itself against the Poles. If the French had taken any action, we would have been easily defeated; our resistance would have been short-lived.'

(*Inside the Third Reich*, Albert Speer, 1970)

EXTRACT E
Czechoslovakia: another small case study, 1938–9

19 September 1938: After meeting Herr Hitler at Berchtesgaden, I told the Czechs to be ready to make sacrifices. The maintenance within their boundaries of the Sudeten Germans cannot continue without imperiling peace which cannot be assured unless these areas are transferred to Germany.
28 September 1939: I met Herr Hitler again on 22 September at Godesberg. He told me that our plans for Czechoslovakia were too slow and that he was prepared to risk a World War over the Sudeten lands.
29 September 1938: This means peace in our time; the Munich agreement is a symbol of our two people's determination not to go to war again.

(Adapted from N. Chamberlain's letters and diaries, 1938–9)

Now test yourself

Knowledge and understanding

Explain how (a) Hitler broke the Versailles Treaty; (b) why most Germans supported him; (c) how other countries' leaders reacted.

Using the sources

1 Do you agree that the evidence suggests that Hitler's foreign policy was a complete success by 1939? Give reasons for your answer.
2 Make a timeline showing how and when Hitler expanded Germany's borders.
3 What can historians learn about Hitler's policies from *pictures 1–3*?

GERMANY AND 'SOLVING THE JEWISH PROBLEM'

1. The front page of *Der Stürmer*, a Nazi newspaper, May 1934.

Hitler blamed the Jews for Germany's defeat (*extract A*). He was appealing to a long-standing anti-Jewish prejudice which was strongest in Poland and Germany where hundreds of Jews were murdered in 1918–19 following the humiliation of Versailles. Germans accepted Hitler's claims that the Jews enjoyed too much success in the professions (law, medicine and education), in banking and in business. Once he came to power in 1933, they welcomed the attacks made on Jewish shops and people by Hitler's Stormtroopers and joined in such attacks on people and property (*picture 2* and *extract B*). They applauded the Nazi-inspired placards outside Jewish-owned cafes, shops and businesses urging people not to support Jewish owners. They put up road signs and hung banners across roads into villages and towns saying 'Jews are not welcome here'.

Thousands of Jews fled the country, many going to Palestine, the USA or Britain, where Jewish scientists contributed to the development of the atomic bomb and other weapons.

In 1935 Hitler addressed a massive Nazi rally at Nuremberg (page 144, *picture 2*), where he announced a series of anti-Jewish laws aimed at making life almost impossible for them. His colleague, Julius Streicher, edited an obscene newspaper, *Der Stürmer*, which attacked Jews and their religion (*picture 1*).

On 7 November 1938 a German Jewish refugee killed a German diplomat in Paris. In reprisal, the Nazis organized a mass attack on German Jews. On 'Crystal Night' (*Kristallnacht*) thousands of windows were smashed in synagogues, businesses and homes and 20,000 Jews were arrested for 'resisting the forces'.

During the war, Jews in occupied countries were sent to concentration camps, which were actually extermination camps (*extract D* and *picture 3*). By 1945 six million Jewish men, women and children had been murdered.

2. Jews are forced to scrub pavements for the amusement of the Nazis.

3. A mass grave at Belsen concentration camp, 1945.

EXTRACT A
Hitler blames the Jews for the German defeat, 1918

If, at the beginning and during the War, someone had only subjected about 12,000 or 15,000 of these Hebrew enemies of the people to poison gas, then the sacrifice of millions at the front would not have been in vain.

(*Mein Kampf*, A. Hitler, 1924)

EXTRACT B
Speedy action against Austrian Jews, June 1938

I met an Austrian yesterday who had just got away from Vienna, and what he said made me ill. They rounded up the people walking in the Prater on Sunday last, and separated the Jews from the rest. They made the Jewish men take off all their clothes and walk on all fours on the grass. They made the old Jewish ladies get up into the trees by ladders and sit there. The suicides have been appalling.

(*Diaries and Letters*, H. Nicholson, 1930–39)

EXTRACT C
Hitler demands an anti-Jewish campaign, 1942

The Fuhrer once more expressed his determination to clean up the Jews in Europe pitilessly. There must be no more squeamish sentimentalism about it. Their destruction will go hand in hand with the destruction of our enemies.

(*Diaries*, J. Goebbels, 1943)

EXTRACT D
The Auschwitz extermination camp, by its Commandant

The 'Final solution' of the Jewish question meant the complete extermination of all European Jews. I was told to set up extermination facilities at Auschwitz in June 1941. There were already three other such camps: Belsen, Treblinka and Wolzek. At Treblinka the Commandant told me that he had liquidated 80,000 in half a year, mainly from Warsaw. He used monoxide gas … not very efficient. At Auschwitz I used Cyclon B, a crystallized prussic acid dropped into the death chamber. It took from three to fifteen minutes to kill the people in the chamber: we knew they were dead when they stopped screaming. After the bodies were removed, special commandos took off the rings and extracted the gold from the teeth of the corpses. We built our gas-chambers to take 2000 at one time.

(Evidence given at the Nuremberg Trials, 1947–9)

EXTRACT E
A British medical officer at Belsen, 1945

I visited the human remains lying on the straw mats, covered with filthy blankets. At first we were unable to define their sex. Their heads shorn, the agony of their sufferings showed clearly in their expressions, their eyes sunken and listless, cheek bones prominent, too weak to close their mouths, their arms extended in an appalling manner. The floor was filthy, straw littered with human excrement.

(Statement made in 1945)

EXTRACT F
SS Commander Himmler praises the exterminators, October 1943

I now want to mention, quite openly, before you all, a difficult subject. Among ourselves it can be discussed, but never mentioned in public. I mean the extermination of the Jews. Any member of the Party will tell you 'the Jews will be exterminated. It's part of our programme'. But not one has seen it done. You will know what it means to have a hundred corpses lying there, or 500 or 1000. To have seen this through has made us hard and is a page of glory in our history.

(Himmler to SS Generals in Poland, 10 October 1943)

Now test yourself

Knowledge and understanding

Explain in detail (a) how Nazi persecution of the Jewish people became increasingly extreme from 1935 to 1945; (b) why many Germans supported these policies.

Using the sources

1 Which sources do you find the most useful in understanding what it was like to be a Jew under Nazi domination?
2 How can we use *pictures 2 and 3* to understand the effects of Nazism?
3 Why did the Nazis use anti-Jewish propaganda as in *picture 1*?

GERMAN SUCCESSES, 1939–42

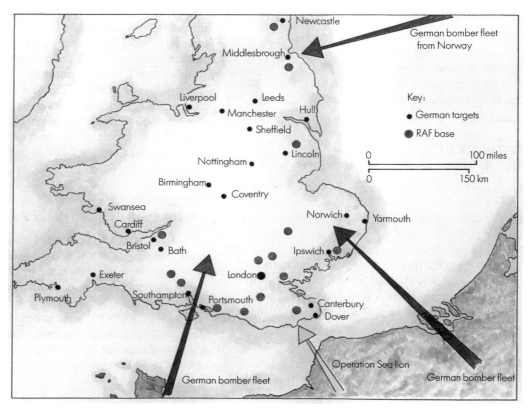

1. The Battle of Britain, August–October 1940.

In 1938 the British and French allowed Hitler to take most of Czechoslovakia (page 149, *extract E*). In doing so, they ignored the Soviet Union, which had an alliance with Czechoslovakia. This may help to explain why Stalin made a pact with Hitler in 1939. Hitler may have seen that pact ('a major turn about') as part of his long-term plans for conquest of the east. That conquest was made easier by his invasion of Poland in September 1939, which plunged Europe into war. The conquest of Poland, like later conquests of Norway and Holland (*extracts B and C*), was speedy – the combined use of air force, tanks and mobile infantry in a 'blitzkrieg' allowing German troops to overcome less-prepared opposition (*extract C*). With the collapse of France in 1940, only Britain remained unconquered: the Battle of Britain (*picture 1*) failed to bring Britain to the negotiating table. In June 1941 Hitler invaded the Soviet Union expecting a quick victory (*extract E*). By December 1941 he seemed to have almost succeeded: later advances in 1942 (*picture 3*) saw his troops march on Moscow and Stalingrad, in spite of the snow (*picture 2*).

2. German soldiers on the Eastern Front.

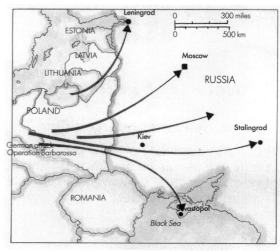

3. German advances into Russia, 1941–2.

EXTRACT A
The 'Phoney' War, September 1939–April 1940

My soul revolted at what was happening. France and Britain stood still while Germany swallowed Poland. We waited to be attacked. If this was war, I did not understand it.

(Field Marshal Montgomery, with the troops in France, 1940)

EXTRACT B
The British, unprepared, defeated in Norway, April–May 1940

The troops lacked aircraft, anti-aircraft guns, anti-tank guns, tanks, transport and training, snow shoes and skis … a ramshackle campaign.

(Churchill on the Norway campaign, 1940)

EXTRACT C
The Germans, prepared, overwhelm Holland in 'blitzkrieg', May 1940

The avalanche of fire and steel rolled across the frontiers, and an overwhelming onslaught was made from the air. The whole country was in a state of confusion.

(Churchill, after speaking to Dutch government ministers, 1940)

EXTRACT D
The first of Churchill's great speeches

I would say to this House as I said to those who had joined the government, 'I have nothing to offer but blood, toil, tears and sweat. You ask what is our policy? It is to wage war, with all our might and with all the strength God can give us. You ask what is our aim? In one word: Victory.'

(Churchill to the House of Commons on becoming Prime Minister, May 1940)

EXTRACT E
Hitler on invading Russia, June 1941

You only have to kick in the door and the whole rotten structure will come crashing down.

(Hitler to the commander of the forces in Ukraine)

EXTRACT F
Have the Germans taken on too much? Russia, August 1941

We reckoned on about 200 enemy divisions: but we have already counted 360. And time favours them, for they are near their own resources, while we are moving further away from ours. Our troops, spread out over an immense front line, without any depth of support, face constant enemy attacks.

(General Halder, in his diary, 11 August 1941)

EXTRACT G
Russia stubborness and 'General' winter, December 1941

Now when Moscow was in sight, the mood of the commanders changed. With amazement we discovered in late October that the Russians were unaware that, as a military force, they had ceased to exist. Then the weather broke and the full force of the Russian winter was upon us.

(General Blumenritt, December 1941)

EXTRACT H
The first months of the siege of Leningrad, 1941

November 1941 arrived; icy wind drove powdered snow through the slits of dugouts and the broken windows of hospitals. The constant shortage of food, the cold weather and nervous tension wore the workers down. Few people paid any attention to the German shells that had shocked them before. In those days death loomed menacingly: lack of food and cold sent 11,000 to their graves in November. But the operetta company remained and the people loved them: the ballerinas were so thin it seemed they must break in two if they moved.

(Pavlova's eyewitness account of the siege, 1941)

Now test yourself

Knowledge and understanding

Show how Hitler's successes were helped by (a) the British and the French; (b) Stalin; (c) Hitler's military forces; (d) his own daring.

Using the sources

1 What do *extracts A–C* and *picture 3* tell us about why the Germans succeeded in 1939–1942?

2 Do you agree that *extract E* gives a different interpretation of the war from *extract G*? Give reasons for your answer.

3 Do *extracts F and H* support *extract E or G's* interpretation? Why?

4 Are *extracts D and F* and *pictures 1 and 2* equally useful as evidence of resistance to the German invaders? Explain your answer.

JAPANESE SUCCESSES, 1937–42

Japan's long-term plans for the conquest of Asia had led to the invasion and conquest of Manchuria (1931) and the invasion of China (*picture 1*) when it signed a pact with Hitler and Mussolini. After the collapse of France in 1940, Japan occupied part of French Indo-China (*picture 2*). The USA stopped trading with Japan in the hope of forcing it out of China and Indo-China. While negotiations about this were taking place in Washington, Japanese forces attacked the US naval base at Pearl Harbor (*extract C*) and brought the USA into the war: even pro-German isolationists such as Lindbergh (*extracts D and E*) saw that this was inevitable. Hitler's declaration of war on the USA made the conflict into a worldwide war.

1. A British cartoonist's view of the failure of Britain and the USA to act when Japan attacked China in 1937.

Even before this, the USA had been friendly to Britain (*extracts A and B*) and supplied it with arms and supplies. This did nothing to stop the headlong advance of the Japanese throughout Asia in 1942 (*picture 2*) from bases in New Guinea and the Celebes they threatened Australia. The allied naval victory at the Coral Sea (*extract F*) prevented an invasion of Australia and marked the high point of Japanese success. In December 1941 Churchill and Roosevelt had agreed that the defeat of Japan would have to wait until Hitler had been defeated – a surprising decision by the USA, considering the reasons for its involvement in the war.

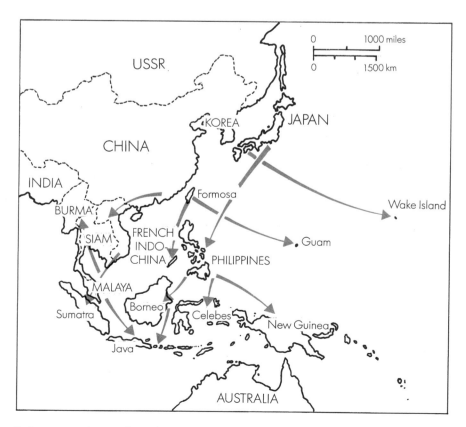

2. Japanese advance through South-East Asia, 1942.

EXTRACT A
President Roosevelt's 'Four Freedoms' for the future, 1941

In the future days, which we seek to make secure, we look forward to a world founded on (1) Freedom of speech everywhere; (2) Freedom of everyone to worship God in his own way; (3) Freedom from want for every nation; (4) Freedom from fear for every nation …

(Roosevelt's speech to the people, January 1941)

EXTRACT B
A summary of the Atlantic Charter, August 1941

The President and the Prime Minister [state] certain common principles on which they base their hopes for a better future for the world: They promise that their countries will try not to seize any land anywhere. They agree that all people have the right to choose their own form of government. All conquered countries should have their independence restored. 'After the final destruction of the Nazi tyranny' all nations should join together to try to ensure greater prosperity for all and to protect peace.

(Adapted from the Joint Declaration by Churchill and Roosevelt, 1941)

EXTRACT C
Japan's plans for the attack on Pearl Harbor, 1941

A gigantic US fleet has massed in Pearl Harbor. This will be crushed with one blow at the beginning of hostilities. The success of our surprise attack will be the Waterloo of the war to follow. The Imperial Navy is massing ships and planes to ensure success. By attacking and seizing all key points at one blow while America is unprepared, we can swing the scale of later operations in our favour.

(Japanese Chief of Staff to Strike Officers, 10 November 1941)

EXTRACT D
An anti-British pacifist on US entry into war, December 1941

Monday, 8th December: I am not surprised the Japs attacked. We have been prodding them into war for weeks. They have simply beaten us to the gun. The President spoke at 12.00, asked for a Declaration of War. Senate passed it unanimously; only one 'no' in the House. If the President had asked for war before, Congress would have turned him down with a big majority. But now we have been attacked. I see nothing to do except to fight. If I had been in Congress I would have voted for war.

(Wartime journals of Charles Lindbergh)

EXTRACT E
Extending the war, 1941

Thursday 11 December: Germany and Italy have declared war on the US. All that I feared would happen has happened. We are at war all over the world.

(Wartime journals of Charles Lindbergh)

EXTRACT F
The first check to the Japanese advance: Coral Sea, May 1942

Friday, 15 May 1942: The Battle of the Coral Sea has resulted in the destruction of many Japanese warships and transports … by aircraft. This action [is] one of the most important which has yet taken place. The Japanese can't replace their losses as Britain and America can; and as their aggressions depend on sea transport, they must come to an end. Burma has fallen, but no move of any kind has taken place this week. The Battle of the Coral Sea may have been preparatory to an invasion of Australia.

(*Journal of the War Years*, A. Weymouth, 1948)

Now test yourself

Knowledge and understanding

1 Show how Japan's expansionist policies affected (a) Manchuria; (b) China; (c) Germany; (d) the USA; (e) Australia.
2 Why did Japanese policies lead to war 'all over the world' (*extract E*)?

Using the sources

1 How reliable do you think *extracts A and B* and *picture 1* are as guides to US and British foreign policies? Give reasons for your answer.
2 How might *picture 2* and *extracts C–F* be used to illustrate the effects of Japan's aggressive policies?
3 Does *extract F* show that *extract C* does not give a fully accurate interpretation of Japanese naval strength? Why?

GERMAN DEFEATS, 1942–5

Churchill called 1942 'the turning point' in the war. The Japanese were defeated at the Coral Sea, and later at Midway. The Russians halted the Germans at Stalingrad in September 1942: the severe Russian winter came to the defenders' help (page 152, *picture 2*) and in February 1943 the Germans surrendered to the Russians (*extract B*) – the first major set-back for the axis powers in Europe. By then the British had won the Battle of El Alamein (*extract A*) and were driving the Germans and Italians across North Africa (*picture 1*). In June 1944 allied forces landed on the beaches of northern France where, in spite of stiff resistance, they were successful (*extracts C and D*). The liberation of France, Holland and Belgium was followed by a drive to Berlin from the west, while the conquering Russians advanced from the east (*extract E* and *picture 1*). German cartoonists tried to show that the Americans were allowing the British and Russians to do most of the fighting (*picture 2*); deliberately ignoring the major role played by US forces in Europe.

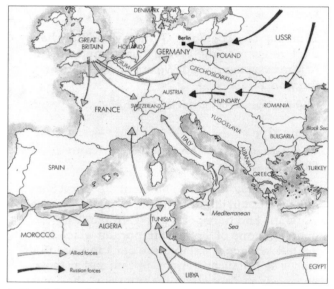

1. The defeat of the axis powers, 1943–5.

Germany had hoped to defeat Britain by attacking merchant ships carrying food, oil and raw materials to Britain. Hitler said that if Britain lost 150 ships a month for only a year, it would have to surrender. So the Battle of the Atlantic was an important one. Germany attacked merchant ships by mines laid around the British coast, by warships, submarine and planes. After the fall of France in June 1940, German planes and ships were able to use ports in northern France to launch attacks on ships in the Atlantic.

British minesweepers were so successful that by the end of 1941, German mines were no longer a major threat. By that time, too, most German planes were being used in the war against Russia, while the threat from British planes forced the Germans to withdraw their warships to port. The major threat came from German submarines – U-boats. In 1942 more than 1,100 of the 1,660 ships sunk at sea were victims of U-boats. This danger was met by the convoy system: merchant ships were gathered into groups which sailed under the protection of warships and planes. The warships used radar to spot submarines which were then attacked either by the ships or by planes. Over half the 750 U-boats which were sunk were destroyed by air attack. Although 22 million tons of shipping were lost during the war, over 42 million tons of new shipping were built, so that Germany lost the Battle of the Atlantic in spite of destroying more than 5000 British ships.

During 1940–2 and again in 1944 German bombers attacked British towns and cities (page 160, *picture 5*). After 1942 British and American planes attacked German industrial and residential areas. Few people in Britain opposed such a policy.

2. A German view of the allied effort, 1944.

EXTRACT A
Turning point 1: El Alamein, November 1942

A real hard bloody fight has gone on now for eight days. I think Rommel is now ripe for a real hard blow that will topple him. If we succeed it will be the end of his army.

(Field Marshal Montgomery to General Alanbrooke, 1 November 1942)

Dearest Lu, very heavy fighting; not going well for us. The enemy's superior strength is slowly levering us out of war positions. That will mean the end. Air raid after air raid after air raid.

(General Rommel to his wife, 2 November 1942)

EXTRACT B
Turning point 2: Stalingrad, January 1943

The Russians are finished. In four weeks they will collapse.

(Hitler, September 1942)

Every seven seconds a German soldier dies; Stalingrad – mass grave

(Moscow Radio, January 1943)

Troops without ammunition, food, dressings or drugs for wounded. Further defence useless. Army requests permission to surrender to save the lives of the remaining troops.

(General von Paulus to Hitler, 24 January 1943)

Surrender is forbidden. 6th Army will hold position to last man and the last round.

(Hitler to von Paulus, 24 January 1943)

Carrying out your orders, on 2 February 1943 we completed the destruction of the encircled enemy forces at Stalingrad.

(General Rokossovsky to Stalin, February 1943)

EXTRACT C
France welcomes the invading allies, 8 June 1944

The first evidence of French feeling came from a village woman. 'God has sent the British and Americans' she said tremblingly. 'The Germans are afraid. They told me as they came through here; "The allies have so many men, so much material the sea is filled with their ships".' Then at Bayeux, men, women and children lining the streets. It was a hysterical welcome. They stood in the cobbled streets, from which the allies had just driven the Germans, with tears streaming down their faces, flags from every balcony. No people were ever more justified in hysteria.

(BBC commentary, 8 June 1944)

EXTRACT D
Rommel advises negotiations with the allies, 15 July 1944

The situation on the Normandy front is becoming more difficult every day. Because of the fierce fighting, the large amounts of material used by the enemy in artillery and tanks, and the impact of the enemy air force which is in full control, our own losses are so high that they seriously reduce the effectiveness of our divisions. The supply situation is also difficult because of the destruction of the railways and the vulnerability of the roads up to 150 km behind the front. The enemy front line receives new forces and supplies every day.

(Rommel, 15 July 1944)

EXTRACT E
Berlin under attack, 9 March 1945

The capital will be defended to the last man and bullet; every building, every house, every floor, every hedge, every shell-crater will be defended to the utmost.

(Order issued by Berlin's Commanding Officer, 9 March 1945)

Now test yourself

Knowledge and understanding

(a) Explain how Germany's defeat was brought about by the following: defeat in Russia; USA's entry into the war; defeat at El Alamein; the Battle of the Atlantic. (b) Place these factors in order of importance and explain your choice. (c) What other factors helped to defeat Hitler?

Using the sources

1 How full an explanation for Germany's defeat is offered in *extract D*?
2 Do you agree that *picture 1*, *the extracts* and text show that *picture 2* is an inaccurate view of the allied war effort? Why?
3 How reliable are the statements in *extracts A, B and E* by the leading soldiers and politicians on both sides in the war?

J APANESE DEFEATS, 1942–5

The German cartoonist (page 156, *picture 2*) used his skill to show a false picture of the US contribution to allied successes. The USA had more factories than any other country – and all free from enemy attack. It also had more raw materials than any other country. During 1941 (while still at peace), America's output of munitions was doubled and over 2000 aircraft produced each month. In 1942 over 60,000 aircraft and 45,000 tanks were produced. By the end of the war the USA had built 86,000 tanks, 296,000 aircraft, 64,000 landing craft, 6,500 naval vessels and 54,000 transport ships. Much of this output was given to the British and the Soviet Union.

It went mainly to ensure the defeat of the Japanese (*picture 1*) whose forces had to be pushed from one island after another in a costly advance by US forces. In August 1945 President Truman ordered the dropping of the first atomic bomb (*extracts B, C and D*) after first warning the Japanese of what was to happen if they continued to fight (*picture 2*). The destruction of Hiroshima (*picture 4*) was followed by the atomic attack on Nagasaki and the Japanese surrender. Few people, in 1945, opposed the use of the atomic weapon against an enemy which had so cruelly treated prisoners of war (*picture 3*).

The end of empires

Before the war, European countries

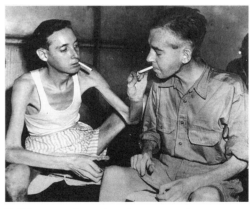

1. The defeat of Japan, 1943–5.

3. Prisoners of war in a Japanese prison camp.

We are in possession of the most destructive weapon ever designed by man. A single one of our atomic bombs equals the explosive power carried by 2000 of our Super-Fortresses … Before using this bomb again and again to destroy every resource which your military leaders have … we ask you to petition your Emperor now to end the war.

2. American leaflet warning of their imminent attack by atomic bomb.

4. After the bomb, Hiroshima, 1945.

held valuable colonies in the Far East. The humiliation of the Europeans by the Japanese, and the self-confidence of peoples of the colonies who had fought guerilla wars against the invader, weakened the power of the Europeans. The French and Dutch fought to hold on to their colonies, but finally had to abandon them. Britain withdrew from India, Burma, Ceylon and, later, Malaya and Singapore.

EXTRACT A
The Japanese (like the Germans) in retreat, 1943

The Japanese are now speaking of the successful evacuation of Salamua in New Guinea. These successful evacuations are getting common with the axis. In the course of one year we have done so much successful evacuating that a large part of our former war potential has been lost.

(*Diaries*, J. Goebbels, 1943)

EXTRACT B
Truman's decision to use the atomic bomb, August 1945

The final decision of where and when to use the bomb was up to me. I regarded the bomb as a military weapon and never had any doubt that it should be used. My military advisers recommended its use and Churchill unhesitatingly told me he favoured its use if it might aid the end of the War.

(*Year of Decisions*, H.S. Truman, 1955)

EXTRACT C
The Hiroshima bomb, 6 August 1945

Suddenly a glaring light appeared in the sky accompanied by an unnatural tremor and a wave of suffocating heat and a wind which swept away everything in its path … thousands in the streets scorched by the searing heat … others screaming in agony from the pain of their burns. Everything standing upright was annihilated and the debris carried up into the air … trams, trains … flung like toys. About half an hour after, a fine rain began to fall caused by the sudden rise of over-heated air to a great height where it condensed. Then a violent wind rose and the fire extended with terrible rapidity. By evening the fire died down. There was nothing left to burn, Hiroshima had ceased to exist.

(*Warrior Without Weapons*, M. Junod)

EXTRACT D
A prisoner of war welcomes the news of Hiroshima

If the atom bombs had not been dropped the War would have dragged on. Those terrible bombs must have seemed as supernatural to the Japanese as they seemed to me when I first heard of them in the darkness and danger of our own prison. For me, selfish as it may sound, there was the certain knowledge that if the bomb had not been dropped, the Japanese would have fought on and hundreds of thousands of prisoners would have been killed. Even if we had not been massacred, we were near our physical end through lack of food.

(*Night of the New Moon*, L. van der Post, 1970)

EXTRACT E
Why did the allies win? Why did the axis powers lose?

They became stretched out far beyond their basic capacity for holding their gains. For Japan was a small island with limited industrial power. Italian incompetence was a constant drain on Hitler's resources.

(The military historian, B.H. Liddel-Hart)

Now test yourself

Knowledge and understanding

1 Explain why the USA was an important ally for Britain.
2 Why did most people in the USA support the dropping of the atomic bomb?

Using the sources

1 How do *extracts B–D* and *pictures 2 and 3* help you to understand (a) why the bomb was dropped; (b) the effects of the dropping of the bomb?
2 Do you think that *picture 1* and *extracts A and E* show that the atomic bomb was not essential for the defeat of Japan?
3 Is *extract B* a reliable source? Give reasons for your answer.

WARTIME BRITAIN

1. A cartoon of 1944.

As in the first World War, the government controlled the nation's economic life – controlling industry as well as labour. When Churchill became Prime Minister in May 1940 he brought Labour politicians into his Cabinet. They 'ran the War at home' so that workers better accepted the loss of trade union power, wages control and higher taxes since they came from 'their' leaders. The severe bombing of many cities (*extract A* and *picture 5*) led to the destruction of millions of homes, factories, ports and business centres, all of which had to be rebuilt after 1945.

But the war brought the people together (*extracts B and C*): better-off people in safer suburbs took in children from bombed cities (*picture 3*) and learned to sympathize with their poverty; soldiers had education classes (*extract D*) in which they called for a post-war unity in a fight against pre-war problems, such as unemployment (*picture 1*). The coalition government produced a series of plans for a better Britain. The most important of these was the Beveridge Report (*extracts F and G*) which called for a major social revolution (*picture 2*). 'From the evil of war, some good came.'

On 5 July 1945, while still at war with Japan, Britain held a general election. Soldiers serving overseas voted and sent their voting papers to their home towns. This meant that the result was not known until 26 July. In 'a most surprising result' Labour won 393 seats to 189 for the Tories. It was the Labour Party which had to deal with Britain's post-war problems.

2. 'Make way for Socialism', *London Express* cartoon.

3. London children were evacuated to the safety of the countryside.

4. Workers could often afford more food in wartime than when unemployed.

5. A London street after an air attack.

EXTRACT A
A destructive war

London people lost much sleep and suffered anxiety and discomfort, but there was no panic except in the small heavily bombed areas. After a few days the first horror of raids wore off and people adjusted to shelter life.

Disorganization was more serious. The network of railways was cut at many places, hundreds of bridges put out of action, roads blocked by craters and debris, water and gas mains broken, telephone exchanges put out of action, factories destroyed or damaged, and millions of homes rendered unfit for use.

(Cabinet Papers 67/9)

EXTRACT B
Togetherness

People were much more together. They met in the air-raid shelters, in the tubes at night, in the Home Guard, or in food queues. When the raids were over they used almost to celebrate in the morning, and this was the spirit that I think a lot of people hoped would continue after the War.

(A. Ling, quoted in *Now the War is Over*, P. Addison, 1985)

EXTRACT C
Evacuees learn new habits – and the sympathy of their host families

My sister whispered for days. Everything was so clean. We were given face flannels and toothbrushes – we'd never cleaned our teeth before. And hot water came from the tap: and there was a lavatory upstairs. And carpets. And clean sheets. It was all very odd. I didn't like it.

(*The World is a Wedding*, B. Kops, 1973)

EXTRACT D
Soldiers learn from one another

As in all wars there were periods of violent action but long periods of boredom during which people had time to read, argue and discuss. Troops were much concerned with what Britain was going to be like after the War … a great deal of discussion about war aims.

(*The Day Before Yesterday*, A. Thompson, 1971)

EXTRACT E
Fair shares of food for all

The War forced us to adopt a food policy based on the needs of the people. Estimates were made of minimum food requirements. Then a scheme was designed to provide the food to meet those needs. The available food was distributed with special measures being taken to ensure that the highest needs of mothers, children and of heavy workers would be met. The poorest part of the population is actually better fed than before the War.

(*Food and the People*, J.B. Orr, 1943)

EXTRACT F
Looking ahead, 1942

Now, when war is abolishing landmarks of every kind, is the opportunity for using experience in a clear field. A revolutionary moment in history is a time for revolutions and not for patching.

(W. Beveridge, 1942)

EXTRACT G
The far-reaching Beveridge Report, 1942

His report was greeted as a blueprint for future society and became a best seller. He noted that there were five giant evils: Want (poverty), Ignorance (poor schooling), Squalor (bad housing), Disease (ill-health) and Idleness (unemployment). He called on the Government to do more for education (which the 1944 Education Act set out to do), for Full Employment, for a National Health Service, for a huge housing programme and for a Ministry of Social Security.

(*Post-War Britain*, P. Lane, 1979)

Now test yourself

Knowledge and understanding

1 Using the text, *pictures 3 and 4* and *extracts A–E* explain how the war affected Britain (a) socially; (b) economically; (c) politically.
2 How were poorer people affected differently from better-off people?

Using the sources

1 Do you agree that the extracts and text show that 'from the evil of war, some good came'? Give reasons for your answer.
2 Are *pictures 1 and 2* useful in helping you to understand the effects of the war on the hopes of many people for the future?
3 Are *extracts F and G* useful as evidence for the long-term effects of the war on the British people? Why?

POST-WAR FRONTIERS

Churchill and Roosevelt held several wartime meetings (page 155, *extract B*). In January 1943 they met in Casablanca and announced that the war would go on until the axis powers had 'surrendered without conditions'. There was going to be no repetition of the mistakes made in 1918–19, which had allowed some Germans to claim that their army had never been defeated. They met Stalin in Teheran in November 1943 and discussed the future of post-war Europe. That discussion continued when the three met at Yalta in February 1945 at what was, perhaps, the most important conference. They agreed to divide Germany between the allied powers, each having a 'zone'. They agreed that the liberated countries would be free to choose the kind of government they wanted and they finalized their agreement on the setting up of the United Nations Organization (page 164).

1. Russian control of Eastern Europe, 1944–7.

Stalin's army liberated eastern Europe (*extract A and picture 1*). But, instead of allowing free elections, the invaders imposed communist governments on most of the liberated countries (*extracts C and E*). This disappointed Churchill, who had defended Stalin's reputation (*extract D*), Labour's Foreign Minister, Bevin (*extract E*), who had hoped that 'left would talk to left', and the Americans, who had hoped to bring their troops home from Europe once the war ended. Instead, Stalin's aggressive policy in Europe and the Middle East led to increased US involvement in post-war Europe (*extract G*). The Iron Curtain (*extract F*) was a symbol of the Cold War in which Germany, and particularly Berlin, were centres of crisis until the 1970s.

For his part, Stalin explained his policy in Europe (March 1946). He argued that Russia had been attacked in 1914 and 1941 through eastern Europe when its governments had been hostile. He wanted to make sure that, in future, governments there would be friendly.

2. The division of Germany and enlargement of Poland.

EXTRACT A
The Red Army liberates eastern Europe – at a price

First came the tank divisions, the guns, the lorries, the parachute divisions, then hundreds of thousands of columns of marching soldiers, men and women. Then the lorries belonging to the Political Commissars and the NKVD [secret police].

(*East Wind Over Prague*, J. Stransky, 1950)

EXTRACT B
The Yalta Agreement and the Polish question

A new situation has been created by the liberation of Poland by the Red Army. This calls for a Polish Provisional Government more broadly based than was possible before this liberation. The Provisional Government now in Poland should be reorganized on a democratic basis with the inclusion of democratic leaders from Poland itself and from Poles abroad.

(Yalta Agreement, February 1945)

EXTRACT C
Yalta – a 'free' agreement?

By February 1945 Poland and all East Europe, except Czechoslovakia, was in the hands of the Red Army. As a result it was not a question of what Britain and the USA would permit, but of what they could persuade the Soviet Union to accept.

(US Secretary of State writing shortly after the signing of the agreement, 1945)

EXTRACT D
Churchill's optimism about Russia's post-war policies

I know of no government which stands to its obligations more solidly than the Russian Soviet government. I decline absolutely to embark here on a discussion of Russia's good faith.

(House of Commons debate on the Yalta Agreement, 27 February 1945)

EXTRACT E
Britain's suspicions of Soviet policy, January 1946

Russia's foreign policy is as imperialistic as Peter the Great's. She is seeking to put around her a group of satellites with the view of controlling every place in contact with her.

(E. Bevin, Foreign Secretary, January 1946)

EXTRACT F
Churchill's 'Iron Curtain' speech, March 1946

From Stettin in the Baltic to Trieste in the Adriatic an iron curtain has descended across the continent. Behind that line lies all the capitals of the ancient states of central and eastern Europe. The Russian-dominated Polish Government has made wrongful inroads upon Germany. The Communist Parties in all these Eastern States have been raised to pre-eminence and power far beyond their numbers and seek to obtain totalitarian control … there is no true democracy.

(Speech at Fulton, Missouri, 5 March 1946)

EXTRACT G
Truman's anti-communist doctrine

At the present moment every nation must choose between alternative ways of life. The choice is too often not a free one. One way of life is based upon the will of the majority. The second is based on the will of a minority imposed on the majority. To ensure the peaceful development of nations, we took a leading part in the establishment of the UNO, to make possible lasting freedom and independence for all its members. We shall not gain our objectives unless we are willing to help free people to maintain their free institutions against aggressive movements that seek to impose on them totalitarian regimes which undermine the foundations of peace and hence the security of the USA.

(President Truman to US Congress, 12 March 1947)

Now test yourself

Knowledge and understanding

1 Using the text and *extract F*, show how and why Stalin changed the map of Europe after 1945.
2 Why did US and British politicians come to be disappointed by events in Europe after 1945?

Using the sources

1 How do you explain the fact that *extract D* gives a different interpretation of the USSR's policies from *extracts A, E and F*?
2 How useful are *extracts C and G* and *pictures 1 and 2* for historians trying to explain and assess US foreign policy?

THE UNITED NATIONS ORGANIZATION, HUMAN RIGHTS AND REFUGEES

The League of Nations had failed in the 1930s (pages 146–9). Allied leaders made wartime plans for a wider-ranging organization (*extract A*). Its Charter was first discussed in January 1942 and approved in June 1945 (*extract B*). The first meeting of the 51 member nations took place in January 1946.

The United Nations Organization (UNO) has three main bodies:

- **The Security Council** has five permanent members (Britain, France, China, Russia and the USA) and ten members elected by the General Assembly (see below) to serve for two years at a time. The Council can order action against an offending nation, either by placing sanctions on trade with that country or by sending in troops provided by member states under a UN flag. In 1950 troops fought against North Korea after it had invaded South Korea. Since then troops have often been used to try to keep warring parties apart (*picture 1*). Each permanent member can stop Council action by voting against such a proposal to act.

- **The General Assembly** consists of one voting delegate from each of the member states. There are now over 150 member states. The Assembly can make recommendations to the Council.

- **The Secretariat**, under the Secretary-General runs the UN's day-to-day affairs.

1. The British cartoonist, Low, showing President Truman of the USA, leading the UNO into a more active role than the one played by the League of Nations.

2. Refugees in Biafra, part of Nigeria, in 1967.

The General Assembly supervises the work of several important agencies, such as the UN International Children's Emergency Fund (UNICEF). Other agencies are linked to UNO – the World Health Organization (WHO), the Food and Agricultural Organization (FAO) and the International Monetary Fund (IMF). These and other organizations are symbols of politicians' hopes for a more united world.

In 1948 the UN produced its Declaration on Human Rights (*extract C*) which extended the idea of 'rights' into many areas other than political and religious. Some people argue that it is not possible to put the Declaration into practice (*extracts D and E*). However, it remains an ideal at which people can aim.

The United Nations Relief and Rehabilitation Administration (UNRRA) was set up in 1943 to plan help for European refugees made homeless by the war. Since then it has had to cope with the ever-growing flood of refugees, from many countries (*picture 2*), which TV and the press have helped many of us to understand.

EXTRACT A
The original idea, August 1941

The President [Roosevelt] and Prime Minister [Churchill] desire to bring about the fullest collaboration between all nations in the economic field with the object of securing, for all, improved labour standards, economic advancement and social security.

(The Atlantic Charter, August 1941)

EXTRACT B
The UN Charter, June 1945

We, the people of the United Nations, determine to save succeeding generations from the scourge of war, and to reaffirm our faith in fundamental human rights, in the dignity of the human person, in the equal rights of men and women and of nations large and small, and to establish conditions under which justice and respect for obligations can be maintained, and to promote social progress and better standards of living, tolerance and peace, promise to unite our strength to maintain peace and to ensure that armed force shall not be used save in the common interest, and to employ international machinery for the promotion of the economic and social advancement of all peoples …

(Signed 26 June 1945 to come into operation 24 October 1945)

EXTRACT C
The Universal Declaration of Human Rights, 1948

23 (1) Everyone has the right to work, to free choice of employment … favourable conditions of work and protection against unemployment.
(2) Everyone has the right to equal pay for equal work.
(3) Everyone has the right to remuneration ensuring for himself and family an existence worthy of human dignity, supplemented by other social protection.

24 Everyone has the right to leisure and holidays with pay.
25 (1) Everyone has the right to a standard of living adequate for the health of himself and his family … food, clothing, housing and medical care and the right to security in unemployment, sickness, widowhood, old age …
26 (1) Everyone has the right to education … free … compulsory.
(2) Education shall be directed to the full development of the human personality … respect for human rights and freedoms … tolerance among nations, racial or religious groups …

EXTRACT D
The absence of human rights in Latin America

'I was born in a small peasant family. None of us children had any schooling. I lost my job when the land went to raising cattle instead of crops. My wife and I lived in a poor hut, and soon after she died of typhoid – drinking polluted water. There was nothing else to do except emigrate to the big city and hope I could pick up work.'

(Quoted in *Rich World, Poor World*, G. Lean, 1978)

EXTRACT E
The fight for human rights

In Latin America today it is not possible to feed, clothe or house the majority of people. Those who are in power are an economic minority that dominates because it controls those who have political and military power. This minority will not make decisions against its own interest. This is called revolution. If it is necessary, the Christian must be a revolutionary. His priestly love for fellow men may force him to this if he is to be true to God.

(*Revolutionary Priest: Camilo Torres*, J. Gerassi, 1971)

Now test yourself

Knowledge and understanding

1 Explain how the setting up of the United Nations was intended to improve the lives of the people of the world.
2 How is the UN organized and how does the United Nations intervene in a war?

Using the sources

1 Do you agree that the text, *extracts* and *picture 2* show that the United Nations has failed? Why?
2 How reliable are *extracts B and C* and *picture 1* for historians writing about the effect of the United Nations after 1945?
3 How do you explain the differences between the ideals set out in *extracts A–C* and the problems shown in *extracts D and E*?

*B*lack peoples of the Americas (study unit 6)

*T*HE FIRST AFRICAN–AMERICAN LINKS

By the middle of the thirteenth century there were well-defined trade routes from Europe to the East. There was the great 'Silk Road' which ran from Beijing across Central Asia and on through the Black Sea to the Mediterranean. There was a longer sea route which ran through the Mediterranean, the Red Sea and into the Indian Ocean.

Both of these routes centred on Venice which, for a while, was the most important city-state in Europe. Goods came there from India, Persia, Arabia and China before being sent on, overland, throughout Europe. From northern Europe goods came to Venice on packhorse or by ships travelling around the coast of Spain. These goods then left Venice on one or other of the eastern trade routes.

In 1453 the Turks captured Constantinople and closed both the traditional routes. This forced Portuguese and Spanish explorers to look for new ways to get to 'the fabled East' with its silks, jewels, tea, porcelain and, most important of all, the spices from the Spice Islands. In their small ships, the Portugese looked for a route around Africa to the East (page 58). As they explored the western coast of Africa, they set up trading posts. In 1444, from one of these posts, came the first black slave – to become a servant in a Portugese home. By 1500, more than 500 black slaves were being 'imported' each year into Europe to serve in rich people's homes.

1. A painting from 1823 showing a white overseer supervising field slaves cutting sugar cane.

2. The mill, where rollers squeezed the juice out of bundles of sugar cane.

Other explorers looked for a westerly sea route to the East. In 1492 Columbus, an agent for the Spanish crown, found the West Indies and the coast of America. This discovery led to the founding of the Spanish and Portugese empires in the sixteenth century. The British and French did not begin colonizing North America and the West Indies until the seventeenth century, but by 1763 Britain had colonies along the east coast of North America and in Canada (page 57, *picture 6*) and had captured most of the islands in the West Indies.

European emigrants could settle and work in the colonies in Canada and in the northern states of North America. But they found it difficult to work in the tropical climates of the West Indies and the southern colonies of North America. In these colonies, rich noblemen and merchants created large plantations, where they were able to grow sugar (*pictures 1–3* and page 168, *picture 1*), tobacco (page 174, *picture 1*), cotton (page 178, *picture 2*) and rice – provided they had the workers (*extract A*). It was this need for plantation workers which led to the development of both the slave trade and of slavery.

In Britain, the Royal African Company was set up with a royal charter which gave it the monopoly of the slave trade, although others fitted out ships to take part in this savage business (page 170, *picture 3*, and *extracts A and B*). In 1713, the Treaty of Utrecht gave Britain the right to carry slaves into Spanish colonies in South America (page 57, *extract D*), so that British slave traders controlled most of the cruel trade.

3. In the boiling house: the slaves are clearing the scum off the juice, which flows into cooling trays under the windows.

EXTRACT A
Sugar, tobacco, slaves – and Britain's wealth, 1729

Our trade with Africa is very profitable to the nation in general. The supplying of our plantations with Negroes is of extraordinary advantage to us; the planting of sugar and tobacco, and carrying on trade there could not be supported without them. All the great increase of the riches of the kingdom come chiefly from the labour of Negroes in the plantations.

(Joshua Cree, a British merchant, 1729)

EXTRACT B
The hypocrisy of some opponents of slavery, 1690

Slavery is so vile and miserable estate of many, and so directly opposite to the generous nature of our nation, that it is hardly to be considered that an Englishman, much less a gentleman, should argue in its favour.

(*Two Treatises of Government*, John Locke, 1690. Locke was a leading philosopher. He was a shareholder in the Royal African Company which had a monopoly in the African slave trade.)

Now test yourself

Knowledge and understanding

1 Explain why the great 'Silk Road' was important to Europe?
2 How were the westerly sea routes to the East opened up and how did this affect people in Africa and Europe?

Using the sources

1 Read *extracts A and B*. What do these extracts tell us about the arguments made in favour and against the slave trade?
2 Study *pictures 1–3*. How can historians make use of these pictures to write about the conditions in which African slaves lived?
3 Do you agree that the *extracts* and *pictures* are completely reliable? Give reasons for your answer.

THE TRIANGULAR TRADE

The 'Negro trade' (*extract A*), which involved the buying, carrying and selling of millions of Africans (pages 170–71), was 'the Middle Passage' of the so-called 'triangle of trade' (page 56, *picture 4*):

- On side 1 of the triangle, ships left Bristol, Liverpool, London and other ports, carrying cotton and metal goods made in Britain (*extract D*). In West Africa, these goods were exchanged for slaves (pages 170–71).
- On side 2 the slaves were carried to the colonies to be sold (pages 170–71).
- On side 3 the ships carried sugar and rum, tobacco and raw cotton, timber and other goods for sale in Britain and Europe.

Many people benefited from this 'triangular' trade:

- Shipyard owners and workers were paid to build ships to carry the slaves.
- Industrialists and workers gained from the production of the goods carried to Africa: over £200,000 of goods were exported each year. They also benefited from the expansion of markets in the West Indies and America. In 1770 one-third of Britain's cotton goods went to Africa to be exchanged for slaves, while one-half went to the colonies to provide clothing for the slaves.

1. The Olivier sugar plantation in Lousiana, painted in 1861

- Slave-ship owners made vast profits from the sale of slaves. Many ships carried over 700 slaves per trip and made the owner over £5000 a voyage.
- Owners of plantations (*picture 1*) profited from the sale of their produce.
- British consumers and workers gained from the growing use of sugar and coffee: in 1753 there were 120 sugar refineries in England.
- British exporters and consumers gained from the availability of cheap cotton goods, made from slave-grown cotton (page 178, *picture 2*).
- Industry as a whole gained from the investment of slave-based profits in many new and growing industries in the eighteenth century.
- Some towns benefited more than others. Bristol (*extract B*; page 57, *picture 5*) and Liverpool (*extracts C and D* and page 61, *extract A*) owed their wealth to the slave trade. London, too, saw the building of many new and large docks specifically built to cater for the colonial trade: West India Docks (1802), London Docks (1805), East India Dock (1806).

EXTRACT A
The slave trade and Britain's wealth, 1746

The extensive employment of our shipping to and from America, and the daily bread of most of our British employers and workers, are owing mainly to the work of Negroes. The Negro trade is the main source of wealth and naval power for Britain.

(*The National and Personal Advantages of the African trade*, Malachy Postlethwayt, economic writer (1707–67), 1746)

EXTRACT B
The slave trade and Bristol's prosperity (page 57, *picture 5*)

There is not a brick in Bristol that was not cemented with the blood of a slave. Sumptuous mansions and luxurious living was made from the sufferings of the slaves bought and sold by Bristol merchants.

(*Bristol Past and Present*, J.F. Nicholls (1818–83), 1881)

EXTRACT C
Liverpool's middle classes and the slave trade (page 61, extract A)

It is well known that many of the small vessels that carry about 100 slaves are paid for by lawyers, drapers, ropers, grocers, barbers and tailors.

(*A General and Descriptive History of Liverpool*, J. Wallace, 1795)

EXTRACT D
A Liberal historian's view of Liverpool and slavery, 1907

The slave trade helped every industry, provided the money for docks, enriched and employed the mills of Lancashire. Beyond a doubt it was the slave trade which raised Liverpool from a struggling port to be one of the richest and most prosperous trading centres in the world.

(*A History of Liverpool*, J. Ramsay Muir (1872–1941), 1907)

EXTRACT E
Did the slave trade benefit the slaves?

In the long run, the triangular trade operation, based on Liverpool, was to bring benefits to all, not least to the transplanted slaves, whose descendants have, subsequently achieved in the New World, standards of education and civilization far ahead of their countrymen whom they left behind.

(*A History of Liverpool over 750 years*, a Liverpool Corporation handbook, 1957)

Now test yourself

Knowledge and understanding

1 Explain how (a) slaves were obtained from Africa; (b) why they were valuable commodities of trade.
2 List and explain in order of their importance the effects of the slave trade on British industry and towns.

Using the sources

1 Read *extracts A–D*. How can each of these extracts be used to explain why the slave trade was such an important aspect of British life?
2 Look at *picture 1*. Do you agree that this source is helpful for historians writing about life on slave plantations? Explain your answer fully.

THE SLAVE TRADE

The slaves in the Americas came from West Africa. Many had been captured in wars between African tribes, with the conqueror selling the prisoners to white traders (*picture 1* and *extract A*). Others were captured by gangs employed by slave traders. Before being packed into the slave ship, the 'prisoners' were branded on the chest with a hot iron, so that each trader would know which were his cargo (*picture 2*).

On ship, the slaves were kept in chains below decks (*picture 3*) in cramped and filthy conditions (*extract B*) for the 100-day journey to the West Indies or the Americas. Many died on the way and, as we shall see on pages 174–5, many were simply thrown overboard while still alive so that slave traders could claim for their loss through insurance policies. It is not surprising that there were many examples of slaves rising up against their treatment.

1. The King of Dahomey arranging a sale of slaves to Europeans, 1793.

Early wood block showing slave branding

2. A slave being branded.

The journey to the Americas was the second leg of the triangular trade (pages 168–9) so that it became known as 'the Middle Passage' (page 56, *picture 4*). Slaves who survived that 'Passage' were sold at the slave markets which operated in the ports of the West Indies and the Americas. People who wished to buy slaves – to work in plantations or as domestic servants – were told of the auction by notices in newspapers and by handbills (*picture 4*). At a slave auction, the bewildered Africans were bought and sold (*picture 5*) just as, in a modern market, people buy and sell cattle or sheep.

3. An 18th-century illustration of slaves being packed below decks for the Atlantic crossing.

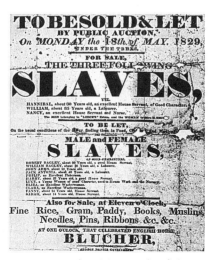

4. A poster advertising a sale of slaves alongside household goods.

5. Slaves were white people's property, traded in open market and families split up to suit the buyers.

EXTRACT A
Collecting slaves on the west coast of Africa, 1791

The general way was that when a ship comes on the coast they send for the traders and make them presents, to encourage them to bring people to sell as slaves. The Black Kings have told me that they were going to war to get slaves. I have seen prisoners brought in, men, women and children, and delivered to the white traders, or else driven down in gangs of two or three hundred to the water side for auction to the best bidder.

(James Towne of *HMS Syren* to Committee on Slave Trade, 1791)

EXTRACT B
Slaves suffer on the Middle Passage

She had taken in 336 males and 226 females on the coast of Africa. After she had been out seventeen days she had thrown overboard 55. The slaves were enclosed under grated hatches between decks. The space was so low that they sat between each other's legs, and they were so close together that they could not lie down or change positions day or night. Over the hatchway stood the slave-driver armed with a scourge of twisted thongs. Whenever he heard the slightest sound below he shook it over them and seemed eager to use it. But the thing that struck us most forcibly was how was it possible for such a number of people to live, packed as tight as they could cram in low cells, three feet high, without light or air with the thermometer in the shade on deck at 89 degrees.

(Evidence to the Committee on Slave Trade, 1791)

Now test yourself

Knowledge and understanding

1 Describe as fully as you can what American slaves experienced (a) on capture; (b) on their journeys in the slave ships; (c) when they arrived in America.
2 Explain the meaning of the phrase, the 'Middle Passage'.

Using the sources

1 Read *extracts A and B*. Are they reliable and useful sources for historians writing about the conditions that slaves suffered on the Middle Passage? Explain your answer fully.
2 Study *pictures 1–5*. Do you agree that historians of the slave trade will find that these sources are equally useful and reliable? Why?

EUROPEANS AND SLAVERY, 1600–1800

Almost as soon as slavery became widespread in Spanish America, the Spanish government passed laws to make slavery 'more lenient': married slaves could not be sold separately – when a slave wanted to marry, his master had either to buy his future wife or sell him to the girl's owner; slaves could buy their freedom at a government-fixed price; slaves had to have plots of land on which to grow crops or rear chickens; they had to have 134 'free days' a year to work their plots.

There were no such laws in the British colonies in the West Indies and the Americas. By 1680 about 600 slaves were being brought in each year and by 1780 over 200,000 slaves were being carried every year in Liverpool-owned ships alone. By 1790 one-third of the population of the southern states of the USA were slaves.

In the West Indies the main crop was sugar (*extracts A–C*, page 168, *picture 1* and pages 166–7, *pictures 1–3*). In the US slave states, a major crop was tobacco (page 174, *picture 1*). On tobacco plantations slaves lived in one-roomed cabins of brick or wood. They worked sixteen hours a day and for six days a week. Once a week they were given four pounds of pork and some corn, but they could rear chickens and grow vegetables on land near their huts.

1. Treadmills like this were introduced to the West Indies as an 'improved' form of punishment.

By 1790, many whites were uncertain about slavery. Was it economic (*extract D*)? Was the cruelty of overseers and masters (*picture 1*) justified? In 1774 the white colonists, in their anti-British campaign (pages 58–9), voted to stop importing slaves. When Jefferson, a slave owner, wrote the Declaration of Independence (*extract F*) he wanted to include a clause to abolish slavery, but his colleagues took it out (*extract G*).

American doubts about slavery were changed by the growth of the cotton trade. Until 1790, most of the cotton used in British factories had come from the West Indies, and in that year, the USA exported only 4000 bales of cotton. In 1793, Eli Whitney invented a machine (the gin) which quickly separated the black seeds from the raw cotton. This revolutionized the US cotton-growing industry. By 1860 the USA exported 4 million bales and, as the number and size of cotton plantations grew, so did the demand for slaves. In 1808, following the British example, the USA abolished the slave trade, so that no fresh Africans would be shipped to America to be bought and sold. However, this led to the growth of slave breeding in the southern states where, by 1861, there were four million slaves, most of them US-born.

EXTRACT A
Slave gangs on a sugar plantation, 1807 (page 168, picture 1)

The slaves are divided into three gangs. The first, consisting of the most healthy and strong, clear and plant the ground; during crop time, they cut the canes, feed the mills and attend to the manufacture of the sugar. The second gang – young boys and girls and pregnant women, weed the canes and do other light work. The third gang – young children guarded by an old woman, collect food for the pigs and sheep and weed the garden.

(*Plantation Work*, 1807; see also pages 166–7, *pictures 1–3*)

EXTRACT B
The slave's day, 1807

5.30 a.m. To the fields carrying breakfast with them; register called; work until 8.00.
8.00 a.m. Breakfast of boiled yam, edoes, okra. Latecomers are whipped.
8.30 a.m.–12.00 noon Work.
12.00–2.00 p.m. Dinner of salted meat or pickled fish. Rest.
2.00–6.00 p.m. Work.
6.00 p.m. Return to huts.

(*Plantation Work*, 1807)

EXTRACT C
Punishing slaves, 18th-century Jamaica (*picture 1*)

For rebellions, burn them by nailing them to the ground with crooked sticks on every limb, and then apply the fire by degrees from the feet and hands, burning them gradually up to the head, whereby their pains are great.

For lesser crimes, castrate them or chop off half of the foot with an axe.

For running away, put iron rings of great weight on their ankles, or put pot hooks about their necks which are iron rings with two long hooks riveted to them; or put a spur in the mouth.

For negligence, let the overseers whip them with laice-wood switches, after they have been tied up.

EXTRACT D
Slavery is uneconomic, 1776

Experience shows that the work done by slaves, though it seems to cost only their keep, is in the end the dearest of any. A person who can acquire no property can have no other interest other than to eat as much and work as little as possible. Work can be squeezed out of him by violence only.

(*The Wealth of Nations*, Adam Smith, 1776)

EXTRACT E
Virginian rebels stop importing slaves – to hurt British trade

During our present difficulties no slaves ought to be imported, nor wines or British manufactures. We take this opportunity of declaring our sincere wishes to see an end forever to the wicked, cruel and unnatural slave trade.

(Fairfax Resolutions, 1774, signed by Washington, Jefferson and 86 other members of the Virginia House of Burgesses)

EXTRACT F
'All men are equal', but some are more equal than others, July 1776

We hold these truths to be sacred and undeniable; that all men are created equal and independent, that from that equal creation they derive rights inherent and inalienable, among which are the preservation of life, and liberty and the pursuit of happiness.

(Jefferson's first version of the American Declaration of Independence, July 1776)

EXTRACT G
Dr Johnson (1709–84) attacks Jefferson's hypocrisy, 1776

How is it that we hear the loudest yelps for liberty among the drivers of negroes?

(Quoted in *William Wilberforce*, R. Furneaux, 1974)

Now test yourself

Knowledge and understanding

1 How did the treatment of African slaves by the Europeans vary between 1600 and 1800? In your answer refer to (a) Spanish America; (b) the West Indies; (c) the USA.
2 List and explain the reasons why Jefferson failed to abolish slavery in the USA.

Using the sources

1 Look at *extracts A–F* and *picture 1*. (a) How could opponents of slavery use the information in these sources to support their point of view? (b) How reliable are these sources? Explain your answer.
2 Read *extract G*. On what grounds is the writer attacking Jefferson?

A BOLISHING THE SLAVE TRADE

A legal decision of 1729 showed that a slave was 'his master's property' (*extract A*). This decision was challenged in 1765–7 by Granville Sharp (1735–1813), a leading Evangelical (page 130). In 1765 he met a former slave, Jonathan Strong, who had been beaten by his master and become a runaway. Sharp nursed him and found him work. In 1767 Strong's master saw him, had him captured, and put on board ship for Barbados. Sharp took the case to court where the Lord Mayor of London ruled that Strong should be freed. In 1771–2 Sharp helped James Somerset, another runaway slave who had been recaptured and was due to be returned to Jamaica. This case was important because it involved the Lord Chief Justice's decision (*extract B*).

Sharp was also involved in the notorious case of the slave ship *Zong* which had left Africa in 1781 with 440 slaves. During the journey many died, and 133 sick slaves were thrown overboard. The owners of the *Zong* claimed the insurance money for 'lost cargo'. Sharp helped the insurance company in its refusal to pay, and in the ensuing court case. However, in this case the Lord Chief Justice ruled in 1783 that the owners had the right to do what they wanted with their 'property. It was just as if horses had been thrown out'. The publicity surrounding the case united all the opponents of slavery.

In 1784, a group of Quakers formed an Abolition Committee which gained an important recruit in Thomas Clarkson (*extract C*), another leading Evangelical as well as a well-known speaker and author. In 1787 Clarkson and some Quakers persuaded an Evangelical MP, William Wilberforce, to act as the Parliamentary spokesman for the Abolition Committee (*extract D*). The Committee produced evidence about the cruelties involved in the slave trade (*picture 2*, pages 170–71, *picture 3* and *extract B*). Wilberforce brought several Bills for Abolition before Parliament from 1789 onwards. It was not until 1807 that Parliament finally agreed to abolish the slave trade throughout the empire.

1. Slaves preparing tobacco leaves for curing. All the work needed was done on the plantation which was almost an industrial estate.

The USA followed Britain's example in 1808, although the demand for US cotton (page 178, *picture 1*) led to slave breeding there. In 1815, the statesmen at the Congress of Vienna outlawed the slave trade, but many nations ignored this decision. Brazil abolished the trade only in 1850, while some Arab states have never outlawed it. There, as in 19th-century Britain and America, too many powerful

2. The slave ships stacked their cargo between decks; each slave had a space about 1.5 metres by 0.6 metre, was taken out once a day for exercise and fed twice. This model was made by Wilberforce in an attempt to force MPs to realize the truth.

people (politicians, landowners, merchants) benefit from slavery and the slave trade. It will need strong-minded individuals to start and lead anti-slave movements before the slave trade and slavery are finally abolished.

EXTRACT A
Slaves are masters' property, 1729

We are of the opinion that a slave by coming from the West Indies to Great Britain, either with or without his master, does not become free, and that his master's property in him is not in any way changed. And Baptism does not give him freedom or make any alteration in his condition. We are also of the opinion that his master may legally compel him to return again to the plantations.

(Decision by Yorke and Talbot, Crown law officers, 14 January 1729)

EXTRACT B
Lord Chief Justice Mansfield and the Somerset case, 1771–2

In 1769 the slave, James Somerset, came from Virginia to London with his master. He escaped but was recaptured and put on a ship for Jamaica. Some sympathizers stopped the ship from sailing and brought the case before the courts. Lord Mansfield had already said that 'I hope the issue of whether slavery can exist in England will never be finally settled'. He agreed that Somerset's master 'owned' him according to the Law of Virginia in America. He asked Parliament to make such laws for England. Parliament refused. So, against his real wishes, he ruled that 'the power claimed by Somerset's owners was never in use in England, or acknowledged by our law. The claim of slavery can never be supported.'

(*William Wilberforce*, R. Furneaux, 1974)

EXTRACT C
How Clarkson became an opponent of slavery, 1785

I won the University prize for my essay on 'Is it right to make men slaves against their will?' As I rode back from Cambridge to London I thought about what I had written. I stopped my horse from time to time, got down and walked. I tried to persuade myself that what I had written could not be true. The more, however, I thought of the authorities on whose work I had relied, the more I saw how right they were. Coming in sight of Wade's Mill in Hertfordshire, I sat down, saddened, by the roadside and held my horse. The thought came to me that, if the contents of the essay were true, it was time that some person should see these calamities to their end.

(*The History of … Abolition*, Thomas Clarkson, 1808)

EXTRACT D
Wilberforce's decision to act for the Abolitionists, 1787

When I had got so much information about the Slave Trade, I talked it over with Pitt. He advised me to undertake the campaign, as a subject suited to my character and talents. At length, I well remember, after a conversation in the open at the root of an old tree at Holwood, just above the steep descent into the vale of Keston, I resolved to bring the subject forward in the Commons.

(Quoted in a biography of Wilberforce by his sons, 1838)

Now test yourself

Knowledge and understanding

1 How did opposition to the slave trade grow in Britain as a result of campaigns by (a) Granville Sharp; (b) the Quakers; (c) William Wilberforce?
2 List and explain the reasons why the abolition of slavery took a long time.

Using the sources

1 Do you agree that *extract D* and the text show that Wilberforce was the most important person in the movement to abolish slavery? Explain your answer.
2 Do you agree that *pictures 1 and 2* are completely reliable as evidence for the history of slaves and their owners in the USA? Explain your answer.

BRITAIN ABOLISHES SLAVERY, 1833–4

Once the slave trade was abolished, Abolitionists campaigned for the abolition of slavery itself. Huge meetings were held (*picture 1*), pamphlets written, and petitions presented to Parliament, where, after Wilberforce became ill in 1824, the Abolitionist case was led by Thomas Fowell Buxton.

Governments passed laws to make slaves' lives less brutal, but these were rarely observed in the West Indies, where slave owners influenced governors. Between 1807 and 1830, the Abolitionists had little success:

- Politicians argued that they didn't understand the issue (*extract A*).
- Opponents offered a religious solution to slaves' problems (*extract B*).
- Most people thought that Britain should face its problems at home sooner than the problem of black slaves in 'some faraway country'.
- Many MPs, including Gladstone (*extracts B and C*), knew that their families' wealth had been made in slave trading and the sugar trade (page 169, *extracts A–E*).

In the end it was economics which decided the issue:

- Cuba and Brazil began to produce cheaper sugar, so that West Indian plantations were forced to shut down.
- Following the successful revolt by slaves on the French island of St Dominique and the island's winning of its independence (1804), West Indian slaves became restless. In 1831 Jamaican slaves rose in revolt and 100 were shot and 300 hanged once the rebellion was put down.

Although the rebellion had failed, Parliament decided to abolish slavery in the British empire so as to avoid further uprisings. The Bill passed through Parliament for its final reading while Wilberforce was on his death bed.

The main terms of the Act, which became law on 1 August 1834, were:

- All slaves under the age of six years were to be freed immediately
- Other slaves were to be 'part slave' and 'part free' for four more years. In that time they had to be paid a wage for work done in the one-quarter of the week when they were 'free'.
- Slave owners were to receive about £37.50 for each slave they 'lost'.

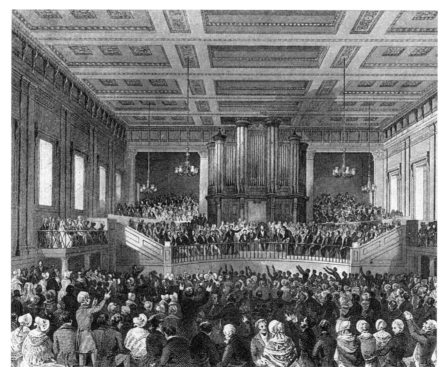

The freed slaves refused to work for the low wages which owners offered so that the sugar trade declined more rapidly. This confirmed the worst fears of opponents of Abolition (*extract D*) and the slave owners of the USA who had followed the work of the Abolitionists (*picture 2*) and who feared that their cotton, sugar and tobacco industries might be ruined if ever their slaves were freed.

1. An anti-slavery meeting.

EXTRACT A
Abolitionists don't understand the problem?

There can be no doubt that a great many of the Abolitionists are actuated by very pure motives; they have been shocked at the cruelties … practised towards slaves, … and they have an invincible conviction that slavery under any form is repugnant to the spirit of the English Constitution and the Christian religion, and that it is a stain upon the national character which ought to be wiped away. These people, generally speaking, are very ignorant concerning all the various difficulties which beset the questions.

(*Charles Greville (1794–1865)*, clerk to the Privy Council (1821–59), *Memoirs*, 1852)

EXTRACT B
A slave trader's Tory son wants religion for the slaves

I come to Slavery. I desire to see an universal and efficient system of Christian instruction, not meant to hinder the work of individual piety now working for the religious improvement of the negroes, but to do thoroughly what such voluntary work can only do partially.

(*W.E. Gladstone in his election address to the voters of Newark, 1832*)

EXTRACT C
Gladstone's opposition to abolition of slavery, 1832

As regards immediate emancipation, whether with or without compensation, there are several minor reasons against it; but that which weighs with me is that it would, I … fear, exchange the evils now affecting the negro for others which are weightier – for a relapse into deeper abasement … for bloodshed and internal war. Let fitness be made a condition for emancipation; let him enjoy the means of earning his freedom through … industrious

habits; and thus, without risk of blood, without violation of property, … and with the utmost speed which prudence will admit, we shall arrive at that exceedingly desirable consummation, the utter extinction of slavery.

(Gladstone, Newark, 1832)

EXTRACT D
British fears of emancipation of slaves

Talking over the matter the other day, Henry Taylor (of the Colonial Office) said that he was well aware of the consequences of emancipation both to the negroes and the planters. The estates of the latter would not be cultivated; it would be impossible, for want of labour; the negroes would not work – no inducement would be sufficient to make them; they wanted to be free merely that they might be idle. They would, on being emancipated possess themselves of ground, the fertility of which in those regions is so great that very trifling labour will be sufficient to provide them with the means of existence, and they will thus relapse rapidly into a state of barbarism; they will resume the habits of their African brethren, but, he thinks, without the ferocity and savageness which distinguish the latter.

(*The Greville Memoirs*, 1852)

2. Josiah Wedgwood, the owner of Britain's most famous potteries, made thousands of plaques like this. He even sent a shipload to the USA. The caption reads: 'Am I not a man and a brother?'

Now test yourself

Knowledge and understanding

1 Explain fully why the Abolitionists found it difficult to persuade Parliament to outlaw slavery in the British empire.
2 Do you think the success of the Abolitionists was due more to their own campaigns *or* the resistance of the slaves? Explain your answer.

Using the sources

1 Read *extracts A–D*. (a) Are they equally useful for historians writing about why many British people opposed abolition of slavery? (b) Do you agree that the statements made in the extracts are reliable? Explain your answers.
2 (a) How do the *extracts* in this topic contrast with *extracts D and F* on page 173?
(b) How do you explain such contrasting views?

THE UNITED STATES – SLAVE OR FREE?

In 1763 two English surveyors, Mason and Dixon, settled a dispute between Maryland and Pennsylvania by fixing the border along the 39° 40' lateral parallel. When extended later, this became the line between the 'slave' states of the south and the 'free' states of the north where slavery had been abolished.

As the USA expanded, Congress created new states in pairs – a 'free' one north of the River Ohio and a 'slave' one in the south. This maintained the 'balance of power' in the US Senate, the more important part of Congress. In 1819 the territory of Missouri asked to be admitted to the Union as a slave state, although it ran both north and south of the Ohio. This led to the 'Missouri Compromise' which:

- allowed Missouri to be a 'slave' state, while a new 'free' state was created in Maine
- fixed the parallel 36° 30' as the new boundary between 'free' and 'slave' (*picture 1*).

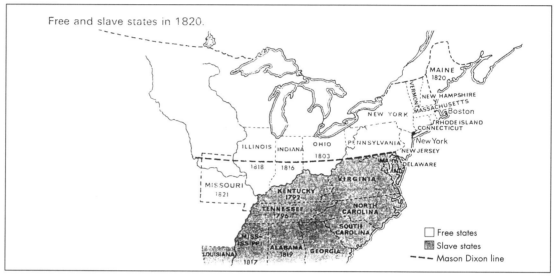

1. Free and slave states in 1820.

In 1854 the 'boundary' was once again threatened when a new state, Kansas – north of the line – asked to be allowed to vote on whether it should be 'free' or 'slave'. Supporters and opponents of slavery packed the new state with followers who fought pitched battles in a local civil war. In the end, Kansas joined the Union only in 1861.

The abolition campaign got under way in 1831 when W.L. Garrison of Boston founded a newspaper, *The Liberator*, in which he claimed that slavery was cruel (*extract A*) and contrary to the Declaration of Independence (page 173, *extract F*).

2. A white 'overseer' and black cottonfield workers.

Slave owners, for their part, argued that northerners did not understand how well they treated slaves (*extract B*) and how essential slaves were to the future of the tobacco, sugar and cotton plantations (*picture 2*).

Southerners feared a slave rebellion, like the one led by Nat Turner in 1831 when 55 whites were slaughtered. They welcomed legal and army support against runaway slaves. In 1857 a slave, Dred Scott, who lived in the 'free' state of Illinois, claimed that he was 'free'.

The Supreme Court decided he was 'his master's property' and that 'no law can take away the master's right to that property'.

Abolitionists feared that Congress would never abolish slavery while the Scott decision implied that slavery might extend to the north. In 1859 a northerner John Brown, who was a fanatical opponent of slavery, attacked a government arms depot, to get arms for a slave rebellion. He was caught (*picture 3*) and hanged. But southerners feared that others might do the same. It was at this critical time that Lincoln became President (page 180).

Many Southerners feared that Abraham Lincoln would be sympathetic to the people who wanted to abolish slavery. This encouraged some southern states to think about breaking away from the northern states.

3. A more fanatical opponent of slavery was John Brown. In October 1859 he attacked the federal armoury and arsenal at Harpers Ferry, Virginia, aiming then to move south stirring up the slave insurrection. But his expedition was quickly overpowered and Brown was sentenced to death.

EXTRACT A
Breaking in slaves, c.1840

'Mr Covey had a high reputation for breaking young slaves, and this was of great value to him. It enabled him to get his farm tilled with much less expense than he would have had without that reputation. I had been at the farm for about a week before he gave me a severe whipping, cutting my back, causing the blood to run. I lived with him for a year. During the first six months hardly a week passed without his whipping me.'

(Quoted in J.M. Chandler, America, 1965)

EXTRACT B
Thomas Dabney, a liberal slave owner

His negroes raised chickens by the hundred. One of them, old Uncle Isaac, reckoned he raised five hundred a year unless the season was bad. His boast was that he was the same age as the master. He would draw himself up as he said; 'I called marster "brother" till I was a right big boy, and I called his mother "Ma" till I was old enough to know better and to stop it myself. She never told me to stop.' Dabney's thrifty negroes made so much on their chickens, peanuts, popcorn, baskets, mats and in other ways that they were able to buy silk dresses and luxuries. Their cabins were clean and orderly, their beds had bright quilts and often the pillows were snowy enough to tempt any head.

(J.M. Chandler, America, 1965)

Now test yourself

Knowledge and understanding

1 Explain (a) why most white southerners opposed Garrison's ideas about slavery; (b) why Garrison opposed slavery.
2 Make two lists showing (a) the extension of slavery after 1819; (b) how slavery was attacked after 1819.

Using the sources

1 Read *extracts A and B*. Do you agree that these extracts are useful because they offer differing accounts of the conditions of slavery in the USA? Explain your answer.
2 Study *pictures 1–3*. Are they equally useful for historians writing about the effects of slavery in the USA? Explain your answer.

THE END OF AMERICAN SLAVERY, 1863

Abraham Lincoln was elected President in November 1860, although he did not take office until March 1861. He was not an Abolitionist (*extracts A and B*), although he hoped that slavery would die out (*extract A*). Prior to the 1860 Congress Election, the Democrats controlled Congress and would have defeated his attempts to abolish slavery.

However, some southern states, ignoring Lincoln's belief in states' rights (*extract B*), decided to break up the Union, which Lincoln could not accept (*extracts C and D*).

South Carolina was the first to declare the Union 'dissolved'. In February 1861 it was joined by six other southern states to form the Confederate States of America. They elected Jefferson Davis as their President. In April–May 1861 five more southern states joined the anti-Union and anti-Lincoln Confederacy (*picture 1*). Clearly, slavery was the main issue dividing north and south. However, there was more to the division than this important issue:

- The South was mainly agricultural, dominated by very wealthy landowners, where whites lived an easy-going life. It had once been the more important part of the Union, providing five of the first seven Presidents.
- The North was mainly industrial, dominated by merchants and businessmen, who had become very wealthy. The recent and rapid growth of industry meant that the North had become the more important part of the Union. Southerners resented this (*extract E*).

The Civil War began in April 1861 when the Confederates demanded the surrender of the port of Charleston (South Carolina) with its Federal troops. The officers in charge refused to surrender until bombardment forced them to do so. Confederate troops had fired on the Union flag: the war had begun. It was the first 'modern' war with powerful rifles and heavy artillery taking many lives and damaging property (*extract G*). The Confederates had the best generals and more experienced soldiers. But the North had the industry to produce new weapons and a larger population from which to recruit armies. However, it was not until the end of 1862 that the North won its first major victory which allowed Lincoln to abolish slavery (*extract F*). It was another two years before the South finally surrendered (9 April 1865) when Lincoln expressed his hopes for a peaceful and united country (*extract H*). His murder on 14 April 1865 killed any such hopes (pages 182–3).

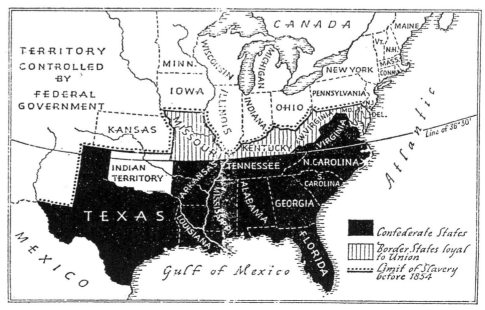

1. The Civil War.

EXTRACT A
Lincoln on 'a house divided', 1858

A house divided against itself cannot stand. I believe this government cannot endure permanently half-slave and half-free. I do not expect the Union to be dissolved; I do not expect the house to fall; but I do expect it to cease to be divided. It will become all one thing or all the other.

(Part of the Lincoln–Douglas debates, 16 June 1858)

EXTRACT B
Lincoln in favour of states' rights, November 1860

We must not interfere with the institution of slavery in the States where it exists, because the Constitution forbids it, and the general welfare does not require us to do so.

(Statement made when elected, November 1860)

EXTRACT C
The Union is more important than slavery: Lincoln, 1862

I would save the Union. If I could save it without freeing any slave, I would do it; and if I could save it by freeing all the slaves, I would do it; and if I could do it by freeing some and leaving others alone, I would also do that.

(Letter to Horace Greeley of the *New York Tribune*, 22 August 1862)

EXTRACT D
Lincoln defends the Union, March 1861

No state upon its own simple motion can lawfully get out of the Union. I therefore consider that, in view of the Constitution and the laws, the Union is unbroken [in spite of what seven States had decided].

(First Presidential address, 1861)

EXTRACT E
What was at stake in the Civil War? A southern view

It is not humanity that influences you. It is that you may have an opportunity of cheating us that you want to limit slave territory within certain bounds. It is that you may have a majority in the Congress and convert the government into an engine of northern aggrandisement. It is that your section may grow in power and prosperity upon wealth taken from the South, like the vampire gorged and bloated with the blood which it has sucked from its victim.

(Jefferson Davis, President of the Confederacy, 1861–5)

EXTRACT F
The Emancipation Proclamation, 1 January 1863

All persons held as slaves within any State, or part of a State, the people of which shall be in rebellion against the United States, shall be then, and forever, free.

EXTRACT G
The destruction made 'while we were marching through Georgia'

There was hardly a fence left standing; fields were trampled down and the roads lined with carcasses of horses, hogs and cattle deliberately killed to starve the people and prevent them making their crops. The houses that were standing all showed signs of pillage and everywhere the charred remains of ginhouses. Hayricks and fodder stacks were demolished, corncribs empty, and every bale of cotton burst. I saw no grain and there was not even a chicken left in the country.

(Eliza Andrews, an inhabitant of Georgia, 1864)

EXTRACT H
Lincoln's hopes for the future, 4 March 1865

With malice towards none, with charity for all, with firmness in the right as God gives us to see the right, let us strive on to finish the work we are in; to bind up the nation's wounds – to do all which may achieve a just and lasting peace among ourselves.

(Second inaugural address)

Now test yourself

Knowledge and understanding

1 Explain how the American Civil War was brought about by (a) the row over slavery; (b) the differences between North and South; (c) the quarrel at Charleston.
2 List and explain (a) the causes of the northern states' victory; (b) the effects of this victory on slavery.

Using the sources

1 Read *extracts A–D and H*. What do they tell you about Lincoln's beliefs about the USA and slavery?
2 *Study picture 1* and *extracts F and G*. Are these sources equally useful and reliable for historians writing about the effects of the Civil War on the USA? Explain your answer.

F REE – BUT UNEQUAL

Lincoln's successor, former Vice President Andrew Johnson, was too weak to control the ruthless extremists and self-seeking northern politicians. They wanted to humiliate white southerners who had previously controlled the US political system. They were responsible for:

- the reconstruction Act, 1867, which suspended the constitutions of the rebel states and placed them under the rule of five northern generals
- the Fourteenth Amendment to the US Constitution, 1868, which took away the right of former rebels to be elected to the USA Congress
- the Fifteenth Amendment, 1870, which gave the vote to black people, many of whom could neither read or write (*picture 1* and page 184, *picture 1*).

1. Blacks and whites were to enjoy political equality.

The southern states were now ruled by a Radical coalition of blacks, 'carpetbaggers', and 'scalawags'. Many former slaves were elected to serve in states' Assemblies and were appointed to various official posts. The 'carpetbaggers' were former Union soldiers, northern businessmen and government agents who came to the South bringing their goods in holdalls made of carpetlike material. Some of these men were honestly seeking to run profitable businesses. Southern whites paid more attention to them, many of whom were as corrupt as were the businessmen and politicians who governed northern states and cities.

President Johnson tried to stop Congress from passing the 1867 Act and the Fourteenth Amendment. But too many northerners wanted even stronger anti-southern laws: indeed, Johnson was brought to trial before Congress accused of 'high crimes and misdemeanours' – and was only just found innocent.

In 1868 former Union General Grant was elected President. He had called for more revenge on the South in a campaign in which he 'waved the bloody shirt of war'. In that year many blacks were elected to represent southern states in Congress and to sit in states' Assemblies. It is not surprising that southern whites mocked a system in which, in South Carolina, only 22 of the 155 members of the Assembly could read or write, while none of the state's judges could do either.

In March 1865, while the southern states were still goverened by their pre-war 'whites only' governments, the federal government set up the Freedmen's Bureau, which:

- provided aid (including food) to the many white and blacks who otherwise would have starved
- set up over 100 hospitals
- started over 4000 schools to educate black children (page 184, *picture 1*).

The bureau was hated by southern whites (*extract A*) who saw that Republican 'schoolmarms and do-gooders' only encouraged black hatred for whites. Even Grant, a Republican, thought that most Bureau officers were 'a useless and dangerous group'. White anger at the northern treatment of southern whites and blacks led to the formation of the Ku

2. The Ku Klux Klan used racial hatred as a political weapon.

3. Whites regained control of the southern political system often by force or the threat of force.

Klux Klan which terrorized, whipped, shot and lynched blacks. The federal government could not protect every black person, and in any case, northern opinion of the South had changed, so that the government had to agree that mistakes had been made after 1867.

In 1877 the last of the 'army of occupation' left and whites were now free to take control of the political system. Votes were given only to those with certain 'qualifications': few, if any, blacks 'qualified'. They also used force to keep blacks from voting (*picture 3*). The result was that, in Louisiana for example, between 1896 and 1904 about 129,000 blacks out of 130,000 lost the right to vote. The southern white Democrats were back in control.

EXTRACT A
Hatred of the North

Oh, I'm a good old rebel! Now that's just what I am;
For this 'Fair Land of Freedom' I do not give a damn;
I'm glad I fought against it. I only wish we'd won,
And I don't want no pardon, For anything I've done.

I hate the Constitution, This great Republic, too.
I hate the Freedmen's Bureau, In uniforms of blue;

I hate the nasty eagle, With all his brag and fuss.
The lying, thieving Yankees, I hate them wuss and wuss.

I can't take up any musket And fight them now no more,
But I ain't going to love 'em, Now that is cartain sure;
And I don't want no pardon, For what I was and am;
I won't be reconstructed, And I don't give a damn.

('I'm a good old rebel')

Now test yourself

Knowledge and understanding

1 List and explain in order of their importance the reasons why the southern whites felt humiliated after the end of the Civil War.
2 Show why and how the southern whites gained their revenge through (a) the Ku Klux Klan; (b) new laws after 1877.

Using the sources

1 Read *extract A*. Is this a useful source for historians wishing to explain how southern whites felt about the 'Yankee' North? Why?
2 Look at *pictures 1–3*. How well does *picture 1* explain what is being shown in *pictures 2 and 3*? Explain your answer.

THE NATURE OF FREEDOM, 1880–1935

The Emancipation Act had abolished slavery. The Fifteenth Amendment gave black people political equality with whites – although the vast majority of southern blacks lost the right to vote soon after 1877 (page 183). However, neither the Emancipation Act, nor the Fifteenth Amendment did anything for the economic or social inequalities facing the freed slaves (*extract A*).

1. School teachers came from the North ('Yankee schoolmarms') once it was legal for blacks to learn to read and write.

There were about 10 million former slaves in the southern states in 1870. Many had been, and remained, servants in rich whites' homes. The majority had worked, as slaves, in cotton plantations (page 178, *picture 2*), most of which had been devastated by the Civil War so that there was little employment opportunity there after 1865. A minority of blacks became sharecroppers, giving a large part of their produce for the rent of a plot of land owned by a white landlord. Some hoped to improve their lives by moving to the 'freer' North. Here, however, they found that they could afford only the worst and overcrowded housing (*picture 2*) and being unskilled, they could only do the lowest paid jobs – if they were lucky.

In the South, all the white governments followed the example of South Carolina, which was the first to bring in 'Jim Crow' laws. These denied blacks equal rights almost everywhere – black people were not allowed to eat in 'whites only' hotels or restaurants; they could not sit in 'whites only' seats on buses and trains; their children were denied entry to 'whites only' schools, colleges and universities. The Federal government accepted such discriminatory laws: even during the Second World War, black soldiers were conscripted into black-only regiments (*extract D*).

In the South, blacks were often physically attacked, with their attackers rarely being arrested or punished. Thousands of blacks were arrested, often for 'having looked at a white woman', and many of them were lynched by white mobs, usually led by Klansmen (page 182, *picture 2*), with the support of seemingly 'decent' white people (*picture 3* and *extract B*).

There was similar discrimination and violence in the North. In July 1919 a black boy, swimming in Lake Michigan, drifted over to waters reserved for whites. He was stoned from the white beach and drowned, which led to a

2. New York housing conditions were without parallel in the civilized world. 'Not in heathen Canton or Bombay are to be found such conditions as prevail in modern, enlightened, 20th-century, Christian New York.'

week-long series of race riots in Chicago in which 40 people died and over 500 were injured.

Some blacks campaigned for improvement in black peoples' lives. A former slave, Booker T. Washington, managed to get on, and in 1881 he founded a college in Alabama and urged blacks to become qualified so that they might have better job prospects. Another gifted black, W.E.B. DuBois had been educated at the élite University at Harvard. He helped set up the National Association for the Advancement of Colored People (NAACP) which campaigned for equal treatment for blacks. However, many influential blacks opposed him (*extract C*).

Neither agitation nor 'patience' had much effect. Roosevelt, the supposedly 'liberal' President, refused to support an anti-lynching Bill in 1935, or to end segregation in the armed forces (*extract D*). 'The Road to Freedom' was still far away when the Second World War broke out in 1939.

3. A lynching, 1935

EXTRACT A
Free – but homeless and hungry

'He was free from the old huts that once gave him shelter, but a slave to the rains of summer and the frosts of winter. He was turned loose, but naked, hungry and destitute to the open sky.'

(Quoted in *The Making of America*, BBC Publications, 1968)

EXTRACT B
Poster written to appear with picture, 1935

Robin Stacy, the Negro, was lynched at Fort Lauderdale on 19 July 1935, for 'threatening and frightening a white woman'. He was already in the hands of the law: hence the handcuffs. But the law could not stop him being lynched. Since 1922, over a half of lynched victims have been taken from legal custody. More than 5000 lynchings have taken place without any punishment of the lynchers. A Federal law is needed, as in the case of kidnapping, to strengthen existing state laws which fail to stop lynching.

(Poster issued by the National Association for the Advancement of Colored People)

EXTRACT C
A black leader opposes campaigns for equality, 1895

The wisest among my race understand that agitation for social equality is the extremest folly.

(Booker T. Washington, in Atlanta, Georgia, 1895)

EXTRACT D
President Roosevelt's wife advises 'patience' to black servicemen, 1935

Trying to change the law on segregation in the forces is difficult. These things come slowly, and patience is required.

(Letter by Mrs Roosevelt, 10 December 1935)

Now test yourself

Knowledge and understanding

1 Make a list of ways in which black people suffered (a) politically; (b) socially; (c) economically.
2 (a) How did black people try to overcome their difficulties? (b) Why did they find it difficult to do so?

Using the sources

1 Read *extracts A–D*. Do you agree that the views expressed in *extract A* are explained by *extracts B, C and D*? Give reasons for your answer.
2 Look at *pictures 2 and 3*. What do you learn from *both* these sources about (a) what life for black people was like; (b) white people's attitudes to black people?

L evel Descriptions

At the start of Key Stage 3 the majority of pupils will have reached at least Level 4 in History. By the end of Key Stage 3 most pupils should be within the range of Levels 4–7. Levels 5–6 are the target for 14-year-olds. Level 8 is the standard reached by very able pupils.

Use our checklist to assess the Level reached, by ticking the skills that have been mastered.

Level 4

- ☐ Demonstrate factual knowledge and understanding of aspects of the history of Britain and other countries, drawn from the Key Stage 3 programme of study.
- ☐ Use the above to describe the characteristic features of past societies and periods, and to identify changes within and across periods.
- ☐ Describe some of the main events, people and changes.
- ☐ Give some reasons for, and results of, the main events and changes.
- ☐ Show how some aspects of the past have been represented and interpreted in different ways.
- ☐ Begin to select and combine information from sources.
- ☐ Begin to produce structured work, making appropriate use of dates and terms.

Level 5

- ☐ Demonstrate an increasing depth of factual knowledge and understanding of aspects of the history of Britain and other countries drawn from the Key Stage 3 programme of study.
- ☐ Use the above to describe and to begin to make links between features of past societies and periods.
- ☐ Describe events, people and changes.
- ☐ Describe and make links between relevant reasons for, and results of, events and changes.
- ☐ Realization that some events, people and changes have been interpreted in different ways and suggest possible reasons for this.
- ☐ Using knowledge and understanding, begin to evaluate sources of information and identify those that are useful for particular tasks.
- ☐ Select and organize information to produce structured work, making appropriate use of dates and terms.

Level 6

- ☐ Use factual knowledge and understanding of the history of Britain and other countries drawn from the Key Stage 3 programme of study, to describe past societies and periods, and to make links between features within and across periods.
- ☐ Examine, and begin to analyse the reasons for, and results of, events and changes.
- ☐ Describe, and begin to explain, different historical interpretations of events, people and changes.
- ☐ Using knowledge and understanding, identify and evaluate sources of information and use these sources critically to reach and support conclusions.
- ☐ Select, organize and deploy relevant information to produce structured work, making appropriate use of dates and terms.

Level 7

☐ Make links between outline and detailed factual knowledge and understanding of the history of Britain and other countries drawn from the Key Stage 3 programme of study.

☐ Use the above to analyse relationships between features of a particular period or society, and to analyse reasons for, and results of, events and changes.

☐ Explain how and why different historical interpretations have been produced.

☐ Begin to show independence in following lines of enquiry, using knowledge and understanding to identify, evaluate and use sources of information critically.

☐ Begin to reach substantiated conclusions independently.

☐ Select, organize and deploy relevant information to produce well structured narratives, descriptions and explanations, making appropriate use of dates and terms.

Level 8

☐ Use outline and detailed factual knowledge and understanding of the history of Britain and other countries drawn from the Key Stage 3 programme of study, to analyse the relationships between events, people and changes, and between the features of past societies.

☐ Explanations and analyses of, reasons for, and results of, events and changes are set in their wider historical context.

☐ Analyse and explain different historical interpretations, and begin to evaluate them.

☐ Drawing on historical knowledge and understanding, use sources of information critically, carry out enquiries about historical topics, and independently reach substantiated conclusions.

☐ Select, organize and deploy relevant information to produce consistently well structured narratives, descriptions and explanations, making appropriate use of dates and terms.

Exceptional performance

☐ Use extensive and detailed factual knowledge and understanding of the history of Britain and other countries drawn from the Key Stage 3 programme of study, to analyse relationships between a wide range of events, people, ideas and changes and between the features of past societies.

☐ Explanations and analyses of, reasons for, and results of, events and changes, are well substantiated and set in their wider historical context.

☐ Analyse links between events and developments that took place in different countries and in different periods.

☐ Make balanced judgements about the value of differing interpretations of historical events and developments in relation to their historical context.

☐ Drawing on historical knowledge and understanding, use sources of information critically, carry out enquiries about historical topics and independently reach and sustain substantiated and balanced conclusions.

☐ Select, organize and deploy a wide range of relevant information to produce consistently well structured narratives, descriptions and explanations, making appropriate use of dates and terms.

GLOSSARY

Abolition   From the verb abolish, meaning to bring to an end.

Absolute monarch   A monarch who has total power, because their country does not have a constitution (see below).

Alliance   A treaty of friendship joining countries together.

Altar   A flat-topped table used during religious ceremonies.

Ancient Régime   French for 'old method of government': name given by historians to France before 1789.

Apprentice   A young person learning a trade or a craft.

Arable   Land which is being used to grow crops.

Archbishop   'A chief bishop': a very important post in the *Church*.

Aristocracy   People with special titles, such as Duke, Earl, Count: Usually very important landowners and *nobles*.

Auction   A public sale in which goods are bought by the person who offers the highest price – or bid.

Bailey   The courtyard, or walled enclosure, of a castle.

Baptism   A religious service and *sacrament* in which someone becomes a Christian, when water is used as a sign of new life.

Baron   An important nobleman (see *aristocracy*).

Besiege   To surround a town or castle in an attempt to capture it.

Bias   Having and presenting a one-sided view about a person or event, sometimes without knowing it, but often deliberately.

Bishop   The person in charge of a large area of the *Church* (see *diocese*).

Black Death   The bubonic *plague*.

Borough   A town which received a royal *charter*, allowing it to have an elected council (corporation) and certain other privileges: these included, later, the right to send two MPs to Parliament.

Burgess   A citizen of a *borough* who had all the rights listed in its *charter*.

Calvinist   An extreme *Puritan* who accepted the ideas of the Swiss Protestant reformer, John Calvin (1509–64).

Cavalry   Soldiers on horseback (see *knights*).

Ceremony   A special occasion, often religious.

Chancellor   (Medieval) An important adviser to the King: (modern) German and Austrian name for Prime Minister.

Charter   A list of rights for a borough or company, or, as in 1215, for the people as a whole.

Chastity   To abstain from sexual relations.

Chronicle   A history of events.

Church   (a) A building where Christians worship; (b) the organization of the people who belong to a certain faith.

Christianity   The religion of those who believe that Jesus Christ is the son of God.

Civil Service   The paid officials who administer the government's laws.

Code Napoleon   A list of French laws drawn up by Napoleon.

Colony   The territory taken by, and used by, a foreign power.

Compensation   A payment made to make up for something else.

Concentric   A castle with more than one set of walls, one inside the other, the outer walls being lower than the inner so that archers from both walls could fire out their missiles.

Confederate States   The states of the South of the USA which allied with each other (confederacy) to break away from the Union, 1860–65.

Constitution   A list of the rules which set out how a country should be run and the rights of its citizens.

Coronation   The crowning and anointing of a *monarch*.

Court   (a) The place where the *monarch* lives; (b) the people among whom the monarch lives and who advise him/her.

Declaration of Independence	A statement drawn up by Thomas Jefferson in June–July 1776 explaining why the American colonists had rebelled.
Deputy	Member of French Parliament or (in the 1790s) Assembly.
Discrimination	Making rules, or keeping customs, which are meant to give one group certain privileges not given to another group.
Dissolution	(a) The ending of a meeting of *Parliament*; (b) the shutting down of *monasteries* (so ending monks' meetings).
Emancipation	Setting free (a) slaves; (b) Catholics in 1829; (c) women in 20th-century Britain.
Emperor	The ruler of an *empire*.
Empire	Countries belonging to a ruling state (see *colony*).
Enclosure	The use of walls, fences or hedges to make separate fields or farms from former open land and commons.
Epidemic	The rapid spread of a disease affecting many people.
Evidence	What we get from a historical source (books, letters, photographs, paintings, houses, objects) when we examine it and ask the right questions.
Excommunicated	To be forbidden to be a practising member of a *Church*.
Faith	A set of religious beliefs (Christian, Islamic, Jewish, Hindu, etc).
Fallow	Land on which no crops are being grown.
Fertilizer	Something put on the land to make it more productive.
Feudal system	Traditional landholding system: in England it decayed slowly in medieval times; in France it was swept away only in 1789.
Freeman	Someone who has political and civil liberties, and, in medieval times, was free from most (or all) duties to a lord.
Frontier	The border between two countries.
Governor	Someone who rules a country (e.g. Roman Britain) or a state (e.g. in Britain's American colonies) on behalf of another *country*.
Guild	An organization or society to which medieval merchants and craftsmen belonged.
Heaven	The home of God to which, believe Christians and members of other faiths, good people will go after death.
Heretics	People who believe (or teach) something opposed to the teachings of the religious belief of the *Church*.
Jacobites	Supporters of Prince James (*Jacobus* in Latin) Stuart and, later, 'Bonnie' Prince Charles Edward Stuart.
Jury	A group, originally of men only, who decided if a prisoner was telling the truth.
Justices of the Peace	People appointed to deal with law and order in a particular area: for many centuries they were also the only form of local government in many areas.
Lawyer	Someone who advises people about the law.
Legend	An ancient story, usually passed down by word of mouth. It often contains a mixture of fact and exaggeration, and is believed by many people to be true.
Lynching	Illegal execution (usually by hanging).
Long-term results	When the effects of an event develop, or take place, a long time after the event.
Mail	Armoured clothing made by linking metal rings together.
Manor	The estate owned by a medieval lord.
Manuscript	Something written by hand (Latin 'manus' = hand).

Martyr	A person who is killed for his or her beliefs (usually religious).
Mass	The main religious ceremony of the Catholic Church.
Masterpiece	A piece of work done by a journeyman which the officers of his *guild* thought good enough to allow him to become a master.
Medieval	Means Middle Ages. Some people say that it refers to the period from the end of the Roman Empire (5th century) to the *Renaissance* (around 1400): others think the starting date may be as much as 400 years later.
Merchant	A person who buys and sells things made or grown by others.
Monarchy	Rule by a king or queen.
Monument	A building to remind people of some historic person or event.
Motte and bailey	A castle on a mound (motte) with a courtyard (*bailey*).
Noble	A lord or lady of the *aristocracy*.
Oath	A very serious promise, usually calling on God as a witness, to tell the truth or to honour an obligation (e.g. to a lord).
Parish	A small area (once the *manor*) which has its own church.
Parliament	Originally the people called to advise the monarch and give him/her the right to collect taxes. The House of Lords was once more powerful than the House of Commons which, at first, was made up of two *knights* from every shire and two *burgesses* from each chartered *borough*. The relative power of both Houses began to change in the 17th century.
Penance	(a) A *sacrament* in the Catholic Church where one expresses sorrow for *sin* and is asked to perform some act of self-denial by way of showing that sorrow; (b) punishment for sins.
Pilgrim	A person making a special journey to a holy place.
Plantation	An estate on which cotton, sugar, tobacco or rubber are grown.
Pope	The head of the Catholic Church.
Priest	(a) A man who leads people in religious worship; (b) a man who organizes and controls the Church in a parish; (c) a Catholic clergyman.
Primary sources	Ones which give us evidence from the period being studied; e.g. eye-witness accounts, pictures made at the time, objects such as furniture coming from the period, letters or diaries. Historians use this raw material to present students with *secondary sources* in the form of books or articles.
Propaganda	(a) information, which may be true or false, given to try to get people to think in a certain way; (b) the method of spreading an opinion (true or false) in an effort to get it accepted by others.
Protestant	(a) Any of the Churches which broke off from the Catholic Church during the *Reformation*; (b) a member of such a Church.
Rebellion	An organized armed resistance to the government of a country.
Reformation	The religious movement of the early 16th century which began in an attempt to reform abuses in the Catholic Church, but which led to the formation of break-away *Protestant* Churches.
Relics	Parts of a holy person's body, or belongings which are kept, after his or her death, as objects of reverence.
Republic	A form of government without a monarch.
Royalist	A supporter of the king.
Revolution	A complete change of methods of production (industrial/agricultural) or of rulers (American, French, English, Russian).
Sacrament	A religious *ceremony* or act which believers see as an outward sign of God's gift of a particular grace. The Eastern and the Catholic Churches name seven sacraments: *Baptism*; *Penance*;